THE OPEN UNIVERSITY

Social sciences: a foundation course

MAKING SENSE OF SOCIETY

BLOCK 7 UNITS 21–24   ATTITUDES AND BELIEFS

PREPARED BY THE COURSE TEAM

The Open University Press

The Open University Press
Walton Hall, Milton Keynes
MK7 6AA

First published 1975. Reprinted 1977

Designed by the Media Development Group of the Open University.

Printed in Great Britain by
COES THE PRINTERS LIMITED
RUSTINGTON, SUSSEX

ISBN 0 335 04558 8

This text forms part of an Open University course. The complete list of units in the
course appears at the end of this text.

For general availability of supporting material referred to in this text, please write
to: Open University Educational Enterprises Limited, 12 Cofferidge Close, Stony
Stratford, Milton Keynes, MK11 1BY, Great Britain.

Further information on Open University courses may be obtained from the
Admissions Office, The Open University, P.O. Box 48, Walton Hall, Milton Keynes,
MK7 6AB.

1.2

INTRODUCTION TO BLOCK 7 *Richard Stevens*

'Attitudes' denote the ways in which people *feel* about aspects of the world in which they live, and 'beliefs' the ways they *think* about them. To understand any man or any society it is necessary to know something about the basic beliefs and attitudes they hold. Behaviour, styles of interaction, social rituals and institutions may appear strange and meaningless unless the feelings and ideas which underlie them are appreciated. If we are to make any sense of society, the significance of understanding the nature of attitudes and beliefs and how they develop and change should not be underestimated. They are an important aspect of many of the dimensions already discussed in the course. The communication technology of a society, for example, will be to some extent interdependent with its prevailing beliefs and attitudes. The kind of work a man does, his willingness to do it and the way he performs it both reflect and shape what he believes and feels. Styles of interpersonal communication and the quality of social relationships depend on and affect attitudes held. The way parents bring up their children will be based on their view of and feelings towards life and other people.

Many of the social problems discussed earlier, such as racial conflict, crime and pollution are, in particular, a direct function of the attitudes and beliefs of society and those concerned. Whether men or nations engage in aggression and men go out to kill and maim each other rests to a considerable degree on particular styles of thought and feeling. As the United Nations Charter puts it 'wars begin in the minds of men'. With a different set of beliefs and attitudes, men will instead risk their own lives to help strangers. Block 2 discussed what is probably the major problem threatening man today – population expansion. The world's population is now approaching 4,000 millions and is increasing at an accelerating rate. Whereas a few hundred years ago the world population took 1,600 years to double in size, it is now estimated that the present day figure may well be doubled to 8,000 millions in about 50 years. The world has finite resources. Whatever the effects of the development of modern technology, the yield of food and resources is inevitably limited. If famine, conflict and suffering are to be avoided, man's reproductive patterns must change. And the key to this is modification of the way in which people feel and think about the need for and practice of birth control. Understanding attitudes, beliefs and the way these evolve and change, both within individuals and cultures is, therefore, of both practical as well as academic concern.

This block illustrates two rather different, although related, approaches to the study of attitudes and beliefs. Units 21 and 22 form a continuous double unit which explores the nature of beliefs and attitudes *in the individual*. It considers the basic question of what these are and the extent to which they are measurable. It goes on to discuss the origins of the attitudes a person holds, their relation with personality factors and behaviour, the reasons why they are often difficult to change and ways in which it may be possible to modify them. As you might expect, the methods, evidence and theories considered here are mostly from psychology, in particular social psychology.

Units 23 and 24, in contrast, illustrate the approach of the sociologist. Here the focus is not so much on aspects of and factors determining attitudes within the individual, as on the *prevailing attitudes within a society*. These units are concerned especially with exploring the interplay of social forces which both produce and, in their turn, are themselves influenced by cultural patterns of beliefs and attitudes. Unit 23 illustrates the interdependence of beliefs, values and the social context by a case study of the development of scientific thinking. It shows how even the development of science, with its seemingly objective methods and independent knowledge, depended on particular kinds of social conditions. The unit argues that one factor of especial importance was the pattern of beliefs and attitudes characteristic of the Protestant religion.

Unit 24 extends this discussion with further illustrations of the ways in which

3

Beliefs/attitudes v.a.v.
social devt.
+ change

(1)

(2)

(3)

(4)

underlying patterns of beliefs and attitudes serve as necessary pre-conditions for social development and change. The first is Weber's thesis that the Protestant religion generated the values, attitudes and beliefs appropriate to the behaviour, patterns and social institutions on which the development of modern capitalism depended. The second illustration is the analogous Halévy thesis which views nineteenth-century Methodism as providing a system of beliefs and values which helped workers to adjust to the new styles of living and working demanded by industrial capitalism and also as providing an outlet for collective feeling other than rebelling against the established order. The third example the unit considers is a study of a contemporary phenomenon – the 'cargo cults' found among primitive groups in New Guinea. Landing strips are built and rituals engaged in designed to entice the white man's planes and boats which are believed to be carrying 'cargo' or goods sent by the natives' ancestors. These cults illustrate a situation where beliefs have evolved in an attempt to interpret and make sense of new and unfamiliar events; also as a means of trying to satisfy the material needs stimulated by the coming of western culture. Finally, the unit views religious beliefs in the context of twentieth-century British society by discussing a study of the nature and function of religious organizations in an area of Birmingham. The study of religion is introduced earlier in the block in the final section of Units 21–22 which examines the psychological bases of religious attitudes. Unit 24 discusses the topic in more detail by looking at the role of religion in society as a whole. Together they provide an introduction to the social psychology and sociology of religion.

interdependence of
cultural belief
patterns and
the social
context ......

The primary aims of this block, then, are to explore the nature and origins of attitudes and beliefs in the individual and the interdependence of cultural belief patterns and the social context. These are inevitably closely intertwined. The cultural context is a most important source of an individual's beliefs and attitudes: yet, as Erich Fromm (1960 p 10) has pointed out 'Man is not only made by history – history is made by man, . . . passions, desires, anxieties change and develop as a *result* of the social process but, . . . man's energies thus shaped into specific forms in their turn become *productive forces, moulding the social process.*'

REFERENCE

FROMM, E. (1960) *Fear of freedom*, London, Routledge and Kegan Paul.

STUDY PROGRAMME FOR BLOCK 7

	TITLE	SOURCE	TIME (hours approx)
1	Block introduction	Correspondence text	$\frac{1}{4}$
	UNITS 21–22		
2	'Attitudes', introduction, study objectives, study guide and section 1	Correspondence text	1
3	Fromm, E. 'The human situation' pp 351–6	Reader[a]	$\frac{1}{2}$
4	'Attitudes', sections 2–5	Correspondence text	4
5	Asch, S. 'Opinions and social pressure' (including SAQs)	Set book[b]	1
6	'Attitudes', sections 5.1–6	Correspondence text	$1\frac{1}{2}$
7	Katz, D. 'The functional approach to the study of attitudes' (including SAQs)	Reader[a]	1
8	'Attitudes', sections 7–8	Correspondence text	$1\frac{3}{4}$

4

9	Festinger, L. 'Cognitive dissonance' (including SAQs)	Set book[b]	1
10	'Attitudes', sections 8.1–11.2	Correspondence text	$2\frac{1}{4}$
11	Fromm, E. 'The human situation' PP 355–9	Reader[a]	$\frac{1}{4}$
12	'Attitudes', sections 11.3–11.5	Correspondence text	$\frac{1}{4}$
	UNIT 23		
13	Beliefs and social change: the scientific revolution', introduction and section 1	Correspondence text	$1\frac{1}{4}$
14	Zilsel, E., 'The sociological roots of science' (including SAQs)	Reader[a]	$1\frac{1}{4}$
15	'Beliefs and social change: the scientific revolution', sections 2–3.1	Correspondence text	$1\frac{1}{4}$
16	Merton, R., 'Motive forces of the new science' (including SAQs)	Reader[a]	$1\frac{1}{2}$
17	'Beliefs and social change: the scientific revolution', sections 3.2–4	Correspondence text	$1\frac{1}{4}$
	UNIT 24		
18	'Beliefs and social strata', introduction, study objectives, study guide and sections 1–3	Correspondence text	2
19	Hill, M., 'The Halévy thesis' (including SAQs)	Reader[a]	$1\frac{1}{4}$
20	'Beliefs and social strata', section 4	Correspondence text	1
21	Talmon, Y., 'Millenarian movements' (including SAQs)	Reader[a]	$1\frac{1}{4}$
22	'Beliefs and social strata', section 5	Correspondence text	$\frac{1}{4}$
23	Rex and Moore pp 173–90 (including SAQs)	Set book[c]	$1\frac{1}{4}$
24	'Beliefs and social strata', sections 6–7	Correspondence text	$\frac{3}{4}$
25	CMA	Supplementary material	2
26	TMA	Supplementary material	5
27	Radio and TV programmes and notes	Supplementary material	4
		TOTAL	40

[a] POTTER, D. and SARRE, P. (eds.) (1974) *Dimensions of society*, London, University of London Press/The Open University Press.

[b] SCIENTIFIC AMERICAN (1974) *Papers in socialization and attitudes*, Reading, Freeman.

[c] REX, J. and MOORE, R. (1967) *Race, community, and conflict*, London, Oxford University Press.

Units 21-22
Attitudes

delinquent ULSTER HOMOSEXUAL
DYEECANGING PORN
INFLATION GOD
ABORTION
OVALIN
Pill birch sex
Pollution
witchcraft
hippie FOOTBALL
NUDISM

Prepared for the course team by Richard Stevens

CONTENTS

INTRODUCTION

'It's rubbish'

'Mini-skirts are marvellous'

'It's about time we abolished the royal family'

'The social contract is the only thing that can get us out of this mess'

'God is love'

'For goodness sake, no more nationalization'

'There's just too much permissiveness these days'

'Mental hospitals are just no good'

'No more abortion'

Our experience of the world is shaped and people identify us by the opinions and attitudes we hold. Men have suffered and died because of their beliefs and, as the Block Introduction has indicated, the well-being and survival of our species may now well depend on the attitudes that prevail. Beliefs and attitudes are of central importance to our understanding of men and society.

STUDY OBJECTIVES

Units 21 and 22 have three kinds of objectives.

Their primary purpose is to explore *the nature and the social and psychological bases of attitudes in the individual*. More specifically, after having studied the units, you should be able to:

1 Discuss how attitudes are formed.

2 Distinguish some of the functions that attitudes serve.

3 Discuss the relationship between attitudes and personality.

4 Describe the basic principles of cognitive dissonance theory and ways in which it has been experimentally tested; predict what is likely to happen as a result of the dissonance aroused by voluntary lying, making a choice, temptation, voluntarily undergoing difficulty or pain in pursuit of some goal, doing someone a favour or doing someone harm.

5 Explain why it is difficult to modify attitudes and suggest procedures likely to be effective in producing attitude change.

6 Discuss the psychological bases of religious belief and prejudice.

7 Distinguish between existential and historical needs.

Secondly, the units consider further the problem of *definition and measurement of psychological and social science concepts*. This is essential to appreciate properly what attitudes are. More specifically, after having studied the units, you should be able to:

1 Define the concept 'attitude' and distinguish it from 'belief' and 'value'.

2 Understand what is meant by a hypothetical construct.

3 Evaluate the degree to which it is possible to measure attitudes; describe some of the basic procedures for constructing attitude scales and assess the likely usefulness of any attitude scale.

Thirdly, interwoven in the exploration of the nature of attitudes is a consideration of *methodological issues* designed to increase your understanding of research methods on which, of course, theories and explanations usually depend. Experimentation and problems of drawing precise inferences from research results are given particular emphasis. More specifically, having studied the units you should be able to:

1　Compare the relative advantages and disadvantages of laboratory and natural experiments.

2　Interpret research, particularly experimental, data more effectively.

3　Interpret an index of statistical significance.

4　Describe and comment on the principal procedures used in the research study 'The Authoritarian Personality'.

STUDY GUIDE

Units 21 and 22 are presented as an integrated double unit. Its eleven sections form into three main groups. 1 Sections 1 and 2 are concerned respectively with the *concept* and *measurement* of attitudes. 2 Then, section 3 considers the *stability* of central attitudes and how this is maintained. The next five sections each explore factors underlying this stability. Section 4 discusses the *formation* of attitudes, section 5 is on *social influence*, section 6 on the *functions* attitudes serve, section 7 on the relationship between *personality* and attitudes and section 8 on the way attitudes are *organized* into interlocking systems and the consequences of this. 3 The three final sections each draw on and thus serve to help you review the preceding material. They consider in turn *persuasion* (how to change attitudes), *prejudice* and *religious belief*.

There are four extracts to be read with Units 21 and 22.

'The human situation' by Erich Fromm is to be read in conjunction with sections 1 and 10.

'Opinions and social pressure' by Solomon Asch with section 5.

'The functional approach to the study of attitudes' by Daniel Katz with section 6.

'Cognitive dissonance' by Leon Festinger with section 8.

The papers by Fromm (1949) and Katz (1960) are in your Course Reader *Dimensions of society* (Potter and Sarre 1974) and those by Asch (1955) and Festinger (1962) in the set text *Papers on socialization and attitudes* (Scientific American 1974). Instruction, comments, notes and/or SAQs on each are given in the unit sections indicated.

In addition to SAQs, you will find occasional activities or questions in the text. Try to formulate an answer to these as you come to them before reading on. It is up to you, of course, how you organize your work but it is suggested that a good way might be to study the unit initially in seven sessions, taking at least a break between each, as follows: sections 1-2, 3, 4-5, 6, 7, 8, 9-11.

1　WHAT IS AN ATTITUDE?

1.1　CHARACTERISTICS OF ATTITUDES

Take a pen and jot down a few examples of attitudes held by people you know. Now briefly list some of the attitudes you hold yourself.

Look back over both sets and note down any general characteristics the attitudes listed share. Write down your definition of attitude.

One feature you may have picked out is that attitudes, either explicitly or implicitly, relate to people, events, actions, things, ideas or institutions. They are about, for example, the Common Market, mini-skirts, the Church, capital punishment. men with red beards, socialism, authority, etc. In other words an attitude has an 'object' (note that the term 'object' will be used to denote any aspect of the world, including people and ideas, towards which we have an attitude).

attitude → object

evaluation

A second characteristic is that attitudes express the way a person evaluates, the degree of positive or negative feeling he has towards the object in question.

Thirdly, attitudes are relatively enduring. If you know a person's attitude you can usually predict what he will think or say in future reactions to that or similar objects. Attitudes, therefore, must be based on some underlying physiological/ experiential system 'inside' us.

1.2 SYMBOLIC THOUGHT

When you have read this sentence, close your eyes and think of two people you know, the place that you have been to which is farthest from your present home and two moral principles which are important to you.

Hockett, you will remember, in discussing the characteristics of human language, used the term 'displacement' to describe the capacity to refer to things and events removed in time and space. Not only were you able just now to 'experience' or imagine people and events not physically present but you could probably even conceptualize a 'moral principle', a concept which has no actual existence anywhere but represents a cluster of key defining features abstracted from particular sequences of behaviour and situations.

For Hockett's discussion of displacement: see Unit 7, section 3.5

Displacement...

(You might care to ponder the extent to which you could have done this had you not possessed a language. This is a problem which has exercised the attention of philosophers, psychologists and linguists though it need not concern us now except to note it in passing. Both section 3.7 in Unit 7 on 'Language and thought' and Unit 19 touch on the issue.)

Your achievement here illustrates your 'internalized world' – the extraordinary capacity of the human brain somehow to represent and store internally aspects of experience, and generalizations and abstractions from that experience. Men can even conceive, as the myths and legends of nearly all cultures amply testify, beings and events which have no existence outside his mind.

internalised world...

SAQ 1

Give some examples of concepts of this imaginary kind.

Answers to SAQs in Units 21–22 are on pp 80–6

It is often instructive in trying to understand behaviour as well as physiology to view man in an evolutionary context. Also, as we saw with Hockett's system, contrasting man's capacities with those of other species often illuminates his characteristics. Man is a very recent animal indeed among life on this planet. If we reduce the 3,000 million year span from the emergence of the first forms of primitive life to the present, to the scale of twenty-four hours, then *Homo sapiens* begins to emerge as a species in the last thirty seconds! One of the key features that characterized the development of the early man apes was the extraordinarily rapid evolution of the brain. The increase was largely in the size of the cortex, the area of the brain which is concerned with thought and conceptualization and which underlies the 'categories' which, as Unit 7 showed, mediate perception and experience. One result therefore was to increase greatly man's capacity for symbolic thinking and lessen his dependence on his immediate sensory environment.

man's great capacity for symbolic thinking...

Low down on the evolutionary scale behaviour is often governed by 'tropisms'. These are relatively fixed, innately determined reactions to specific stimuli. So a sunflower turns throughout the day to face the sun and a moth is attracted to light (see Figure 1).

Tropisms (innate reactions)

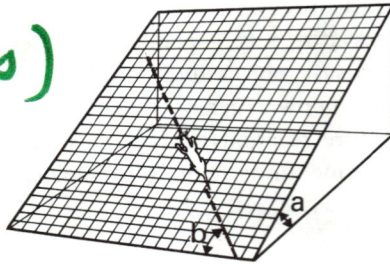

Crozier and Pincus have demonstrated how baby rats respond tropistically. The angle at which they climb an inclined plane was found to be directly related to the steepness of the plane. As the gradient (angle a) is increased so the angle at which the rat creeps (angle b) increases.

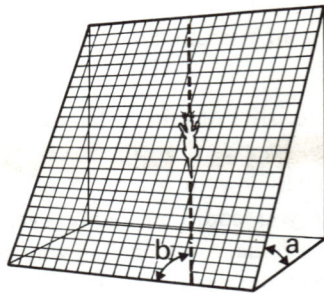

Gradient (angle a)	Angle at which rat creeps (angle b)
20°	44°
30°	57°
40°	70°
50°	78°
60°	85°

Figure 1

(Based on Crozier and Pincus 1926)

Generally speaking, the higher up the evolutionary scale they are, the less organisms depend on such innate responses to stimuli and the more variability there is between the behaviour of different members of the same species. The way a man, for example, reacts to a stimulus will depend very much on how he experiences it and this will depend in turn on the internalized world of concepts and categories he has built up through earlier learning and experience. It is unlikely that two men's experience of and reactions to the same situation are ever identical. Quite often they are not even similar.

Capacity for symbolic thought has been a vital factor in the evolutionary success of man, an otherwise not very effectively equipped organism. It permits the planning and anticipation of long term projects, the co-ordination of group action and the communication of ideas between people and over generations, on which the evolution of culture depends. Erich Fromm argues in his paper 'The human situation', which can be found in your Reader, that it also generates problems of a particular kind. You might like to read the first half (pp 352–6, line 9) of this paper now and answer the following SAQs.

planning; anticipation; co-ordination; communication

Read Fromm in Reader pp 352–6, line 9

SAQ 2

Briefly distinguish between historical and existential dichotomies.

SAQ 3

Why does man have existential dichotomies?

SAQ 4

Give two examples of the existential dichotomies that Fromm cites.

Existential dichotomies

Fromm points out that capacity for conceptual thought makes us painfully aware of 'existential dichotomies', for example that although we live we will die, that although we may have potentialities we can realize but few of them, that although we are

14

separate we depend on others. Fromm's argument is essentially philosophical. He offers thought-provoking and interesting ideas about the implications of the nature of man's experience and his power of symbolic thought. He does not, as most psychologists and social scientists endeavour to, support his case with empirical evidence. But it is difficult to see how he could do so for assertions such as these. His appeal is to reason and to your own experience. How far does his account make sense to you?

We use many terms to denote aspects of symbolic and conceptual thought, e.g. 'ideas', 'thoughts', 'feelings', 'values', 'categories', 'contructs', and also, of course, 'attitudes' and 'beliefs'. These are the means by which we make sense of, order, organize and predict, and which shape our reactions to the world about us.

1.3 DEFINING 'ATTITUDES'

Gordon Allport has produced perhaps the most widely quoted definition of *attitude*. 'A mental and neural state of readiness, organized through experience, exerting a directive or dynamic influence upon the individual's response to all objects and situations with which it is related' (Allport 1954 p 45).

Similar is that of Krech and Crutchfield. 'An attitude can be defined as an enduring organization of motivational, emotional, perceptual and cognitive processes with respect to some aspect of the individual's world' (Krech and Crutchfield 1948 p 173).

Both definitions state or imply the characteristics we have already noted:

1 Attitudes are related to an object – some aspect of the individual's world.
2 They are part of the general way the individual experiences and reacts to his world.
3 They are relatively enduring.
4 They imply evaluation and feeling (Allport talks of 'directive and dynamic influence' and Krech and Crutchfield of 'motivational, emotional . . . processes').

The vitally important thing to realize is that attitudes are not tangible. We cannot see or study directly the 'organization of motivational, emotional, perceptual and cognitive processes' or a 'mental and neural state of readiness'. They are only inferred. The concept of attitude is an abstraction. We use it to denote certain consistencies in a person's behaviour, statements and, we assume, experience. In other words 'attitude' is a hypothetical construct, or, as English and English (1958 p 9) define that, 'an inferred entity . . . conceived as actually existing and as giving rise to measurable phenomena, including phenomena other than the observables that led to hypothesizing the construct'. We observe that a person is a member of a certain political party. We note the views he expresses. From this we infer that he has a particular kind of 'political attitude' and we can anticipate, often quite effectively, his views and reactions on other issues (i.e. 'phenomena other than the observables that led to hypothesizing the construct').

One important implication of the fact that it is a hypothetical construct is that there is no one absolute and correct meaning or definition of the concept 'attitude', any more than there is of the abstract terms 'beauty' or 'justice'. The definitions given will depend on what observables are selected as a basis for inference. Definitions are useful, however, as a means of clarifying usage. Although distinctions between concepts like 'attitude', 'belief' and 'value' are to a large extent arbitrary, it is necessary to clarify what is meant when the word is used.

Most social scientists view attitude as a complex, multidimensional concept. Like Krech and Crutchfield, they see it as having an emotional or *affective* aspect – that is, it embodies positive or negative feelings about the object in question; a *cognitive* aspect – beliefs or ideas about it; and a *conative* aspect – a tendency to behave in a particular way towards it. Most of the studies discussed in the unit use 'attitude' in this more global sense. There are some psychologists, however, who

state of readiness influencing our responses to objects/situations.

abstractions

hypothetical construct

multidimensional concept...
cognitive
conative

15

prefer to restrict the use of the concept to denote affect. Attitude for them refers to 'the amount of affect for or against a psychological object' (Fishbein and Coombs 1974). They use the term 'belief' for the cognitive aspect and 'behavioural intention' for the conative. They point out that their formulation is more useful because feelings, beliefs and behaviour relating to the same object are not necessarily correlated. Two people may both have positive feelings about a person but have different ways of reacting to him and believe different things about him.

The term *belief* denotes an assertion about some aspect of the world or the relation between two such aspects: for example, Jones and Gerard (1967 p 158) define belief as expressing 'the relation between two cognitive categories when neither defines the other'). In linguistic terms, a belief can be expressed as a statement with a subject and a predicate, such as *smoking leads to ill health*, *the social contract is the best way to ensure justice for all*, *the Conservative party is opposed to nationalization* etc. *Opinion* is used in various ways but usually means a verbal statement of an attitude or belief. *Value* is also used variably but most often to denote what is believed to be good and desirable. It tends to be a higher order concept in that it may subsume a whole host of related attitudes. For example, a person whose basic value is humanitarian will have positive attitudes towards measures he believes to be instrumental in promoting human happiness and wellbeing but will be negative towards objects he believes lead to suffering. *Ideology* is another higher order concept generally denoting a cluster of related values, attitudes and beliefs.

2 MEASURING ATTITUDES

Verbal definitions are not sufficient. The progress of social science depends, like any science, on being able to describe and record the phenomena under investigation as precisely as possible. Studying immigration, for example, might require comparing the attitudes of one individual with those of another. For the last fifty or more years, social psychologists have expended much time and energy attempting to devise sophisticated techniques for measuring attitudes. The problems involved are formidable. One of the difficulties of psychology in particular and social science in general is that some of the most important factors influencing behaviour and society are not easily observable, let alone measurable. How can you observe and measure, for example, experience, feelings or a 'mental and neural state of readiness'?

2.1 ATTITUDE DIMENSIONS

To assess a person's physique you can rate him on a number of *dimensions* – height, weight, strength of grip etc. What *dimensions* do attitudes have? Write down any you can think of.

A number of different attitude dimensions have been suggested. The most significant of these are:

Valence   The degree of positive or negative feeling the object of the attitude evokes; in other words, the way it is evaluated. As will be seen, this is what is usually measured by attitude scales.

Multiplexity   The degree to which an attitude is differentiated. You may have a host of feelings and ideas about the Open University compared to a friend who is not a student. He may still have an attitude towards it but it will be less multiplex.

Breadth   This is a term I have coined to refer to the number of criterial attributes which characterize the object of the attitude. Some attitudes are related to very specific objects, e.g. people who sneeze on buses; others relate to much broader concepts which subsume a whole range of different attributes, e.g. war.

For the meaning of 'criterial attributes': see Unit 7, section 3.3.1

16

Intensity   The strength of feeling about the object. This tends to relate to valence (i.e. extremes of positive and negative feeling are usually associated with greater intensity) but need not necessarily do so. For example, it would be possible to have weak but positive feelings about something.

Stability   The degree to which an attitude is resistant to change.

Centrality   The degree to which an attitude is part of the individual's self-concept and to which he feels it reflects his identity.

Salience   The degree to which an attitude occupies a person's awareness, ranging from total preoccupation to complete absence.

Interrelatedness   The degree to which an attitude is interrelated with other attitudes (the consequences of interrelatedness are explored in detail in section 8).

Behavioural expression   The degree to which an attitude is acted upon.

Verifiability   The degree to which an attitude's cognitive aspects can be checked against evidence. Religious attitudes often have cognitive aspects (e.g. assertions about the nature of an after-life) which are impossible to subject to direct test.

Note that these dimensions are not necessarily 'independent' but are likely to co-vary. For example, an attitude which is central is also likely to be multiplex, stable and fairly salient. Note also that the more multiplex and broad an attitude, the more likely it is that the person holding the attitude may feel *ambivalent* (i.e. have both positive and negative feelings) towards the attitude object.

Look back over the dimensions you thought up and see how far they are the same or similar to those listed.

2.2   ATTITUDES AND BEHAVIOUR

An attitude is a hypothetical construct. We cannot therefore measure it or its dimensions directly. We can measure only its 'operational expression', i.e. the observable phenomena it gives rise to; in other words, what an individual does or says.

can only measure its operational expression ..

To measure the direct *behavioural* expression of an attitude (i.e. what a person *does* in relation to the attitude object) poses substantial problems. Such behavioural expression is likely to be elicited only by very specific situations – and these may occur only on rare occasions, if at all. Observation would be difficult and time consuming. Even if we succeeded in observing relevant behaviour, such data would be likely to have limited value as an index of the individual's attitude as measured by other means such as verbal statements.

Can you suggest reasons why this should be so?

Observer bias   As we saw in Unit 7, perception, particularly person perception, is a highly subjective affair and what is seen depends as much on the perceiver as what or who is observed. Variations would be likely to occur even between two observers viewing the same situation. However, it might be possible to achieve some degree of reliability by using a form of category analysis as demonstrated in the television programme in Block 3 on the 'Analysis of Interaction'.

Different situations not comparable   Secondly, even if we succeeded in devising some effective category analysis system, data taken from different real life situations would not be comparable .There would be very many uncontrolled variables differing in the two situations which could affect the result, such as the social roles adopted by the participants at the time, the length of their interaction etc.

Observer effect   A third problem is that if the subject is aware of being observed, and it would probably be difficult to avoid this, his behaviour may be inhibited or modified so that it is no longer representative of his normal pattern. (Similar problems arise in substantially different. IQ scores are another example of an interval scale. They indicate how one person performs on an intelligence test in comparison with others or with the average level for the general population which is arbitrarily defined as an IQ of 100. You can determine whether one IQ is higher than another and to some extent how far apart they are, but it makes no sense to describe a person with an IQ of 140 as twice as intelligent as a person with an IQ of 70. Multiplication and division cannot be applied to interval scales.

A *ratio scale* is the most powerful form of measurement. It indicates the order of and the interval between items and also has a true zero. Height and weight are examples of ratio scales. Any arithmetical operation, multiplication, division, addition and subtraction can be used with numbers on a scale of this type.

Now look or think back to section 2.3 where the construction of Thurstone and Likert scales was described. What kind of measurement do you consider scores on these attitude scales to be?

The careful attempts made to discard irrelevant, ambiguous and inconsistent items ensure that both types of scale achieve at least the level of *ordinal* measurement. They aspire to *interval* status but it is doubtful whether they fully succeed. For a Likert scale to be a good interval measure, we would need to make the questionable assumption that the degrees of difference between each of the seven response categories (Strongly Agree to Strongly Disagree) are always constant and the same. In fact, when comparing total scores, we cannot be sure that the units of the scale are equivalent at different points along it. We cannot necessarily assume, for example, that an increase from a score of 50 to one of 55 represents an equivalent degree of attitude change as an increase from a score of 30 to one of 35.

The Thurstone method of equal-appearing intervals is probably more effective in this respect. An attempt at ensuring an interval scale is made by asking the judges to sort the statements into eleven categories, *equally spaced* in terms of the degrees of positivity or negativity they represent. The problem is that the judges' own attitudes may, to some extent, influence this process. Although the ordering of statements tends to remain relatively constant from one group of judges to another, there is some evidence that which statements are adjudged as neutral and the amount of difference attributed between them varies depending on the judges used.

Other construction techniques, more complex than those described here, have been developed which can lay stronger claim to produce an effective interval scale (e.g. Coombs 1964, Thurstone's method of paired comparisons, 1927). No attitude scale, however, is a *ratio* measure. There is no true zero. They usually indicate only the positivity or negativity of a person's attitude relative to that of others.[1] An attitude score of sixty does not represent an attitude twice as favourable as that represented by a score of thirty.

2.6 THE ATTITUDES THAT SCALES MEASURE

If you want to get some idea of the enormous variety of attitude scales available, look at *Scales for the measurement of attitudes* by Shaw and Wright (1967) though note that this is *not* required reading. Their list of 176 scales is a small sample of those which have been constructed. Examples of attitudes for which scales have been devised are:

attitudes towards the Church, war, divorce, patriotism, capital punishment, birth control, vivisection, death, the police, probation officers, disabled people, intensive competition in team games, the use of fear as a means of controlling the behaviour of children, Sunday observance, and mental hospitals; ethnocentric, radical/conservative, intolerant/tolerant, authoritarian, tough/tender-minded and humanitarian attitudes.

[1] *The semantic differential is possibly an exception here in that 0 on any scale may be presumed to indicate absence of both positive and negative feelings.*

atomic physics. Energy transmitted by an electron microscope used to observe a particle may also serve to move the particle itself, thus affecting what is observed – the so called Heisenberg uncertainty principle.) For an observer to remain undetected in the kinds of situation he would need to record, would not only be likely to impose insuperable difficulties, but ethical problems as well.

Possible discrepancy between overt behaviour and attitude   A number of studies have demonstrated that there may be little relationship between the verbal expression of an individual's attitude and his overt behaviour towards the object of the attitude. In a classic study (La Pière 1934) a white American sociologist travelled, with a smartly dressed, young Chinese couple who spoke fluent English, several thousand miles across the USA. In the course of the journey they stayed or ate at over 200 hotels and restaurants. Surprised to be refused service only once in view of survey data which had suggested the likelihood of greater racial discrimination, he sent a letter to each of the 250 places which had received them asking whether they would be prepared to serve Chinese (and, in some cases, mentioning other ethnic groups as well). Of the 128 replies he received, over ninety per cent were negative. Just in case this was a result of the proprietors' experience of La Pière and his friends earlier in the year, he sent similar questionnaires to other establishments which they had not visited. The responses were almost identical. Similar results were found in other studies (e.g. Kutner *et al.* 1952).

How would you explain the discrepancy between the proprietors' behaviour and their written reply?

Possible reasons might be:

Proprietors' interpretation of La Pière's enquiry   A query of this kind may well have been an unusual event. They possibly feared a positive reply might generate a flood of foreign and minority group visitors – a very different situation from receiving two well-mannered Chinese customers.

Different cues available in the two situations   From the letter, the proprietors had only the cue of ethnic identity and could respond only in terms of their stereotype of Chinese etc. In the interpersonal situation, however, they had other cues available. The couple were Chinese, spoke well, were well dressed, polite and had expensive luggage. Even though La Pière tried to lurk in the background (to avoid observer effects!) the proprietors probably observed that they had an upper-class American as a companion.

Situational constraints   To refuse by letter would be likely to have few repercussions. Refusal in a face-to-face situation could lead to an embarrassing scene.

Competing attitudes   To confront potential customers face-to-face with a refusal to serve would be likely to be construed as a much greater act of rudeness than would a refusal by letter. Thus, to act on prejudice then would be more likely to conflict with other aspects of the proprietors' self-concept such as being a civilized person, a welcoming host etc.

Different people involved   Of course, it is possible that, whereas the proprietors may have been responsible for answering the letters, the people receiving La Pière and his friends may have been receptionists, waiters etc.

We have seen then several reasons why direct observation of natural behaviour towards an attitude object is not only difficult and time consuming but only provides a measure which, because of the influence and constraints imposed by other factors, is likely to be difficult to interpret as well. One solution might be to measure response to standard situations set up under controlled laboratory conditions. While this is a technique sometimes used, it has serious limitations such as artificiality and (usually) the need for deception. (These problems are discussed in section 3 and elsewhere in the unit.) It is not surprising, therefore, that psychologists concerned with attitude assessment tend to resort to measures based on verbal and written responses. The next section discusses some of the difficulties involved here and the techniques developed to attempt to overcome them.

2.3 ATTITUDE SCALES

Attitude scales consist of sets of statements or words relating to an attitude object or class of objects. They almost always measure *valence*. On the basis of his responses, an individual is assigned to some point along a scale representing degrees of positive to negative feelings towards the attitude object concerned.

valence

Constructing an attitude scale, however, involves more than just thinking up a set of statements reflecting positive and negative evaluations of appropriate people, institutions and issues.

Can you suggest why such a procedure alone would be unlikely to produce an effective attitude measure?

You cannot necessarily rely on the judgement of the person constructing the scale as to the degree of positivity or negativity a statement expresses; or indeed, even as to whether other people are likely to regard it as positive or as negative. First, then, we need to be sure that each item will actually discriminate between people who are high and those who are low on the attitude in question. This is not always immediately obvious. For example, in the construction of a scale to measure attitudes towards the Church, the statement 'I am interested in a church that is beautiful and that emphasizes the aesthetic role of life' had to be omitted because it failed to discriminate between people with positive attitudes and those more negative. Secondly, it is also useful if we know what degree of positivity or negativity agreement with a statement indicates.

Several techniques have been developed to construct effective scales. They tend to be lengthy and are technically complex but a description of the basic steps involved in two widely used construction methods – *Thurstone* and *Likert* scales – will give you some idea of the kind of procedures used.

Thurstone & Likert Scales

Thurstone's method of equal-appearing intervals L. Thurstone developed one of the earliest and still, perhaps, most widely used construction techniques. The basic procedure is as follows:

1 A large number of statements expressing as many variations as possible of positive and negative feeling towards the attitude object in question are collected. These may be derived from ideological or literary sources, interview data or may be thought up by the constructor.

2 A group of people are then asked to judge the positive or negative value of each statement by sorting it into one of eleven piles representing equal gradients of evaluation from very negative through neutral to very positive.

3 The piles are numbered from one to eleven and the median value assigned by the 'judges' is computed for each statement. This is the 'scale value' of that item.

The median is the middle measure, i.e. the measure half-way up counting from the bottom or half-way down counting from the top

4 Each statement is checked for the consistency of the reaction it elicited from the 'judges'. One measure of this is Q or interquartile range which shows the amount of variation in the various judgements made for any item. A statement which received consistent and highly similar ratings from the judges will consequently have a low Q score, while an ambiguous statement which is likely to be assigned to widely varying categories by different judges, would receive a high Q score.

Consistency of responses elicited by each statement may be further checked by administering them to subjects (other than the judges) who are asked this time to indicate whether or not they themselves agree with each statement. Any statement which fails to discriminate between those subjects with high and those with low total scores (i.e. based on all items) is then discarded.

5 The final scale is made up of a small number of items which elicit consistent responses and which represent as wide a range of scale values as possible. Sample items together with their scale values from Thurstone's scale measuring attitudes towards the Church are given in Table 1.

TABLE 1 SAMPLE ITEMS FROM THURSTONE'S SCALE ON ATTITUDES TOWARDS THE CHURCH

16 of the 45 items from Thurstone's scale for measuring attitudes towards the Church. The scale value of each item is indicated in brackets.

2   I feel the church services give me inspiration and help me to live up to my best during the following week.   (1.7)

3   I think the church keeps business and politics up to a higher standard than they would otherwise tend to maintain.   (2.6)

5   When I go to church I enjoy a fine ritual service with good music.   (4.0)

8   I believe in religion but I seldom go to church.   (5.4)

9   I am careless about religion and church relationships but I would not like to see my attitude become general.   (4.7)

13   The paternal and benevolent attitude of the church is quite distasteful to me.   (8.2)

17   I think the church is a parasite on society.   (11.0)

18   I feel the need for religion but do not find what I want in any one church.   (6.1)

19   I think too much money is being spent on the church for the benefit that is being derived.   (7.5)

21   I think the church is hundreds of years behind the times and cannot make a dent on modern life.   (9.5)

26   I feel the church is petty, always quarrelling over matters that have no interest and importance.   (8.6)

29   I enjoy my church because there is a spirit of friendliness there.   (3.3)

32   I believe in sincerity and goodness without any church ceremonies.   (6.7)

33   I believe the church is the greatest influence for good government and right living.   (0.4)

40   The church represents shallowness, hypocrisy and prejudice.   (10.4)

44   I believe the church is a powerful agency for promoting both individual and social righteousness.   (1.0)

Subjects given the scale are asked merely to tick the statements with which they agree.
A subject's score is the average of the scale values of all the items he has ticked.

Likert's method of summated ratings   This alternative technique was designed by Rensis Likert.

1 Statements are collected. For a Likert scale, each is formulated so that a subject can indicate, not just whether he agrees or disagrees, but the extent to which he agrees. A sample item might be:
'Laws which provide the death penalty for crimes are morally wrong.' Subjects are asked to indicate the extent to which *they themselves* agree or disagree with each statement by circling one of five categories:

STRONGLY AGREE   AGREE   NEUTRAL/DON'T KNOW   DISAGREE   STRONGLY DISAGREE

SAQ 5

How does this differ from the judges' role in the construction of a Thurstone scale?

2   Total scores are then calculated for each subject (strong agreement receiving five marks, agreement four marks etc., with scoring reversed on negative items). The discriminatory usefulness of each individual item is then checked by correlating subjects' scores on that item with their total score. This process is known as *item analysis*. Statements with the highest correlations are measuring most effectively what the rest of the items collectively are measuring and so are included in the final scale. One value of this procedure is that each statement is evaluated not by its content but by the effectiveness with which it measures.

The form in which the Likert items were expressed may have aroused memories of the semantic differential procedure which was described in Unit 7 as a measure of the connotative values of concepts. The *evaluative* scales of the semantic differential represent, in fact, a form of attitude scale. Osgood and his associates found that subjects' responses on attitude scales towards, for example, the Church, capital punishment and negroes, were highly similar to their responses on five bipolar, semantic differential scales, *favourable-unfavourable*, *valuable-worthless*, *pleasant-unpleasant*, *clean-dirty* and *good-bad* (Osgood *et al.* 1957). Yet another and not dissimilar form of attitude measure is a *checklist* like the Wilson-Patterson Conservatism Scale. This is given in full in Table 2 on page 22 and you might like to try it. Scoring instructions and further details are given in the Appendix.

The semantic differential is described in Unit 7, section 3.3.2 and the Appendix.

2.4   THE RELIABILITY AND VALIDITY OF SCALES

Two important considerations of any kind of measurement procedure are *reliability* – the extent to which it provides a consistent measure, and *validity* – the extent to which it is measuring what it is intended to. A well constructed attitude scale will certainly provide data on reliability and probably some information on validity, though assessing this is a difficult operation.

Validity and reliability are usually expressed in terms of a *correlation coefficient*. This is an index of the degree of correlation or relationship between two variables. A completely positive correlation is where two sets of scores given by a group of subjects show exactly the same order and relationships, the person who is top in one set being top in the other. An example of an inverse or negative correlation, on the other hand, is the amount of sand in two halves of an egg timer: where it is high in one it is low in the other and *vice versa*. There are statistical tests which can be applied to two sets of data to yield correlation coefficients. A completely negative relationship is expressed as -1, a random relationship as 0 and a completely positive relationship as $+1$. Degrees of correlation are indicated by numbers in between 0 and -1, 0 and $+1$. So a coefficient of $+.5$ would indicate a medium positive correlation. It would be the kind of correlation you would expect, for example, between the scores of the same class of children in English and in French. The two sets of scores yielded by the Crozier and Pincus experiment described in Figure 1 on page 14 correlate together to the extent of $+.98$ which is very high indeed.

One method of assessing *reliability* is to administer the scale, retest the same subjects a little later with the same scale and then correlate the two sets of scores (the *test/retest* method). If a scale is providing a consistent measure, the correlation should be very high. The problem with this method, however, is that there could be a genuine fluctuation in the attitudes of the subjects between the two administrations. This would result in a lowering of the correlation which was not due to inconsistency in the scale itself. Alternative methods which avoid this difficulty are the *split-half* method where the total scores of a group of subjects on half the items are correlated

TABLE 2 CONSERVATISM SCALE

Which of the Following do you Favour or Believe in?
(Circle 'Yes' or 'No'. If absolutely uncertain, circle '?'. There are no right or wrong answers; do not discuss; just give your first reaction. Answer all items)

1 death penalty	Yes	?	No	26 computer music	Yes	?	No
2 evolution theory	Yes	?	No	27 chastity	Yes	?	No
3 school uniforms	Yes	?	No	28 fluoridation	Yes	?	No
4 striptease shows	Yes	?	No	29 royalty	Yes	?	No
5 Sabbath observance	Yes	?	No	30 women judges	Yes	?	No
6 beatniks	Yes	?	No	31 conventional clothing	Yes	?	No
7 patriotism	Yes	?	No	32 teenage drivers	Yes	?	No
8 modern art	Yes	?	No	33 apartheid	Yes	?	No
9 self-denial	Yes	?	No	34 nudist camps	Yes	?	No
10 working mothers	Yes	?	No	35 church authority	Yes	?	No
11 horoscopes	Yes	?	No	36 disarmament	Yes	?	No
12 birth control	Yes	?	No	37 censorship	Yes	?	No
13 military drill	Yes	?	No	38 white lies	Yes	?	No
14 co-education	Yes	?	No	39 birching	Yes	?	No
15 Divine law	Yes	?	No	40 mixed marriage	Yes	?	No
16 socialism	Yes	?	No	41 strict rules	Yes	?	No
17 white superiority	Yes	?	No	42 jazz	Yes	?	No
18 cousin marriage	Yes	?	No	43 straitjackets	Yes	?	No
19 moral training	Yes	?	No	44 casual living	Yes	?	No
20 suicide	Yes	?	No	45 learning Latin	Yes	?	No
21 chaperones	Yes	?	No	46 divorce	Yes	?	No
22 legalized abortion	Yes	?	No	47 inborn conscience	Yes	?	No
23 empire-building	Yes	?	No	48 coloured immigration	Yes	?	No
24 student pranks	Yes	?	No	49 Bible truth	Yes	?	No
25 licensing laws	Yes	?	No	50 pyjama parties	Yes	?	No

Source: Wilson and Patterson (1968)

with their totals on the other half, and the *alternate forms* method where subjects' scores on two versions of the same scale are correlated. To be accepted as reliable, an attitude scale should have a reliability coefficient of at least + .8. The Wilson-Patterson Conservatism Scale has a reliability coefficient, based on the split-half method with 244 subjects, of + .94.

The *validity* of many attitude scales is, to some extent, built in with their content. Their statements will be about a particular kind of attitude object so that, presumably, is the attitude they are measuring. Some further attempt, however, is usually made to assess validity. One method is to see how well the scale distinguishes between groups of people who are known to hold either strongly positive or strongly negative attitudes of the kind being measured. We would expect atheists, for example, to score significantly lower than regular church attenders on a scale measuring attitudes towards the Church. So Wilson and Patterson applied their Conservatism Scale to Socialist and Conservative student political groups. The results given in Figure 2 show that the scale distinguished clearly between the two groups in that there was little overlap between their two sets of scores. This *known groups* method cannot guarantee a scale's validity for it does not tell us whether the scale would be equally good in distinguishing among those with more moderate attitudes. Nor is it always possible to find for many attitudes two groups who can be assumed to have strongly negative and positive attitudes respectively. Another method of validating a scale is to correlate subjects' scores on it with their response on another scale measuring a similar attitude. However, this depends on an appropriate comparison measure being in existence.

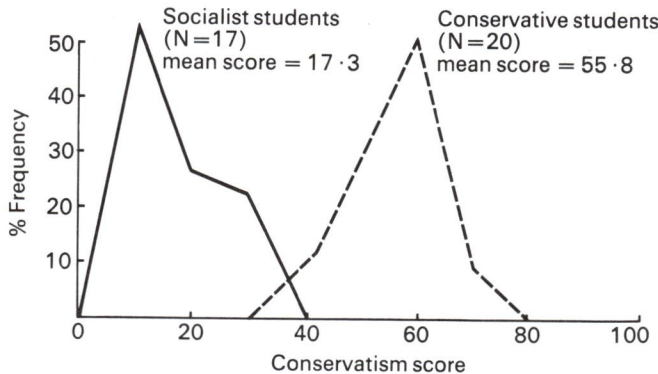

Figure 2 Distribution of conservatism scores for two 'known' groups

Source: Wilson and Patterson (1968)

Note that validity presupposes reliability. Unless a scale is a consistent and reliable measure, it cannot be measuring *anything* effectively. Although they are not entirely satisfactory, it is difficult to find more effective means of ascertaining validity. Knowing that a scale can consistently and effectively distinguish between people who can be assumed to have positive or negative attitudes and that the scores yielded by the scale correlate with scores of a similar kind, is not a bad beginning. The important implication of this section is that before you can assess the effectiveness of any attitude scale, you need information as to the method by which it was constructed, its reliability and, if possible, its validity.

2.5 LEVELS OF MEASUREMENT

Attitude scales are designed to *measure* attitudes. Measurement is 'the assignment of numerals to objects or events according to a rule or set of rules' (Shaw and Wright 1967). Not all kinds of measurement are equally powerful. S.S. Stevens has usefully distinguished four types (Stevens 1951).

A *nominal scale* uses numbers merely to name or identify a person or object, as with telephone numbers or numbers on football jerseys.

An *ordinal scale* indicates rank order, that is to say, first, second, etc. It tells us the order in which each item appears but no more. We do not know, for example, how far apart any item is from another. Note that arithmetical procedures such as addition, subtraction, multiplication and division cannot properly be used with nominal and ordinal scales.

An *interval scale* provides information about not only the order of items, but also the distance between them. Temperature is an example of an interval scale. From their temperatures we know not only that one place is colder than another but by how much. Note, however, that temperature scales do not have a *true* zero. Zero does not indicate a state of 'no temperature'; it is merely allocated to an arbitrary point. In the case of the centigrade scale, for example, this is the melting point of ice. Had the melting point of some other substance been selected, zero point might well have been

23

Note that these attitudes vary considerably in terms of the *breadth* or degree of specificity of their objects. These may be relatively specific institutions, kinds of people or issues, such as disabled people, divorce and Sunday observance etc., or they may be more complex concepts containing a variety of components and attributes. 'Patriotism', for example, might include as component concepts 'my country', its government, typical ways of life, physical characteristics, cultural and artistic traditions and history.

Breadth was discussed in section 2.1

As will be discussed in section 7 on personality and attitudes and in section 8 on the organization of attitudes, many attitudes co-vary. A person who is prejudiced against hippies is quite likely to be prejudiced against other minority groups and to be patriotic as well. Thus the Ethnocentric Scale which is described in section 6, includes items which reflect attitudes of all these kinds. Some scales then are of a 'higher order' type and measure attitude clusters rather than attitudes related to specific kinds of people, object and issue.

2.7 THE DIMENSIONS THAT SCALES MEASURE

Look back over sections 2.1 and 2.3 and decide for yourself what dimensions of attitudes are being measured by attitude scales.

The attitude scales described measure *valence*. Techniques have also been devised for assessing *multiplexity*. In one method, subjects are required to comment on statements of a vague and general kind related to the attitude in question. Responses are scored in terms of the degree to which they refine and explore the implications and alternative meanings of each statement. Merely paraphrasing a statement or commenting irrelevantly would score no marks.

Although *stability* is not measured directly by scales, difference in scores yielded by the same scale administered both before and after an attempt to modify the attitude concerned would provide some index of this dimension. Scales do not measure *salience*. One might anticipate that a person for whom an attitude was not salient would produce a neutral score on a scale measuring that attitude. However, it is not possible to distinguish such cases from other middle range scores which reflect a salient and genuinely neutral attitude. So it is possible to obtain the same score from one person who has considerable interest in the attitude in question and from another who has never thought about the issue before. Other dimensions noted in section 2.1, *intensity*, *centrality*, *interrelatedness* and *behavioural expression* are also not measurable by attitude scales currently available. *Breadth and verifiability* are characteristics of the attitude object rather than the attitude held.

Finally, it is worth noting that it is possible to get a valid and reliable measure of the strength of a *belief* or the cognitive aspect of an attitude by asking subjects to evaluate their belief on a series of bipolar probabilistic scales such as *probable/improbable*, *likely/unlikely*, *possible/impossible*, etc.

2.8 SUMMARY

Section 1 attempted to clarify what attitudes are. We saw that, although we assume it to have some mental and neural basis, an attitude is essentially a hypothetical construct. Section 2 has looked at the way psychologists have tried to 'operationalize' attitudes by devising scales to measure their observable manifestations. Do note, in this context, that when the attitudes of a population or large group of people are being assessed, scales are usually administered for practical or economic reasons to only a sample of the total group. In such a case, it is necessary to ensure that the sample is *representative* and does not have a 'built-in bias' so that the results can be generalized validly to the rest of the population. Some of the pitfalls to be avoided are discussed in the first chapter of the set book by Darrell Huff, *How to lie with statistics* (1973 pp 13–36).

Chapter 1 of Huff's book was set as required reading for Unit 2

The rest of the unit now goes on to consider what research studies have demonstrated and revealed about the nature of attitudes.

SAQ 6

'I work for a marvellous firm'. What dimension of the speaker's attitude towards his or her employers can you infer from this statement?

SAQ 7

Is an attitude scale with a reliability coefficient of $+ .45$ likely to be a good attitude measure?

SAQ 8

'Put a mark against those statements you agree with'. Does this instruction indicate a Thurstone or a Likert scale?

SAQ 9

What is meant by *multiplexity*?

SAQ 10

Briefly distinguish between the *stability* and *centrality* of an attitude.

SAQ 11

Why is it necessary to carry out an *item analysis* in constructing a Likert scale?

SAQ 12

Is the cost of bread likely to co-vary with the cost of flour?

3 THE STABILITY OF ATTITUDES

Krech and Crutchfield, you will remember from section 1.3, define an attitude as 'an *enduring* organization of motivational, emotional, perceptual and cognitive processes' (my italics). You will almost certainly be able to supply from your own experience numerous examples of the resistance of central attitudes and beliefs to change. It takes a great deal to undermine a party worker's belief in the political views he supports, to change the views of an ardent supporter of capital punishment, opponent of birth control or divorce or of a person who is either for or against immigration. Evidence that runs counter to strongly held views tends to be disputed and its source or interpretation questioned. Rational argument is likely to be discounted or ignored. We begin this section with an account of a study which illustrates the extraordinary resistance of beliefs to change even in the face of disconfirmatory evidence and go on to consider the means by which we manage to keep our beliefs and attitudes intact.

3.1 LABORATORY AND NATURAL EXPERIMENTS

Section 1 of Unit 18 described some of the methods used in the study of social behaviour. The advantage of the *laboratory experiment* is that it gives the experimenter some control over the situation. He can reduce or allow for the influence of extraneous factors and so increase the probability that the results he observes are a direct consequence of the variables he has manipulated. A disadvantage, however, is that the situation is artificial and it is often difficult to know how far results observed under laboratory conditions are generalizable to real life situations. It may be impossible to

Test artificial

26

reproduce in the laboratory the essential characteristics of the natural situation and subjects may give the response they think the experimenter wants rather than reacting spontaneously to the stimulus provided (anyone interested in this problem should see Orne 1962).

A method of investigation which is sometimes called the *natural experiment* circumvents these difficulties. The essence of this procedure is that the investigators take advantage of some event which is known will occur and change the normal or predicted course of events. This serves as a naturally occurring independent variable which requires no manipulation by the investigator. He merely observes the effect produced by the event. Examples of situations with potential for a study of this kind might be a change in the law, a confrontation between two opposing groups or the integration of black pupils into a previously all-white school. (Note that in the *field* experiment which is also carried out in a real life setting, the experimenter, in contrast, *manipulates* some aspect of the situation.)

Natural — "real" site …

Field experiments and the meaning of 'independent variable' are discussed briefly in Unit 18, section 1

Provided the experimenter can avoid 'observer effects' by remaining unobtrusive and unobserved, the natural experiment has the advantage of allowing observation of spontaneous reactions to a genuine situation.

Can you see what *disadvantages* natural experiments have in contrast to laboratory experiments?

In natural experiments detail and precision in the recording of data, and the control of extraneous factors are usually much reduced. Naturally occurring events which are relevant to the investigator's research interests may be few and far between. There may also be ethical difficulties. People observed without their knowledge may, perhaps rightfully, regard this as an intrusion of their privacy.

The investigation described below is of the natural experiment type.

3.2 THE RESILIENCE OF BELIEF

A few years ago, an American newspaper the *Lake City Herald*, carried a report about a Mrs Marian Keech. Mrs Keech claimed to have received messages from 'superior beings' from outer space who communicated to her by means of 'automatic writing'. Mrs Keech would sit with pen in hand and with an empty pad in front of her. Eventually her hand would begin to write without her conscious involvement as if moved by some outside agency. In this way, the beings told her that they came from the planet Clarion and that, in the course of their visits in flying saucers, they had noticed faults in the Earth's crust which they realized would inevitably lead to a flood which would engulf most of the western side of the American continent from Seattle to Chile. The Clarionians were even so good as to predict the exact date on which this flood would occur – 21 December.

Mrs. Marian Keech …

Mrs Keech had made no attempt to court publicity. The newspaper report which appeared in September was the result of a press release by Dr Thomas Armstrong, a physician from a nearby town who was a regular attender at meetings held by Mrs Keech and a few friends who believed in the messages she had begun receiving nine months earlier. The story attracted the attention of three social psychologists, Leon Festinger, Henry Riecken and Stanley Schachter who were particularly interested in the effect of disconfirmation on beliefs. They had little doubt that Mrs Keech's predictions would not be fulfilled. By posing as committed believers and without revealing their true purpose, the three investigators, together with a few graduate students, managed to infiltrate Mrs Keech's group. One of the investigators' problems was to maintain their pose while remaining as neutral as possible in order to avoid affecting the course of events in any way. As 21 December approached, the small band of believers held numerous meetings. Some gave up their jobs and others gave away their possessions. Dr Armstrong was dismissed from his College Health Service post as a result of rumours about his involvement with this group, an event which was given considerable space by local newspapers. In spite of her own reserve, therefore, Mrs Keech's views not only received support from her fellow believers but also attracted widespread publicity.

On the morning of 20 December, Mrs Keech received her final instructions. A flying saucer would arrive at midnight to take the believers to safety in outer space. All metal was to be removed from pockets and clothing. That evening, fifteen people gathered in Mrs Keech's living room. Several of the investigators were present in addition to Mrs Keech's group. Her 'patient but sceptical husband' had retired to bed. Passwords for boarding the flying saucer were rehearsed, coins, keys, watches and even the tinfoil from chewing gum packets were removed.

At 11.15 p.m. Mrs Keech received a message for the group to get their overcoats and to stand by. At 11.35 one of the psychologists suddenly announced that he had forgotten about the metal zip of his trousers. It was hurriedly slashed out with a razor blade by a near panic-stricken Dr Armstrong and the gap sewn up with a few rough stitches.

Tension in the last few minutes before midnight ran high. One of the two clocks in the room reached 12 o'clock. A member pointed out that it was fast. A few minutes later the second clock chimed twelve. More minutes passed. No one spoke. One member moved across to lie down on a sofa. The rest sat still. At 12.30 a.m. there was a knock at the door which, to the group's irritation, proved to be only some boys playing a joke.

Eventually, disillusion and despair crept in. The believers desperately re-examined earlier messages, anxiously searching for some explanation. Just after 4 a.m. Mrs Keech broke down and cried.

Then, at 4.45 a.m., Mrs Keech announced that she had received a message. The group by their belief and behaviour had 'spread so much light' that God had called off the flood and saved the world. By such elegant reinterpretation of the situation, the beliefs of Mrs Keech and her group could remain intact in the face of stark disconfirmation.

3.3 STABILITY MAINTAINED BY CONSENSUS

cognitive Dissonance

The reason Festinger and his colleagues joined the group was to test out the predictions of his theory of *cognitive dissonance* as to the way the discomfort which had been produced by disconfirmation would be resolved. This theory is discussed in detail in section 8. The Keech study serves here to demonstrate the high resistance of central beliefs to change, and how stability is achieved by the capacity of beliefs and attitudes to filter and to influence the way events are perceived.

Attitudes and beliefs constitute evaluations and/or assertions about events or the way events are causally interrelated. It is not possible to verify evaluations as to what is good and bad by recourse to direct evidence. The most one can hope to do is to demonstrate how an attitude is instrumental in achieving desired goals. This, like many assertions of belief, will depend on the way causal relationships are interpreted; such relationships are often difficult to establish with any certainty. So there is sufficient latitude for Mrs Keech to provide a 'causal explanation' of why the flood did not occur which was quite consistent with her belief.

The influence of consensus on attitudes and beliefs is discussed in section 4

supporters; followers; believers ...

'Verification' of attitudes and beliefs tend to come as frequently from consensus as from evidence. As Unit 19 and section 1.3 of Unit 7 pointed out, much of the way that we perceive reality and the way we construe and evaluate our social world is defined by the judgements and views of others. Immediately after Mrs Keech had formulated her solution she began, for the first time, actively to seek converts. Her solution had given the group a means of keeping their shaken beliefs intact but they needed support. A most potent form of support is that others believe as we do.

In normal circumstances, we may not need actually to convert others to our way of thinking. Associating with those who share similar views and actively avoiding the

28

presentation of opposing ideas may provide quite sufficient impression of consensus for us to maintain our beliefs and attitudes intact. Political broadcasts by the other party can be switched off. We need go only to meetings which support the views we already hold.

3.4 THE INFLUENCE OF ATTITUDES ON PERCEPTION

Section 5 of Unit 7 has already discussed the active nature of perception. We select from the many cues that confront us the few that our limited channel capacity can assimilate. The way we categorize these depends on our expectations, personality, motivation and attitudes. Therefore, even when we are exposed, by choice or chance, to evidence or arguments opposing our views, they may well have little impact. Numerous experiments have demonstrated the extent to which people perceive events in accordance with their beliefs and attitudes. As you will remember from Unit 7, Allport found that many prejudiced subjects, required to recall from memory a picture which included a white man holding a razor, transposed the razor to the hand of the black man he was talking to. Hastorf and Cantril (1954) in the study described below, found a similar effect.

A football match between two American universities, Princeton and Dartmouth, had aroused considerable controversy. Reports about the game indicated that, while both sides had clearly engaged in rough play, Dartmouth had been particularly aggressive. Students from both universities were shown a film of the match and asked to note the number of fouls committed by each team. The results are shown in Table 3.

TABLE 3

	Number in group	Average number of fouls seen as committed by	
		Dartmouth team	Princeton team
Dartmouth students	48	4.3	4.4
Princeton students	49	9.8	4.2

Dartmouth students saw both sides as committing approximately the same number of fouls. Princeton students, however, saw the Dartmouth team committing twice as many fouls as their own side. Thus the two groups interpreted the game in a significantly different way. The investigators concluded that the 'game' actually was many different games and that each version of the events that transpired was just as 'real' to a particular person as other versions were to other people. They argue that it is not so much a question of attitudes *affecting* perception of something 'out there' but that the attribution of meaning and significance is an intrinsic part of the perceptual process. From the complex of events that constitutes a game we tend to see only that which has meaning and significance for us. They also point out that 'it is inaccurate and misleading to say that different people have different "attitudes" concerning the same "thing". For the "thing" simply is *not* the same for different people whether the "thing" is a football game, a Presidential candidate, Communism, or spinach.' In other words people with different attitudes actually *experience* the object of the attitude differently.

Hastorf and Cantril's results are hardly new to any of you who spend Saturday afternoon on the terraces cheering on your local team in between roaring at the ref. to buy a new pair of spectacles! You may wonder whether the investigation was worth the time and effort involved. As has been pointed out previously, much of social science involves testing out commonsense assumptions. Sometimes, like here, they work out as expected. On other occasions, they don't, as Block 1 in particular has illustrated. One advantage of a controlled study is that we can apply statistical techniques to the careful observations made and, with their help, distinguish between results which are likely to represent genuine effects and those which could have been due merely to chance. With a small sample of observations we may get what appears to be a consistent effect which is, in fact, due to chance alone and not representative of results which we would have obtained had we taken a larger sample. Toss a penny four times and it is not that unlikely that it will come up heads every time, even though, if you toss it enough times, you will nevertheless (provided it is unbiased) obtain a more or less equal distribution of heads and tails. A measure of statistical significance is based on the number, size and consistency of the effects observed and indicates the likelihood of the result arising through chance and, therefore, the reliance we can place on it. The difference between the 4.3 fouls which Dartmouth students, on average, saw their own team as committing and the 9.8 attributed to the same team by Princeton students is significant at the .01 level. This means that there is less than one chance in one hundred of such a difference occurring as a result of chance alone. Significance levels higher than .05, i.e. odds of more than 5 in 100 or 1 in 20 that the result could be due to chance, are generally not considered as an acceptable result, though this criterion of significance is, of course, arbitrary and merely a convention.

Statistical significance is discussed in Huff, Chapter 3

3.5 EXPERIMENTS ON ATTITUDES AND THE ASSIMILATION OF INFORMATION

I would like to conclude section 3 by discussing two experiments which demonstrate that the relationship between attitudes and the way information is assimilated operates in a complex way, and also highlight a few of the problems of designing experiments and of drawing inferences from experimental results.

In an experiment by Jones and Aneshansel (1956), white undergraduate students at Duke University in the southern states of the USA were allocated to two groups by means of a specially constructed Likert type attitude scale according to whether or not they favoured the segregation of blacks and whites. Subjects from both groups were then asked to learn eleven statements arguing *against* segregation (e.g. 'the Negro points up the greatest disparity between the theory and practice of democracy'). Each subject was required to read the set of statements aloud and then attempt to recall as many of them, or the basic ideas underlying them, as possible. This procedure was repeated five times. A subject's score was represented by his recall performance over these five 'trials'. The results showed that on every trial the group of students who were opposed to segregation recalled more of the anti-segregation statements than did subjects favouring segregation.

SAQ 13

Can we conclude, therefore, that material which is congruent or in line with a person's attitudes is more effectively assimilated? If you think we cannot conclude this, on the evidence given, briefly note down why not.

Although the anti-segregation students score better than the pro-segregation students on every trial, the differences, in fact, are not large enough to be significant at the .05 level. Thus there is sufficient possibility that the differences, although consistent within this sample of subjects, may be due merely to chance.

Note that, even if they were significant, we cannot necessarily draw the conclusion suggested above. The subjects were not assigned *randomly* to the two groups but according to whether they favoured or were opposed to segregation. It is quite possible, if not likely, that the anti-segregation subjects were more familiar with the anti-segregation arguments given. As suggested earlier, people tend to seek out ideas and evidence congruent with their attitudes and avoid opposite views. Many experiments have demonstrated that familiar material is more easily recalled than unfamiliar.

30

The results found, then, could be due merely to differential familiarity with the statements given rather than being due to differences in attitudes *per se*. Also, as we shall see in section 6 on personality and attitudes, there is evidence that attitudes are related to the level of a person's intelligence and educational achievement. So another possibility might be that the difference observed is due to students who favour segregation being less efficient at remembering things. For all these reasons, we cannot conclude that the results described so far necessarily indicate that material congruent with attitudes is more effectively assimilable. It may be, but we cannot be sure on the basis of these results alone.

An experimenter must be alert to other ways in which it is possible to explain the results he obtains. Though this is not always easy, an experiment should be designed ideally to rule out all, or as many as possible, alternative explanations. Jones and Aneshansel tried to assess the possibility of differences in intelligence or in reading and retention skill between the two groups influencing the results. They found that 'antis' did obtain significantly higher scores on an intelligence test though there were no differences in measures of reading skill between the two groups. The next and key phase of their experiment, however, produced results which would seem to rule out the possibility of the results they obtained being a function of either differential ability or differences in familiarity with the arguments. Another group of 'antis' and another groups of 'pros' were asked to learn the eleven anti-segregation statements, but they were told that this was merely a prelude to a further task in which they would be asked to provide counter-arguments (i.e. arguments against) to statements which favoured segregation. It was pointed out that the initial learning of anti-segregation arguments was likely to be of some considerable help to them in the later task. In other words, learning the anti-segregation statements *now had some value* for pro-segregation subjects. Under these conditions, the pro-segregation students actually learned the anti-segregation arguments, even though they were opposed to their own views, more effectively than the anti-segregation students, the differences being significant at the .01 level. Jones and Aneshansel argue that the pattern of results indicates that where learning is congruent with the achievement of valued ends then it will be performed more effectively. In the first part of the experiment, the statements were learned more effectively by those subjects for whom they were co-valuent (i.e. in line with subjects' own views) than by those for whom they were contra-valuent (i.e. opposed to their own views). In the second phase, however, the 'pros' had a reason to learn the contra-valuent statements because they could expect that this would equip them to perform more successfully on the task which they were told they would be required to do later. Under these rather unusual circumstances, learning contra-valuent material becomes instrumental in achieving a valued end. One might expect, however, that, if the investigators' explanation was correct, then there would be *no* difference in the performances of the two groups under these conditions, for *both* groups would anticipate that learning the arguments would be useful to them later. Jones and Aneshansel suggest that the curious result found that 'antis' actually performed better than the 'pros' was due to the former group assuming that, as they were already familiar with the arguments, there was less need to learn them in order to ensure effective performance in the later task.

For all their ingenuity and the complexity of their design, the investigators ended up with a main conclusion which, while plausible, was still not demonstrated entirely satisfactorily by their results, for you may remember that the differences obtained in the first phase of the experiment were not statistically significant. This all goes to show not only some of the trials and tribulations of research, but that the results listed in text books are not obtained as easily as sometimes may appear!

In a later experiment with Kohler, Jones was able to obtain further results which he considered confirmed his earlier interpretation (Jones and Kohler 1958). Using a similar procedure, they compared recall scores for a list of twelve statements by subjects allocated to one of three groups, for segregation, against segregation or neutral. The twelve statements consisted of six which argued for segregation and six

31

which argued against. Three statements of each set of six were plausible and three were implausible. Examples of each type of statement are given below:

Plausible pro-segregation 'Southerners will have to pay the price of lower scholastic standards if they yield to the pressures to integrate their schools.'

Implausible pro-segregation 'If Negroes and whites were meant to live together, they never would have been separated at the beginning of history.'

Plausible anti-segregation 'The present inferior condition of the Negro is the result of long and effective suppression by the Southern whites.'

Implausible anti-segregation 'The real reason why most Southern whites oppose integration is their realization that the Negro is more capable than they are.'

The results are summarized in Figure 3.

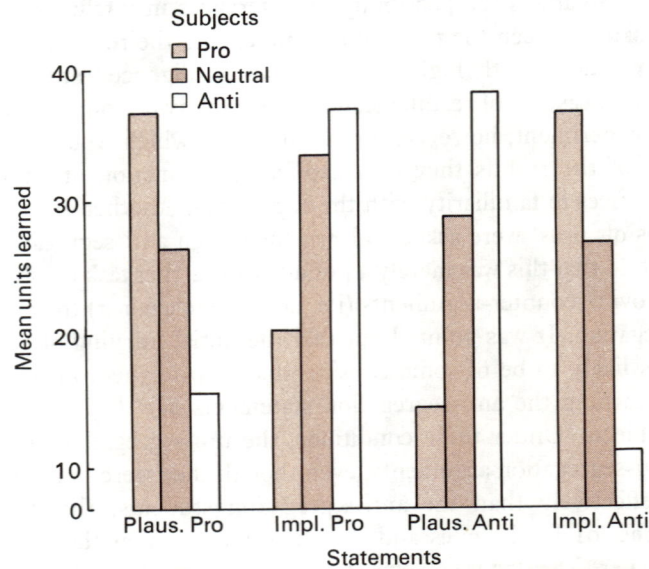

Figure 3 The relation between plausibility, direction of statement and attitude in the learning of controversial material

Source: Jones and Kohler (1958)

As can be seen, when the statements are plausible, co-valuent statements are learned significantly more effectively (i.e. pro-segregation subjects learn pro-segregation arguments better and anti-segregation subjects learn anti-segregation arguments better). When the arguments are implausible, however, contra-valuent statements are learned significantly more effectively. The recall scores of 'neutral' subjects fall in every case, as one would expect, between the 'pros' and 'antis'. Table 4 shows the significance levels of the differences between each group of subjects (pro, neutral and anti) for each type of statement (plausible, implausible).

TABLE 4 COMPARISONS BETWEEN SCORES OF SUBJECTS HOLDING DIFFERENT ATTITUDES, ON DIFFERENT TYPES OF STATEMENT

Statement Type

Pro Plausible		Pro Implausible		Anti Plausible		Anti Implausible	
Direction	P	Direction	P	Direction	P	Direction	P
P > N	.05	A > N	.50	A > N	.10	P > N	.05
N > A	.10	N > P	.01	N > P	.01	N > A	.001
P > A	.001	A > P	.01	A > P	.001	P > A	.001

Note: P, N, and A stand for pro-segregation subjects, neutral subjects and anti-segregation subjects respectively.

The P column indicates the probability of a particular result being due to chance.

Source: Jones and Kohler (1968)

32

Jones and Kohler conclude 'while the results show the learning of a controversial statement cannot be predicted solely from the direction of the argument, they still support the functionalist's basic assumption that cognitive processes operate so as to promote the constancy of attitude and belief'.

Now answer the following SAQs, all of which are based on the Jones and Kohler experiment just discussed.

SAQ 14

In the Jones and Kohler experiment, the person actually running the experiment was not told to which of the three groups the subjects had been assigned. Why was this necessary?

SAQ 15

The experimenters ensured that each of the twelve statements were of similar length. Why?

SAQ 16

How many of the twelve comparisons shown in Table 4 can be considered as significant (accepting the criterion level of .05)?

SAQ 17

Is it possible that these results could be due to differences between the learning capacity of subjects in the anti-segregation and those in the pro-segregation groups?

SAQ 18

Is it possible that the results could be due to differences between the groups in their familiarity with the arguments?

We have seen how attitudes are able to remain intact even in the face of contradictory views and evidence by means of differential, cognitive processing of co-valuent and contra-valuent material. Each of the following five sections which comprise most of the remainder of this double unit, helps, among other things, to make clearer *why* central attitudes and beliefs have such remarkable stability. The foundations of central attitudes are laid in childhood and in our basic relationships with others. The next section takes a look at *how attitudes are formed* and section 5 considers the ways in which *other people can influence* the kinds of attitudes we hold. Attitudes and beliefs give meaning and stability to our world and allow us to predict events. This and the other *functions attitudes serve* form the subject matter of section 6. The way attitudes are closely interlinked with *personality characteristics* and the different methods used to investigate this relationship are discussed in section 7. Finally, section 8 focuses on the key issue of *attitude organization*. Attitudes do not exist in isolation. They form a balanced and interlocking system. If this balance is disturbed there are often surprising effects.

4 THE FORMATION OF ATTITUDES

As we have seen, attitudes represent the ways in which we order and give meaning to our experience. They indicate how we will predict and evaluate events and sometimes how we will react. They reflect, therefore, a person's general cognitive and emotional development and, like cognitive and emotional development, their foundations will be laid in early experience and socialization.

Think back to Unit 18 and note down aspects of socialization which you consider would be particularly relevant in the formation of attitudes.

Some of our concepts are based on experience. A child learns the meaning of the concept 'hot' by abstraction from a series of experiences which have a common (and in this case probably painful) characteristic. Perhaps most of the concepts which form part of our significant attitudes and beliefs, however, are developed not on the basis of direct experience, but by contact with the beliefs and attitudes of other people. We may either adopt the opinions expressed by others or base our reactions to the object concerned on their reports as to its nature and characteristics or on our observations of their reactions to it. A child who has never been to China is nevertheless quite likely to develop from parents, teachers, television and books, some impression of what kind of place it is. The influencing sources may be various and the concepts that a child develops may not match those from any one source precisely but the point is that many, perhaps most, of his concepts and beliefs derive from those of people around him, from his social environment rather than from his direct experience.

Write down four adjectives which you think characterize Australians and four which characterize Danerians.

Different social environments may produce different stereotypes and different 'norms'. In a study of Nottingham school children, for example, it was found that working class mothers would quite often use the threat of fetching the police as a means of controlling their children's behaviour. Middle class mothers, on the other hand, presented the police as a potential source of help when lost or in need (Newson and Newson 1970). The importance of cultural mediation in the development of concepts and attitudes is illustrated by studies of stereotyping. Gilbert found an amazingly high degree of consensus in the way a group of subjects from a similar background perceived peoples of other cultures, even where the amount and kind of contact that the subjects had had with the other cultures concerned must have been highly variable and in some cases non-existent. For example, when asked to pick from a list of 84 adjectives the 5 which they considered most characteristic of Turks, 48 per cent of a large group of American subjects selected 'cruel' (Gilbert 1951). Reactions to one kind of concept are sometimes generalized to related ones. In one experiment, it was found that many subjects were quite willing to ascribe characteristics (usually unfavourable ones) to Wallonians, Pirenians and Danerians, even though these 'peoples' do not in fact exist. The adjectives which you listed in response to the question above will reflect your stereotype of Australians and also, if you responded to the invitation to characterize Danerians, whether you are, perhaps, too prone to generalize. In this

See also sections 7 and 10   instance, the trap was not too difficult to detect, so those of you who didn't generalize, don't congratulate yourselves too much – you may well do so in more subtle situations.

In Unit 7, the demonstration of the Semantic Differential technique showed how easy it was to rate almost any concept as good or bad. Evaluation is, perhaps, as much an intrinsic dimension of our world of social experience as brightness is of our visual world. The concepts and attitudes assimilated from others inevitably incorporate evaluation. Even the words a child learns as labels for concepts carry evaluative implications in their connotations. Using the term 'pig' instead of 'police' intrinsically conveys a different attitude towards the constabulary! The concepts and attitudes a child learns serve to delimit areas of significance for him. They colour his social experience and shape his reactions. To have power over what a person assimilates through social learning is a potent means of controlling his behaviour. Governments seeking to control the behaviour and attitudes of their people psychologically, therefore, place high priority on regulating education, the press, broadcasting and literature.

Which of the following concepts have you built up mostly on the basis of direct experience and which mostly on the basis of what other people have communicated to you about them?

Whisky, pain, Mars, the Communist Party, Japan, smoking marijuana, heaven, Arabs, coal miners, pornography, the Common Market.

4.2   PROCESSES OF SOCIAL LEARNING

The kind of attitudes formed will also depend on *reinforcement*, *imitation* and *identification*, processes discussed earlier in Unit 18. Positive valence is likely to develop towards objects associated with reinforcement. If Christmas and Santa Claus are always linked with the idea or actuality of feasting and presents, they will come to be evaluated in positive terms. Actual expression of attitudes may also be shaped directly by reinforcement: a boy in Northern Ireland may receive approval and admiration from peers or even parents for jeering at or stoning British soldiers, Nazi parents may have smiled indulgently as their child mocked Jews.

See also section 6 on the instrumental function of attitudes

Although, as pointed out in Unit 18, we do not know precisely how, children clearly assimilate by imitation and identification the expressed values of parents and of other people who are significant and emotionally important to them. Identification is likely to be particularly important in the development of central attitudes. It is interesting to note in this context that the best predictor so far found (though by no means infallible) of the way a person will vote is the political preference of his or her parents (Butler and Stokes 1969). Parents and significant others may sometimes also serve, especially in later childhood, as 'negative shapers', in that some adolescents may specifically adopt attitudes or positions different from those they believe their parents have.

See section 6.3 for a more detailed discussion of identification

4.3   COGNITIVE DEVELOPMENT

As you saw from discussion of Piaget's work in Unit 18, one important basis of cognitive development is *maturation*. A child goes through a series of developmental stages before attaining the power of conceptual and symbolic thought that characterizes adults. The kind of attitudes held and the basis on which they are formed will depend both on *cognitive capacity* and on the stage of cognitive development the individual or child has reached. The *multiplexity* of an attitude and the relationships between attitudes, in particular, will be a function of this. Before he has attained the level of symbolic thought, for example, a child will be less capable of perceiving inconsistency between attitudes. Piaget studied how moral attitudes and the basis on which they are made change as the child grows older. He claimed that there is a gradual shift away from what he called 'moral realism' which is characteristically found in young children. Piaget described moral realism as 'the tendency. . . . to regard duty and the value attaching to it as self-subsistent and independent of the mind, as imposing itself regardless of the circumstances in which the individual may find himself' (Piaget 1932 p 106). Moral rules are seen as absolute and wrongdoers are thought to deserve punishment just because they have broken them. Moral transgressions are judged in terms of the degree of harm done and not in terms of the intention of the wrongdoer. Older children, in contrast, are more likely to adopt a 'morality of co-operation or reciprocity'. They come to realize that moral rules are not externally imposed absolutes but are agreed principles for achieving mutually desired ends. The moral evaluations a person makes will depend on the stage of development he has reached. Vestiges of 'moral realism' underlie the judgements made by many adults. For example, a positive attitude towards corporal or even capital punishment sometimes depends on a belief in *expiatory* punishment, i.e. that people deserve to be punished just because they have 'done what they should not have done'. In Piaget's terms, a belief in expiatory punishment is part of the more immature system of moral realism. Other theorists (e.g. Kohlberg 1968), inspired by Piaget's approach, have attempted to set out in greater detail the developmental

moral realism

reciprocity

sequence of different ways in which moral judgements are made. The point to note here, however, is that the kind of attitudes a person holds and the way in which he makes moral evaluations are likely to be a function of the stage of cognitive development attained and his cognitive capacity.

This section which has considered how attitudes and beliefs are formed, helps us to understand how they can be so resilient in the face of logical contradiction and opposing argument. Attitudes and beliefs are not founded on logic. Their origins lie in early experience and social learning, hence in cognitive development and the norms, customs and beliefs of the culture and people among whom the child is reared. He comes to see the world through the concepts, attitudes and beliefs they provide. To him these beliefs and attitudes are not arbitrary, they represent to him the way things *are*. Even though intangible, a man's experience of his god is as real to him as the experience of his house. Belief that thunder is an expression of God's anger, that red-haired people have quick tempers, and that pornography is bad may be as strong as the belief that fire burns paper. To change a person's central beliefs and attitudes is to undermine an aspect of reality as perceived by him. It may also involve cutting away the props provided by the norms, customs, concepts and even language of the sub-culture in which he lives.

5 SOCIAL INFLUENCE

Their foundations may be laid in early experience but attitudes don't just stop developing after childhood. One of the most potent factors for maintaining stability and creating change is *social influence*.

5.1 CONFORMITY

Read Asch in Scientific American set text pp 29–33

A number of experiments testify to the remarkable degree to which many people will conform to the views of others. One of the classic studies is by Solomon Asch on the effects of social pressure on opinions. You will find an account of this in your set text *Papers on socialization and attitudes* (Scientific American 1974 pp 29–33). Read this now and when you have finished, test out your understanding of the extract by completing the SAQs given below. Note the Study Guide to this paper given on page 45 of the set book. You may find the Summary and Glossary provided there useful in helping you assimilate the content of the paper. The 'Essay Study Questions' there do *not* have to be answered but you may find them useful for self help or study groups.

SAQ 19

According to the chart at the top right hand corner of page 33 of *Papers in socialization and attitudes*, how many unanimous opponents are required to produce maximum conformity effects?

SAQ 20

What is the effect on subjects of the presence of one person who gives accurate responses?

SAQ 21

What happened to subjects' responses when a person who had initially given only accurate responses began to go along with the majority?

Note that Asch found from interviews with his subjects after the experiments that all those who had given way to group pressure underestimated the extent to which they had conformed. Asch points out that subjects who yielded did so in different ways and for different reasons. In a more detailed paper on the same experiments, he describes the three main categories of *yielding* subjects (those who went with the majority during one half or more of the trials):

Distortion of perception under the stress of group pressure. In this category belong a very few subjects who yield completely, but are not aware that their estimates have been displaced or distorted by the majority. These subjects report that they came to perceive the majority estimates as correct.

Distortion of judgement Most submitting subjects belong to this category. The factor of greatest importance in this group is a decision the subjects reach that their perceptions are inaccurate and that those of the majority are correct. These subjects suffer from primary doubt and lack of confidence; on this basis they feel a strong tendency to join the majority.

Distortion of action The subjects in this group do not suffer a modification of perception nor do they conclude that they are wrong. They yield because of an over-mastering need not to appear different from or inferior to others, because of an inability to tolerate the appearance of defectiveness in the eyes of the group. These subjects suppress their observations and voice the majority position with awareness of what they are doing. The results are sufficient to establish that ... yielding (is) not psychologically homogeneous, that submission to group pressure. .... can be the result of different psychological conditions. (Asch 1959 pp 178–9)

The Asch experiments reveal the remarkable degree of conformity of which many individuals are capable. On a simple perceptual task on which subjects not under pressure make fewer than one per cent mistakes, a substantial proportion were prepared to go along with the responses given by a majority of as few as three or four other people, even though these responses were contrary to the evidence of their own eyes. If conformity effects can exert such influence on judgements which, as in the Asch experiments, permit straightforward sensory verification, what is their influence on beliefs and evaluations for which this is not possible?

Another American social psychologist, Richard Crutchfield, devised a procedure which allowed conformity effects to be assessed without the cumbersome procedure of using several 'stooge' helpers for each subject. His system involved seating five subjects each at one of five booths. They were required to indicate their responses to a series of stimuli projected on the wall opposite by pressing one of a set of choice buttons. Each subject was led to believe that an array of lights on the desk in front of him indicated the responses of the other four subjects. In fact, they were completely under the experimenter's control. Close questioning after the experiments indicated that only a small proportion of the subjects had any doubt that the lights represented genuine choices made by the others.

In this way, Crutchfield examined conformity effects in many kinds of situations. In general, he found that the more ambiguous and difficult to verify the stimulus, the more conformity increased. For example, when the stimulus required the completion of a number series which was actually insoluble, he found that as many as 79 per cent of mature male subjects were prepared to go along with an arbitrary response purportedly given by all four of the other subjects. The only main exception to this general trend was where differences could be considered to be essentially a matter of taste as, for example, when a subject is asked which of two drawings he prefers. In such cases, Crutchfield found that conformity effects were negligible.

One of Crutchfield's experiments is particularly pertinent to the discussion of attitudes. He presented subjects with a series of controversial statements. Examples of two of the items are:

Do you agree or disagree with the statement: 'Free speech being a privilege rather than a right, it is proper for a society to suspend free speech whenever it feels itself threatened?

Which of the following do you feel is the most important problem facing our country today? Economic recession; educational facilities; subversive activities; mental health; crime and corruption.

Crutchfield found only 19 per cent of control subjects who had not been subjected to group pressure indicated agreement with the first statement. However, where respondents were led to believe that all four 'other subjects' agreed with it, the percentage agreeing was as high as 58 per cent. On the second item, only 12 per cent of control subjects chose 'subversive activities' as most important. However, 48 per cent of experimental subjects who thought that the rest of the group had selected that item as most important, made the same choice. So even in the relatively artificial conditions of an experimental laboratory, conformity effects on the expression of attitudes are seen to be substantial.

Crutchfield, like Asch, noted that some subjects almost always yielded to group pressure whereas others never did. He tried to find out in what ways independent subjects differed from conformers. He devised a conformity measure based on a subject's performance in the experimental situation over a large number of items.

The split-half method of assessing reliability was discussed briefly in section 2.4

This measure had a split-half reliability of more than +.8. Subjects were then assessed on a variety of traits by psychologists who had no knowledge of their conformity scores. The independents (those with low conformity scores) tended to be more intelligent (the correlation between an IQ test and the conformity score was −.51), more self-confident, more likely to show leadership ability and more free from compulsion about following rules. The yielders, on the other hand, tended to be more anxious, more conventional in values, behaviour and dress, more authoritarian and found it more difficult to tolerate uncertainty and ambiguity. They also had less self-esteem and self-insight. Crutchfield also found differences in the attitudes held by those subjects who were fathers (as many were) towards their children; conformers being more likely to be restrictive and independents permissive. Conformers also tended to paint a more idealized picture of their own parents whereas the independents were more likely to give a more 'balanced picture of praise and criticism' (Crutchfield 1955 p 254). In general these kinds of differences have been confirmed by other studies. The two kinds of subject also tend to describe themselves somewhat differently: 'Independents see themselves primarily as original, emotional and artistic; Yielders characterize themselves as obliging, optimistic, efficient, determined, patient and kind. Yielders tend to be practical-minded, somewhat physicalistic in their thinking and group oriented; Independents placed higher values on creativity, close inter-personal relations and the individual as opposed to the group' (Barron 1950 p 297). In discussing the characteristics of conformers, however, it is necessary to distinguish from habitual conformers those whose occasional conformity is based on realistic appraisal of a situation. Where there is reason to believe that others have better information or skill than oneself, it may be sensible to give more weight to their judgements than to one's own.

Social groups are not all equally effective in moulding the views of their members. A useful distinction here is that discussed in Unit 19 between *membership* and *reference* groups. The influence a group is likely to exert on an individual will correspond to the degree to which it constitutes a *reference* group for him; in other words, the extent to which he values or aspires to membership of it. In an extensive study of a small college community, for example, Newcomb (1959) showed that whether or not students adopted the college norm of non-conservatism was closely related to the strength of their desire to integrate into the community and the extent to which it was used in preference to home and family as the primary positive point of reference.

SAQ 22

Why were the psychologists who were asked to assess the personality characteristics of Crutchfield's subjects not given their conformity scores?

SAQ 23

What does Crutchfield's finding that the correlation between IQ and conformity scores is *negative* indicate?

5.2 KINDS OF SOCIAL INFLUENCE

Herbert Kelman has explored the ways in which a group or individual may influence another person and has distinguished three fundamental forms of social influence. Each stems from a different kind of relationship between the influencing agent and the person influenced.

3 forms

1. *Compliance* can be said to occur when an individual accepts influence from another person or a group because he hopes to achieve a favourable reaction from the other. He may be interested in attaining certain rewards or in avoiding certain specific punishments that the influencing agent controls. (Kelman 1961 p 422)

Saying the right thing in order to be accepted by a particular group or set, or to impress a client or employer, or to avoid antagonizing an assailant or prison warder would all be examples of compliance.

2. *Identification*, in contrast, can be said to occur when an individual adopts behaviour derived from another person or a group because this behaviour is associated with a satisfying self-defining relationship to this person or group. By a self-defining relationship I mean a role relationship that forms a part of a person's self-image. Accepting influence through identification, then, is a way of establishing or maintaining the desired relationship to the other, and the self-definition that is anchored in this relationship. (Kelman 1961 p 422)

Kelman uses the term 'identification' not only in the classical sense of the adoption of the behaviour and attitudes expressed by a person with whom there is a significant, emotional relationship (as a child with his parents) but also to refer to the assumption, often in a conscious and intentional way, of attitudes and behaviour seen as appropriate for a work or professional role. Kelman further uses identification to include not only the adoption of the characteristics of the person identified with, but also the adoption of attitudes and behaviours which fit an individual's role in his relationship with the person identified with. So a person may assume attitudes appropriate to 'reciprocal' roles (i.e. roles defined in relation to the person identified with) like those of 'friend' or 'patient', if these form part of a satisfying relationship.

Note that under certain circumstances, identification may take place even when the relationship with the person identified with could hardly be described as positive. Bruno Bettelheim, a psychoanalyst who survived a year in the concentration camps of Dachau and Buchenwald, observed a phenomenon which Anna Freud has called 'identification with an aggressor'. Some prisoners did their best to adopt the expressions, mannerisms, appearance and aggressive actions of their guards.

For discussion of this use of the term identification see Unit 18

> Old prisoners tended to identify with the Gestapo, not only in respect to aggressive behaviour. They tried to arrogate to themselves old pieces of Gestapo uniforms. If that was not possible, they tried to sew and mend their uniforms

so that they would resemble those of the guards. When asked why they did it they admitted that they loved to look like one of the guards.

The satisfaction with which old prisoners boasted that, during the twice daily counting of the prisoners, they had stood well at attention can be explained only by their having accepted as their own the values of the Gestapo. Prisoners prided themselves on being as tough as the Gestapo members. This identification with their torturers went so far as copying their leisure-time activities. One of the games played by the guards was to find out who could stand to be hit longest without uttering a complaint. This game was copied by old prisoners. (Bettelheim 1943 p 309)

3. The third form of social influence, *internalization*, refers to adoption of another person's attitudes or behaviour because they are perceived as valid, legitimate or likely to result in the achievement of desired ends.

> The individual adopts (the induced behaviour) because he finds it useful for the solution of a problem, or because it is congenial to his own orientation, or because it is demanded by his own values – in short, because he perceives it as inherently conducive to the maximization of his values. (Kelman 1961 p 44)

The key feature of the relationship in this case is not control over desired ends (as with compliance), nor yet emotional involvement or satisfying self-definition (as with identification), but credibility. What is important is that the attitudes adopted be perceived by the person accepting them as valid in themselves and congruent with his pre-existing values.

SAQ 24

Will attitudes adopted as a result of (a) compliance, (b) identification and (c) internalization, continue to be held and/or expressed in the *absence* of the influencing agent and when he has no knowledge of the behaviour of the person influenced? (Give three separate answers.)

SAQ 25

If the relationship between the influencing agent and the person influenced *terminates*, are the attitudes which have been adopted likely to be maintained in the case of (a) compliance?; (b) identification?; (c) internalization?

SAQ 26

Give one word each to express the key characteristic of the influencing agent in the case of (a) compliance; (b) identification; (c) internalization.

The three different kinds of social influence are not always clearly distinguishable. In the Bettelheim observation of identification with an aggressor, noted earlier, what began as compliance eventually took on something of the quality of identification. A similar shift from initial power by compliance to influence by identification or even internalization is sometimes shown in cases where hostages are seized. One of several hostages held at gunpoint for a week by a Palestinian and three other convicts in Scheveningen Prison in Holland in October 1974, was reported as saying afterwards: 'It sounds silly but we all grew to like the convicts over the days. They had been so good to us and none of us wanted to turn Koudache in.' Other cases like this have also been cited.

The best known example ... was the Stockholm siege where one of the female hostages came out at the end saying she would marry the man who had held her hostage. What is not generally known is that, as the siege went forward, the hostages' values changed so much that one girl actually started stealing money from the bank – 80,000 Kr. in all. On one occasion a girl hostage not merely stole money from the bank where she was being held, but as they all came out at the end, she voluntarily positioned herself in front of the criminal so that the police would not shoot him. (Insight 1974 p 15)

Patty Hearst, the American heiress who appeared to be kidnapped by a political group in California in 1973, was thought to have been seen subsequently, actively participating in the exploits of the group who had presumably abducted her (see Figure 4). This may be an example of a shift from compliance to internalization if, after her capture, she had become convinced of the aims and values of the group who held her.

Figure 4 Patty Hearst in action. The photo was taken by a security camera during a bank raid

Experiments in cognitive dissonance theory, which will be discussed in section 8, show that there is a tendency to modify attitudes so that they are congruent with behaviour. Behaviour engaged in and attitudes expressed as a result of compliance (provided there is some element of volition on the part of the person influenced) may, in this way, produce a degree of genuine change and not merely an act produced in order to induce the right response from the agent.

5.3 ROLE INFLUENCE

One form of identification involves adopting attitudes and values appropriate to a particular *role* played or aspired to. As you saw from the discussion of the concept of role in Unit 19, roles carry with them expectations and obligations to behave and conduct oneself in particular ways. The roles we play are likely therefore to exert substantial influence on the attitudes we both express and hold. The influence exerted may be one of compliance, identification or internalization.

A person in the role of Member of Parliament may express certain views because (a) he believes that they represent the best means of achieving values which are important to him or (b) because he sees such views as characteristic of the political party of which he is a devoted member, or (c) merely because he believes that if he doesn't express them, he may be jeopardizing his chances of re-election.

Indicate in each case (a), (b) and (c), whether he is adopting the views because of compliance, identification or internalization.

Consider some of the roles played and attitudes held by yourself and two or three people you know well who are rather different from each other. Roles can include occupation, marital and family status, roles adopted in social situations, at local meetings etc. Do the attitudes they hold in any way seem to correspond to the roles they play?

It is quite probable that you will perceive some degree of correspondence.

SAQ 28

If there is a correspondence, can we then assume that the role a person plays influences his or her attitudes?

The problem of inferring causality from correlation is discussed in Huff, Chapter 8

We cannot infer causality merely from observing that two factors correlate together. Either one could influence the other or both could be the result of some third factor that we have not observed. Where there is an element of choice available as to which roles can be adopted, we do not know merely from perceiving a correspondence between them whether roles influence attitudes or whether they are chosen because they are congruent with a person's beliefs and values.

A series of interesting experiments by Stanley Milgram illustrates the surprising degree to which people will behave in a way their role requires. Subjects were recruited by advertisements in local newspapers to take part in an experiment investigating the effects of punishment on learning (see Figure 5). On arrival at the psychology laboratory, each subject met a person who was introduced as another subject but who was actually an accomplice of the experimenters. The experimental procedure was explained to them and they ostensibly drew lots to determine which part each would play. One was to act as the 'teacher' and to administer the material to be learned, and the other was to be the 'learner'. The draw was rigged by the simple method of writing 'teacher' on both slips of paper so that the genuine subject was always allocated the role of teacher. He then saw the other man strapped in a chair, electrodes attached to his wrist and paste applied to, as the experimenter put it, 'avoid blisters and burns'. The learner began to look a little worried and murmured something about having a heart condition some years ago and that he hoped it would be all right. The experimenter reassured him that 'although the shocks can be extremely painful, they cause no permanent tissue damage'.

The real subject was then taken into the next room and shown a shock generator with a bank of switches running at 15 volt intervals from 15 to 450 volts (see Figure 6). Each group of four switches was also labelled from 'slight shock' to 'extreme intensity shock', 'danger', and 'severe shock'. The last two switches were simply marked XXX. If any switch was pressed, lights flashed, needles deflected and a buzzer sounded. Subjects were each given a sample shock and, on the basis of interviews after the experiment, it was clear that all believed in the authenticity of the generator.

The teacher's task was first to read a series of pairs of words to the learner and then to give him the first word only of each pair together with four alternatives. The

Figure 5   The advertisement placed by Milgram in local newspapers to recruit subjects

Figure 6   The Milgram experiment : photos taken in the laboratory at Yale University

© Copyright 1965 by Stanley Milgram. From the film 'Obedience', distributed by the New York University Film Library

a. Shock generator

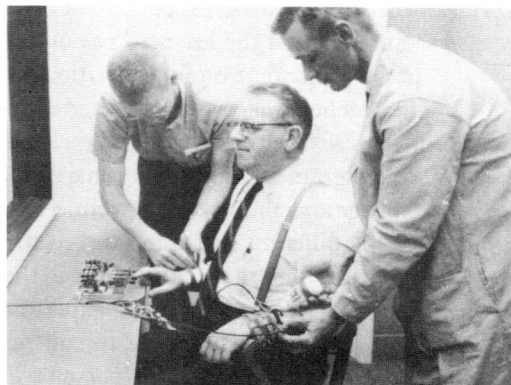

b. Victim is strapped into chair

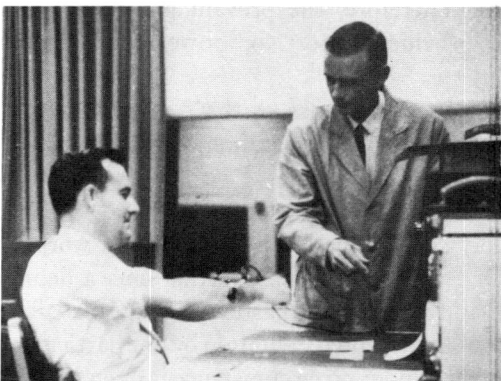

c. Subject receives a sample shock

d. Subject breaks off experiment

learner had to select which of them had been originally paired with the first word. If the learner made a mistake, he was to be 'punished' by being given an electric shock. Subjects were instructed to 'start at fifteen volts and increase the shock level by one step each time the learner gives a wrong answer' (Milgram 1963 p 143).

The learner went through a pre-arranged sequence of right and wrong answers. When the shocks reached the 300 volt level, the teacher heard pounding on the wall separating him from the learner. In some versions of the experiment he actually heard the learner cry out. From that point on there was no further response. The experimenter instructed the teacher to treat no response as a wrong response and to continue to administer and increase the level of shocks accordingly. Any expression of unwillingness to continue on the part of the teacher was countered by the experimenter saying 'please go on'; or, in the case of continued reluctance, the use of stronger phrases such as 'the experiment requires that you continue' or 'it is absolutely essential that you continue'.

SAQ 29

Under these conditions, note down the percentage of subjects who you consider would be likely to continue to shock the learner up to the top 450 volt (XXX!) level.

In subsequent experiments, Milgram tried a number of variations in procedure. He found that the amount of feedback a subject received affected his behaviour. Hearing the learner cry out, for example, or actually seeing him being shocked, both reduced the likelihood that subjects would continue. Under the standard conditions described above, however, 26 out of 40 subjects were prepared to carry on shocking to the 450 volt level. Most of those who continued showed signs of extreme tension and made verbal protests to the experimenter but, nevertheless, they went on to the end. This 65 per cent is well above most people's estimation of the obedience likely in such circumstances but results of this kind have been found in other places and at other times with great consistency. Even in the experimental variation where subjects actually heard the learner cry out, 62.5 per cent were still prepared to continue, and 40 per cent went on in a variation where they saw him being shocked. In one study, the teacher was required to actually hold the learner's hand down on the electrode plate. Even in this situation, nearly one-third soldiered on to the maximum voltage.

Milgram explains this remarkable degree of obedience in terms of the role expectations the situation produces. Our culture stipulates specific styles of behaviour for the different situations and relationships in which we engage. In many aspects of our life, we are required to defer to the control of those who are given authority by the roles that they play. In an experiment authority is assigned to the experimenter's role; in a school situation, in contrast, to the teacher's role. Authority in a military situation will rest with the person who occupies the role of highest rank. Which roles are designated to have legitimate authority in which situations will depend on the values, norms and ideology of a culture. Therefore, the prevailing ideology will

Power is the topic of Block 8   exert an important influence on and/or provide support for power relationships among individuals of that culture.

Milgram cites Goffman to argue that the behaviour of the obedient subject arises largely from the nature of his relationship with the experimenter, which is prescribed by their respective roles.

> Goffman (1959) points out that every social situation is built upon a working consensus among the participants. One of its chief premises is that once a definition of a situation has been projected and agreed on by participants, there shall be no challenge to it. Indeed, disruption of the accepted definition by one participant has the character of moral transgression. Under no circumstance is open conflict about the definition of the situation compatible with polite social exchange.

44

More specifically, according to Goffman's analysis, 'society is organized on the principle that any individual who possesses certain social characteristics has a moral right to expect that others will value and treat him in a correspondingly appropriate way. . . When an individual projects a definition of the situation and then makes an implicit or explicit claim to be a person of a particular kind, he automatically exerts a moral demand upon the others, obliging them to value him and treat him in the manner that persons of his kind have a right to expect.' Since to refuse to obey the experimenter is to reject his claim to competence and authority in this situation, a severe social impropriety is necessarily involved.

The experimental situation is so constructed that there is no way the subject can stop shocking the learner without violating the experimenter's self-definition. (Milgram 1974 p 150)

Milgram argues then that roles can influence the behaviour we engage in not only by providing particular patterns of behaviour and attitude which we adopt as part of playing that role but also, in the case of some roles like that of experimental subject, by requiring us to accept more readily the influence of others.

An extract from Goffman's book, *Presentation of self in everyday life*, from which this statement is taken, is included in the Reader pp 324–35 and was prescribed reading for Block 6

SAQ 30

Do Milgram's results demonstrate conclusively that the role a person plays influences his behaviour and attitudes?

Milgram describes both the overt behaviour of his subjects and the emotional distress that many of them showed in the experimental situation. He does not specifically suggest, however, that the subjects' evaluation of and emotional feeling towards the learner was affected by what they were required to do. A recent experiment by Philip Zimbardo, however, suggests that this may well happen. Zimbardo asked subjects to play out the roles of prisoners and warders (the different roles being allocated randomly by drawing lots). He constructed a makeshift prison and planned to run the experiment continuously for a week or two. In the event, he claimed that the 'warders' became so aggressive, the 'prisoners' so disturbed and the situation in general so out of hand that it had to be terminated after a few days. Subjects interviewed afterwards admitted surprise at the strong emotions aroused in them in relation to the other people involved in the experiment. Some warders confessed, for example, to experiencing something akin to hate for their prisoners. Zimbardo interprets his observations as indicating the degree to which roles played may influence not only behaviour but also feelings and attitudes towards others (Zimbardo 1973).

5.4   INCONSISTENCY AND AWARENESS

Section 5 then has tried to show the degree to which and how our behaviour, attitudes and beliefs are shaped by the social influences to which we are exposed and the roles we play. Attitudes and beliefs developed in this way are likely to remain stable and to resist attempts at modification unless the supportive social context and roles themselves are changed.

The stress in this section on social influence, conformity and the impact of the norms and roles provided by our reference groups may tend to generate the impression that our attitudes and experiences are totally dominated by these factors. We should not leave this section, however, without noting that cultural and social influence is not usually monolithic and uniform. Our complex culture exposes us to many different ideologies, attitudes and norms; to many roles and to people with varying values and styles of behaviour. We have to integrate, select and work through

Diversity

Group psychotherapy is illustrated in television programme 21

inconsistencies. Our own awareness plays a part in this process. Psychotherapy and education are both processes whose goal is to change the awareness of the individual. In the 'non-directive' therapy of Carl Rogers, the therapist, by acting as a 'mirror', tries to show the 'client' the inconsistencies and lack of fit in his awareness of his relationships and experiences. For example, a mother may be helped to recognize feelings of aggression stimulated by her interaction with her child – feelings which she may have hitherto denied and not been prepared to admit to herself because they conflicted with her self-concept of being a 'good mother'.

Education may involve exploring the intricacies of a process or situation and bringing evidence to bear in an effort to understand them. In doing this, it may serve to show up inconsistencies in and undermine values and attitudes developed as a result of socialization and role playing. Perhaps this discussion of social influence and conformity has led you to a greater awareness of their potential effects on your own attitudes and behaviour; perhaps it may even help to reduce their influence on future occasions. The questionnaire provided at the beginning and end of each unit in Block 1 will have given you some idea as to how far these units succeeded in their educational process of 'enlarging awareness'. At the end of the course too, you might care to think back to the effects of its total impact on your values and attitudes.

6 THE FUNCTIONS ATTITUDES SERVE

A further reason why the beliefs and attitudes which we hold are so resistant to change is that usually they have personal and functional significance. Believing and feeling in the ways that we do may result in the attainment of various satisfactions. Changing our attitudes may mean risking the loss of such benefits.

There have been a number of analyses of the functions which attitudes may serve.

Read Katz in Reader pp 360–9

Read now one of these which is given in a paper in the Reader by Daniel Katz, called 'The functional approach to the study of attitudes'. You may find the following notes on this extract useful.

1 Katz begins by analysing the nature of attitudes and distinguishing between attitudes, opinions and values. His analysis is similar to that given in section 1 of this unit.

2 The main body of the paper then discusses what Katz considers to be the four major functions of attitudes, namely *instrumental*, *ego-defensive*, *value-expressive* and *knowledge* functions.

3 The *adjustment* or *instrumental* function is based on the concept of *reinforcement* which you will remember was discussed in Unit 18 and in section 4.2 of this unit.

4 In discussing the *ego-defensive* function of attitudes, Katz refers to the defence mechanisms of rationalization, projection and displacement (NB English spelling is usually defen*ce* and American defen*se*). Projection has already been referred to briefly in Unit 7 (sections 5.5 and 6.4). The term displacement here means displacing emotions and feelings from one object or person to another. A man who finds it difficult to express feelings of resentment which he harbours against his boss might take them out on his wife instead. Rationalization is said to occur when a person re-interprets his own behaviour so that it seems reasonable, favourable or does not arouse anxiety. The reasons he gives, however, do not reflect the real motivations underlying it. The whole question of the ego-defensive function of attitudes is explored in more depth in the next section of this unit.

5 Katz points out that attitudes may also serve a *value-expressive* function; in other words they may allow a person to express the concept he has of himself. Self-concept may well be modelled on other people who are identified with. So Kelman's analysis of identification as a process of social influence, described in section 5.2 of this unit, is

relevant here. Note, however, that Katz uses the term *internalization* in a rather different and less specialized way than Kelman, to refer to the adoption, for any reason, of the values and attitudes of other people. Thus Katz's use of the term includes both the processes that Kelman distingushes as *internalization* and *identification*. Social scientists (and, of course, other writers) often use the same terms in slightly different ways. This problem is particularly likely to arise in an interdisciplinary course like D101 which draws on theories from a variety of disciplines. Look out for this. Such variations illustrate the need for careful definition of major concepts used in essays etc.

6   Katz's *knowledge* function has already been implied and discussed in earlier sections of the unit (1.2 and 4.1, for example). Attitudes and beliefs are the means by which we order, make sense of and are able to react consistently and meaningfully to the world about us.

7   Finally, Katz briefly considers the implications of this functional approach for attitude change. Communication and information are unlikely to change attitudes which serve a useful function for an individual unless some attack is also made on the functions which underlie them. This may be done by making the function no longer attractive, by destroying the attitude's capacity to fulfil that function, or by ensuring that a modified attitude is able to provide equivalent satisfaction.

The topic of attitude change is taken up in more detail in section 9

SAQ 31

There is an example, in addition to *internalization*, in section 6 above of a term which has been used in a different sense elsewhere in this course. Can you spot it?

SAQ 32

Indicate which of Katz's functions is most probably served mainly by each of the four attitudes which are implied in each sentence of the passage below, (a), (b), (c) and (d).
   (a) Because Jim Hennessy had managed to get salaries raised by thirty per cent last year, John voted for him at the Union meeting   (b) Nevertheless he had come to have a growing regard for the Middle Class Party because he realized it epitomized his own basic values   (c) In particular, he had become very concerned at what he regarded to be the flood of permissiveness around him; it disturbed him to see so frequently open displays of kissing and flagrantly sexual interaction in public   (d) John believed that if only people were prepared to work harder and play less then both the economy and the general quality of life in this country would immeasurably improve.

7   PERSONALITY AND ATTITUDES

A theme which has emerged in a number of places in the unit so far is that a particular attitude or belief does not exist in isolation. Attitudes tend to co-vary. As was pointed out in section 2.6, attitudes towards concepts as diverse as hippies, capital punishment and patriotism are quite likely to be interrelated and scales, like the Conservatism Scale you tried earlier, can be devised to assess higher order attitude 'clusters'. Katz's functional theory also indicated the close relationship that attitudes have with self-concept, inner conflicts, guilt and anxiety. Section 7 explores in more depth the question of how attitudes are linked to personality factors.
   Like *attitude*, *personality* is a hypothetical construct. How it is defined will depend on which one of the very different theories of personality which are available, is adopted. Two research studies which suggest some possible links between personality and attitudes are discussed in this section. As the theoretical traditions on which they are based differ, so also do the conceptualizations of personality which they adopt.

The first study is of the Authoritarian Personality and was carried out by a group of distinguished American and European social scientists, the most prominent of whom were Adorno, Frenkel-Brunswick, Levinson and Sanford. They adopt essentially a psychoanalytic orientation. Their research is interesting in that, not only does it illustrate possible ways in which personality factors may be related to attitudes and beliefs, but it also employs a variety of research techniques, demonstrates the interplay of theory and data, and shows the problems involved in and the difficulties of drawing precise conclusions from an investigation of this kind.

It began in 1943 as a study of prejudice against Jews, motivated by the atrocities that were taking place in Germany. It finished seven years and over 2,000 subjects later. The study was published in a volume running to nearly 1,000 pages. Its main finding might be expressed in the phrase 'anti-semitism has little or nothing to do with Jews!'. In other words, prejudice is determined more by the personality of the prejudiced individual than by the characteristics of the person or group who form the target of the prejudice. The research generated literally hundreds of follow-up studies and commentaries. It has been rightly described as 'truly a land-mark in the history of social psychology' (Wrightsman 1968 p 127).

The study is in two main parts. The first phase involved the administration of questionnaires and attitude scales to over 2,000 subjects from organizations ranging from trades unions to schools, universities and hospitals. Almost all subjects were native-born, white Americans, minority group members being intentionally excluded. The researchers began, as you might expect, by devising a scale to measure anti-semitism. The Likert type scale they constructed used six response categories only, the neutral category being purposely omitted. For each item, then, subjects had to indicate whether they strongly agreed, moderately agreed, slightly agreed, slightly disagreed, moderately disagreed or strongly disagreed. There were fifty-two items, most of which reflected one or more of the five main themes listed below.

Offensive items which attribute to Jews characteristics like extravagance, sensuality, over-aggressiveness, nosiness and unattractiveness, e.g. 'A major fault of the Jews is their conceit, overbearing pride and their idea that they are a chosen race'.

Threatening items which view Jews as potentially dangerous, powerful and corrupting, e.g. 'Jewish power and control in money matters is far out of proportion to the number of Jews in the total population'.

Items which *recommend discrimination*, e.g. 'It is sometimes all right to ban Jews from certain apartment houses'.

Items which *attribute seclusiveness and clannishness*, e.g. 'The Jews keep too much to themselves, instead of taking the proper interest in community problems and group government'.

Items which *attribute intrusiveness*, e.g. 'There are too many Jews in the various federal agencies and bureaux in Washington and they have too much control over our national policies'.

Other items were more subtle, not necessarily expressing overtly negative attitudes but, nevertheless, reflecting a concern for the significance of an individual's ethnic identity, e.g. 'The trouble with letting Jews into a nice neighbourhood is that they gradually give it a typically Jewish atmosphere'.

The reliability of the scale was assessed by administering initially half of the items to a group of subjects then, a week later, giving them the remaining items. The sets of scores based on these two administrations correlated +.92.

What does this reliability coefficient indicate?

You may have noticed the paradoxical nature of the different kinds of items used. Some, for example, attribute intrusiveness and others seclusiveness. Some items describe Jews as rich and powerful, others as poor and dirty. Yet correlations between scores on the separate subscales were high, ranging from $+.74$ to $+.94$. These indicate that subjects tend to react in a similar way on the different kinds of items. People attributing one characteristic are also likely to attribute the others. The feature they have in common, of course, is that they reflect negative feeling. This underlying 'psychological' rather than logical consistency suggests that the attitudes expressed are more a function of the respondent rather than of the target group. Gordon Allport has devised an imaginary conversation to show this consistent yet illogical negativity which often underlies prejudice.

MR. SMITH: The trouble with Jews is that they only ever care about their own people.

MR. BROWN: But studies have shown that they tend to give more generously to general charities than non-Jews.

MR. SMITH: That just shows how they are always trying to buy their way into other people's favour and poke their noses into other people's affairs. They think of nothing but money – that's why there are so many Jewish bankers.

MR. BROWN: The percentage of Jews in banking is smaller than in the general population.

MR. SMITH: Just what you would expect. They don't go in for more respectable business – it's all gambling houses and night clubs.

The investigators hypothesized that anti-semitism was only one manifestation of a general 'ethnocentric' attitude. The best definition of *ethnocentrism* is probably 'a tendency. . . to be rigid in the acceptance of the culturally "alike" and in the rejection of the "unlike"'. (Adorno *et al.* 1950 p 102). Their hypothesis implied that an anti-semite would also be likely to be prejudiced against other minority groups. His prejudice would not depend so much on actual contact with the groups concerned but a general tendency to perceive and react to minority groups in a negative way. In order to test this hypothesis, they constructed an Ethnocentrism Scale. This was a thirty four item Likert scale with a split half reliability of $+.91$. It contained items expressing negative feelings towards minority groups, including 'Japs', 'Filipinos' and 'Negroes'. An example of an item used is 'we are spending too much money for the pampering of criminals and the insane, and for the education of inherently incapable people'. Approximately one third of the items were designed to measure 'patriotism', the term being used in a rather special way to indicate blind attachment to national cultural values and the rejection of outsiders. Two items of this kind were 'America may not be perfect, but the American Way has brought us about as close as human beings can get to a perfect society'; and 'Certain religious sects who refuse to salute the flag should be forced to conform to such a patriotic action or else be abolished'.

The investigators administered the E scale to a large group of subjects and found that not only did the 'patriotic' items correlate $+.83$ with the anti-minority items, but that the E scale itself correlated $+.80$ with the Anti-semitism Scale. In other words, the results were beginning to yield what Brown (1965) has called 'the widening circle of co-variation'. Someone who is negative towards one minority group is also likely to be negative against others and blindly patriotic as well. Those of you who are familiar with the predilections and *bêtes noires* of Alf Garnett may not be so surprised!

These results suggested that both attitude scales were assessing a general personality orientation rather than feelings based on actual realistic contact with the attitude objects in question.

The next significant phase of the project was the construction of the Potential for Fascism or F scale (subsequently known as the Authoritarian Scale), which was designed to measure the fundamental features of the general personality orientation underlying ethnocentrism.

> The idea of the F scale was a product of thinking about the A–S and E scales. An effort was being made to abstract from the A–S and E scale items, the kinds of psychological dispositions – fears, anxieties, values, impulses – being expressed, the thought being that systematic covering of this ground might suggest additional E items. There were certain general themes in the item content: e.g. Jews were 'extravagent', or 'sensual' or 'lazy' or 'soft'; or Jews were mysterious, strange, foreign, basically different; or minority groups generally failed to come up to ordinary standards of middle-class morality. It was as if the subject in agreeing with these scale items, was not so much considering Jews or other minority group members as expressing concern lest other people 'get away' with tendencies which he himself had to inhibit, or anxiety lest he be the victim of strange forces beyond his control, lest his moral values, already somewhat unstable, be undermined. And since, apparently, items expressing these kinds of preoccupation were agreed with consistently by some subjects regardless of the minority groups involved, would not these subjects agree with such items even though no minority group were mentioned at all? In short, why not have a scale that covered the psychological content of the A–S and E scales but did not appear to be concerned with the familiar phenomena of prejudice? (Sanford 1956 p 267)

The thirty eight items of the F scale were derived from fascist writings and speeches and from extensive clinical investigations and interviews with ethnocentric subjects. However, they all essentially depend on a conceptualization of personality in psycho-dynamic terms. Sanford describes in the passage below how construction of the F scale was based on an assumption which had guided the group's thinking for some time.

> The essence of this assumption was that some of the deeper needs of the personality were being expressed by agreement with prejudiced statements. If this were true, then these needs should express themselves in other ways as well. If, for example a subject's tendency to attribute weakness to Jews sprang from his own underlying fear of weakness, that fear might also express itself in an over-accent upon his own strength and toughness. Thus, scale items having to do with the supposed weakness of Jews or of other people and items expressing exaggerated strength and toughness would correlate positively in a population of men because agreement with both kinds of items commonly sprang from the same underlying source, fear of weakness. All of us were accustomed to this kind of thinking in terms of levels of functioning in the personality; it is, of course, essentially psychoanalytic. (Sanford 1956 p 268)

Freud's psychoanalytic theory, which was briefly discussed in Unit 18, essentially conceives personality as a system of interacting pressures. The 'id' forces stem from biological needs, 'ego' forces from realistic perception of the situation and the need to integrate the varied influences acting upon the person, and 'superego' forces or con- science from constraints and principles internalized from other people. Conflicts and interaction between these, particularly during childhood, provide the bases of personality. Anxiety created by such conflict may be alleviated by perceiving and reacting to the world in a biased way.

Each of the nine separate subscales which make up the F scale are based on one or more hypotheses relating prejudice to personality dynamics. The essential characteristics of items in the nine subscales are listed below with examples.

1 *Conventionalism*. Rigid adherence to conventional, middle-class values, e.g. 'A person who has bad manners, habits, and breeding can hardly expect to be liked and accepted by decent people'.

2 *Authoritarian submission*. Submissive, uncritical attitude toward idealized moral authorities of the in-group, e.g. 'Obedience and respect for authority are the most important virtues children should learn'.

3 *Authoritarian aggression*. Tendency to be on the look out for, and to condemn, reject, and punish people who violate conventional values, e.g. 'Sex crimes, such as rape and attacks on children, deserve more than mere imprisonment; such criminals ought to be publicly whipped, or worse.' (Adorno *et al.* 1950 p 228)

As Sanford (1956) points out, these three characteristics suggest a strict superego or conscience, a high level of repressed aggression which can be 'legitimately' expressed against those who contravene moral rules, and a weak ego which requires the support of externally imposed constraints.

4 *Anti-intraception*. Opposition to the subjective, imaginative, the tender minded, e.g. 'When a person has a problem or worry, it is best for him not to think about it, but to keep busy with more cheerful things'.

5 *Superstition and stereotypy*. The belief in mystical determinants of the individual's fate; the disposition to think in rigid categories, e.g. 'It's a mistake to trust anybody who doesn't look you straight in the eye'.

6 *Power and 'toughness'*. Preoccupation with the dominance – submission, strong – weak, leader – follower dimension; identification with power figures; exaggerated assertion of strength and toughness, e.g. 'What the youth needs most is discipline, rugged determination, and the will to work and fight for family and country'. (Adorno *et al.* 1950 p 228)

Sanford claims these represent manifestations of a relatively weak ego. Anti-intraception serves to shield the individual from awareness of his own impulses which conflict with superego demands and therefore cause anxiety. Superstition shifts responsibility and control to events outside the self and stereotypy is an inadequate attempt to deal with complex events by the use of oversimplified categories. The emphasis on power and toughness is to cover up feelings of inadequacy and weakness by an overdisplay of and concentration on strength. This is what a psychoanalyst would term a 'reaction formation'.

7 *Destructiveness and cynicism*. Generalized hostility, vilification of the human, e.g. 'Familiarity breeds contempt'.

8 *Projectivity*. A disposition to believe that wild and dangerous things go on in the world; the projection outward of unconscious emotional impulses, e.g. 'Nowadays when so many different kinds of people move around so much and mix together so freely, a person has to be especially careful to protect himself against infection and disease.'

9 *Sex*. Exaggerated concern with sexual 'goings-on', e.g. 'The wild sex life of the old Greeks and Romans was tame compared to some of the goings-on in this country, even in places where people might least expect it.' (Adorno *et al.* 1950 p 228)

Essentially, these last three kinds of item permit expression of and concern with repressed impulses like aggressiveness and sex in a form which does not arouse undue anxiety. For example, Sanford explains the psychological significance of agreement with the item in the sex scale cited above; '... underlying sexual tendencies, inhibited because of a strict superego, have found... some expression in fantasies, which, however can be enjoyed or tolerated only when other people, and not the self, are the actors and when the fantasies are accompanied by ... indignation'.

Although construction of the scale is based on a theory of personality which lacks firm evidence of its validity, subjects' responses on the different items and different subscales did, in fact, correlate highly which suggests that the scale was certainly measuring some overall, psychological variable. The final refined version of the F scale also correlated highly (+.75) with the E scale, thus supporting the investigators' hypothesis that ethnocentrism and prejudice could be measured without any reference to specific groups. It is perhaps also worth noting that psychiatric patients produced the lowest and San Quentin convicts the highest E and F scores of all groups tested.

7.2 CHARACTERISTICS OF THE AUTHORITARIAN PERSONALITY TYPE

Selection of research methods in the social sciences often poses something of a paradoxical problem. As we saw in section 3.1 on laboratory and field experiments, the advantages of one method tend to bring with them disadvantages not inherent in another. Taking large groups of subjects may rule out the bias possible when only a few individuals are used; but it does tend to make difficult the intensive study of the interplay of multiple variables that focusing on one or two individuals renders feasible. An example of a similar dilemma is choice of assessment technique. The objectivity and reliability of attitude scales largely depend on their pre-set form and on the fact that scoring is straightforward and not dependent on interpretation.

See discussion of salience in section 2.7

However, this structured form makes them also less sensitive in picking up characteristics which may have special significance for a subject. In contrast, projective techniques (which essentially depend on presenting a subject with an ambiguous stimulus, for example an ink blot, and interpreting the varied responses a subject will produce) and interviews are far less *reliable* assessment procedures but they do allow more scope for characteristics particularly relevant and significant to the individual to express themselves.

An interesting feature of the Authoritarian Personality study is the way in which the investigators were able to use and to integrate data yielded by a variety of approaches and techniques. A few individuals were selected on the basis of their high and low E scores and subjected to intensive psychological exploration by means of interviews and projective tests. The latter included projective questions like 'If you knew you had only six months to live, but could do just as you pleased during that period, how would you spend your time?' and the Thematic Apperception Test in which subjects are asked to make up stories about each of a series of pictures (see Figure 7). In this way, the researchers gradually pieced together the key characteristics which distinguished high from low ethnocentric subjects.

Prejudiced subjects, for example, had a tendency to over-idealize their parents. Parents were 'wonderful, couldn't make them better', 'always willing to do anything for you', 'most terrific person in the world'. The investigators point out the effusive, stereotyped and somewhat unreal quality of such descriptions and contrast them with those of unprejudiced subjects which appeared to represent more objective appraisals. High scorers also tended to present themselves in an idealistic self-satisfied way. They typically boasted of their fine qualities – 'I've never done things behind peoples' backs', 'always dependable', 'I know I'm a favourite', and many of the men talked proudly of their sexual prowess. What is interesting in view of the psychodynamic interpretation suggested by Sanford is that where criticisms of either themselves or their parents do creep in they tend to be 'ego-alien'. In other words, aspects of themselves or their parents which they recognize as negative are regarded

52

Figure 7 One of the Thematic Apperception Test pictures used in the research on the Authoritarian Personality. Subjects were asked to make up stories about what was happening in the picture

as not really being part of the genuine self. They are explained away, for example, as 'letting my carnal self get the better of me' or 'I guess I just got that from the other side of the family'. This tendency to deny unwelcome aspects of themselves and their parents also reflects the general difficulty prejudiced subjects seem to find in coping with ambivalence, i.e. having both positive and negative feelings about the same person or object. In their personal relationships, high scorers were concerned with status rather than intimacy and men tended to separate sex from tenderness. Differences in cognitive style between high and low scorers were also noted. Prejudiced subjects made little use of qualifications and reservations and tended to have clear-cut, rigid ideas. They disliked ambiguity, preferring to see things 'clearly' in black and white terms.

7.3 CHILDHOOD FOUNDATIONS

Psychoanalytic theory considers early parent/child relationships to be the major source of personality characteristics. The researchers could only build up a picture of the childhood and family life of high and low scorers on the very indirect basis of the reported recollections of their adult subjects. We cannot assume that these will *necessarily* represent an accurate account of what actually happened though they will probably, in most cases, reflect something of the way in which the situation was viewed by the individuals themselves. There were certainly clear differences in the accounts given by high and low scorers.

Discipline in the homes of authoritarian subjects was reported as relatively strict and requiring obedience to specific rules based on conventional values. Parents of low scoring subjects were reported more frequently as basing discipline on principles which they made some attempts to explain to their children. Prejudiced men described their fathers as distant and stern and their mothers as self-sacrificing and

53

submissive. Conflict between parents was rarely reported. Men who were low scorers, on the other hand, described their fathers as relaxed and mild and their mothers as warm, sociable and understanding.

After reviewing the contrasting descriptions in detail, Sanford argues that the family backgrounds reported by the high scorers are likely to foster authoritarian personality characteristics. 'When the child is not allowed to question anything, to participate in decisions affecting him, nor to feel that his own will counts for something, the stunting of the ego is a pretty direct consequence' (Sanford 1956 p 307).

Because he is required to submit to unexplained rules rather than principles and because there is insufficient warmth in parent/child relationships to foster effectively the strong identification on which internalization depends, the child who will become an authoritarian adult fails to develop a strong superego. (Note that psychoanalysts use the term internalization in a similar way to Katz rather than Kelman – see section 6, note 5.) His upbringing has made him, nevertheless, anxious 'to do the right thing', hence his reliance on the external criteria of conventional values. The resentment and hostility built up by the punishment he has received and which he was not free to express directly against his parents, can later find an outlet in harsh and punitive condemnation of those who are assumed to break the conventional standards that he accepts, particularly if his targets have little power to retaliate. Psychologically, this process is similar to that described by Bettelheim in section 5, of identification with the aggressor. The process of projection will lead him to see in others, particularly those people selected as the target of his aggression, the impulses of sex and aggression and the awareness of inferiority which he himself has been forced to repress. By indulging in intensive condemnation of their supposed iniquities, he also has opportunity for vicariously gratifying his own repressed needs in a 'legitimate' way.

7.4 CRITICISMS OF THE AUTHORITARIAN PERSONALITY STUDY

There is no space here to review the many criticisms which have been inevitably provoked by a project so mammoth and which utilized such a variety of research techniques. It is worth noting a few of the more important comments made on methodology, however, as they illustrate the great care needed in good research.

1 One criticism is of the fact that all the attitude scale items used were in one direction, so that agreement always produced high scores.

SAQ 34

Why is this a criticism?

In fact, the investigators had purposely decided to use uni-directional items because they considered that such items were more discriminating and allowed for greater subtlety. Subsequent research has indicated that, although acquiescence response sets probably did help to raise the correlations between A/S, E and F scores slightly, the effect was negligible.

2 In the investigation of selected high and low scorers, interviewers were told the kind of information to elicit and given sample questions, but were allowed considerable latitude as to what questions they actually asked. Not all subjects, therefore, were asked exactly the same questions. Interviewers also knew the scores of their interviewees on the attitude scales they had been given.

SAQ 35

Why are these criticisms?

The interviews were, in fact, initially only part of an informal exploratory study. The data were only analysed subsequently when striking differences had been found between the different kinds of subjects, in order to make more precise comparisons possible. In any case, it could be argued that in order to elicit maximal information, some flexibility in questioning is necessary. Subjects vary in the amount and kinds of prompting they require. Some latitude to react to the individual characteristics of each interviewee might, in fact, be more likely to produce a consistent impression in each subject's mind than a standard set of questions. Knowledge of the subjects' questionnaire responses also enabled interviewers, the investigators considered, to question and probe more efficiently.

3   Authoritarianism appears to be associated with lower socio-economic status. Correlation coefficients between education and F scores and IQ and F scores have been estimated at around $-.5$ (Christie 1954). The investigators, who had noted this relationship, argued that anxiety and concern over status were likely to be more prevalent in lower socio-economic groups and that such concern was very likely to lead parents to act in an authoritarian way, thus influencing the development of their children in the way described earlier. However, it has been argued that this relationship suggests that authoritarian traits, rather than being the results of personality dynamics, are merely a reflection of the assimilation of the norms of a subculture. This criticism then is one of interpretation rather than methodology and you might like to consider which explanation you think holds most weight on the evidence you have.

It is certainly necessary, as with any study, to consider the results and conclusions offered with caution. As we shall see in section 10, not all prejudice can be viewed as a function of authoritarianism. However, although critics may conclude 'the authors' theory has not been proved by the data they cite' (Hyman and Sheatsley 1954), what study of social behaviour of this complexity can hope to produce watertight proof? Their findings were generally gathered with care and their interpretation of them makes sense. They demonstrate how seemingly unrelated variables go together and present a plausible explanation of their cohesion. As Sanford points out:

> The research reported in *The Authoritarian Personality* makes maximum use of hypothetical constructs. The 'correctness' or one might better say the usefulness, of the psychoanalytic formulation is gauged by its service in making sense of a great diversity of material and in predicting what a patient will do next. And it is the same in such research as this: Does the formulation explain the relationships observed and does it permit the prediction of responses in particular types of situations? The truth of such formulations may rarely be demonstrated to the satisfaction of all, but one may hope to creep up on it. (Sanford 1956 p 279)

Sanford concludes 'it is doubtful that greater methodological purity or rigour, or adherence to the advice of the most advanced experts – even Hyman or Sheatsley – would have made any crucial difference in the general results and conclusions of our work'.

There have been many subsequent studies since the original investigation which have clearly demonstrated that significant differences do exist between subjects who score high and those who score low on the F scale. It has been shown, for example, that high authoritarians have less ambiguity tolerance for visual stimuli and are also less willing to volunteer for psychological experiments. Authoritarian teachers are more likely to adopt an autocratic style and authoritarian mothers more likely to be domineering and possessive. Not only are high scorers less effective at assessing the personality of the people they interact with, but they are also significantly more likely than low scorers to utilize 'external' cues (e.g. status and position held and material objects possessed) than 'internal' cues (e.g. personal traits, mannerisms and expressed values) in making their evaluations (this result in an experiment by Scodel and Mussen in 1953 was significant at the .0005 level). In the Milgram experiment too, high F scorers were found to obey significantly more often than low scorers (Elms 1972). Note, however, that there are also indications that, although they may be initially generated by family relationships and early childhood, authoritarian characteristics may be significantly modified by later experiences in interpersonal relationships and education and as a result of social and cultural influence.

SAQ 36

What is meant by 'the results were significant at the .0005 level?

SAQ 37

Describe briefly the key psychodynamic processes assumed to underlie the prejudice of the authoritarian personality?

7.5 OTHER APPROACHES

Factor analysis was introduced briefly in Unit 7, section 3.3.2

Co-variation of attitudes has also been explored by H. J. Eysenck of the University of London, using a statistical technique known as factor analysis. A selection of items from various attitude scales is given to a large group of subjects and their responses analysed to see which items co-vary. For example, people who agree that 'the death penalty is barbaric, and it was right to abolish it', are also likely to agree that 'the dropping of the first atom bomb on a Japanese city, killing thousands of innocent women and children, was morally wrong and incompatible with our kind of civilization', and to disagree that 'it would be a mistake to have coloured people as foremen over whites'. Those who agree with the statement 'the idea of God is an invention of the human mind' are likely to disagree that 'sex relations except in marriage are always wrong' (Eysenck 1971). In this way, it is possible to show how one item relates to another and to extract the primary factors or attitude clusters. With the help of factor analysis Eysenck has elicited what he considers to be the two fundamental dimensions of political attitudes, tender-mindedness – tough-mindedness and radicalism – conservatism.

The way attitude dimensions are related to personality variables will depend, as mentioned earlier, on the theoretical approach adopted by the investigator. Eysenck's view of personality is in the learning theory tradition (see Unit 18). He argues that the two factors he has extracted relate to classical and instrumental conditioning respectively. For example, he claims that individuals who hold aggressive or what he calls 'tough-minded' attitudes have been ineffectively conditioned or socialized, either as a result of lack of training or because of lowered conditionability due to inherited temperament. Eysenck finds support for this assertion in the fact that extraverts, who condition less well than introverts, are somewhat more likely to hold tough-minded attitudes. You may remember from Unit 2 that Eysenck explains criminal behaviour as being often the result of inadequate conditioning. In this context, it is interesting

The E scale was discussed in section 7.1

that many of the E scale items are similar to items measuring Eysenck's tough-minded dimension and that San Quentin prisoners scored high on this scale.

There are difficulties in Eysenck's approach as his results will depend on the kinds of attitude items initially selected for factor analysis and on the composition of the group of subjects to whom they are administered. Other investigators using different items and different subjects have extracted rather different patterns of attitude dimensions.

There has not been space here to consider Eysenck's work in detail but the discussion will, I hope, have been sufficient to demonstrate that the ways in which attitudes are found to relate to personality will depend on the theoretical perspective adopted and the methods employed. The research problems in this area are formidable but the Authoritarian Personality study, Eysenck's work and other studies in the same area (e.g. Wilson 1973), while providing somewhat different analyses of the form that the relationship is likely to take, strongly suggest that many central attitudes and beliefs are rooted in the personality of the individual holding them.

8 THE ORGANIZATION OF ATTITUDES

Section 7 has demonstrated how attitudes co-vary and are organized in a psychologically meaningful way. Several theories have been put forward concerning the implications of attitude organization. Most have emphasized the concept of *balance*. If one attitude or aspect of an attitude is disturbed then other changes are likely to occur in order to restore balance in the overall pattern of attitudes. This idea of balance has been applied in different ways. Heider (1958), for example, has used it in an analysis of interpersonal relations. He argues that balance would be disturbed in a case where person X likes Y and also Z but where there are negative feelings between Y and Z themselves. Hence, in such a situation, X will attempt to restore this balance by seeing the relationship between Y and Z as more positive than it really is. Rosenberg (1960) has applied the idea of balance in a rather different way, to the relation between attitude components. He demonstrated that when valence towards an attitude object was changed (he used hypnosis to do this) then beliefs about it spontaneously changed also so that consistency was maintained. Osgood and Tannenbaum (1955) in yet another approach, showed that if someone whose opinion is valued expresses a dubious statement, then there will be a tendency to even up the imbalance this creates by evaluating the statement more highly and evaluating the person as an information source less.

Attitude components or aspects: see section 1.3

8.1 COGNITIVE DISSONANCE THEORY

The theory which offers the widest application and which has received the most attention is Leon Festinger's theory of cognitive dissonance. An attempt to test out a prediction of this theory has already been described in section 3.2. There is a paper by Festinger (1962) in your Scientific American set text. This introduces the basic tenets of his theory and describes some experimental tests of its often surprising predictions.

Read Festinger in Scientific American set text pp 34–40

The following SAQs are designed to test the effectiveness of your assimilation of Festinger's paper.

SAQ 38

In the Jecker experiment, which girls subsequently re-evaluated the record they had chosen in a more favourable way:

A   those asked to re-rate the records *after having been given the record of their choice?*

B   those asked to re-rate the records *after having been given both the records they had chosen?*

C   those asked to re-rate the records *before knowing whether they would receive both records or only the one they had chosen?*

SAQ 39

In the Festinger and Carlsmith experiment, which subjects regarded most favourably the experimental session in which they had taken part:

A   those receiving $20?   B   those receiving $1?

SAQ 40

Why?

SAQ 41

Although not quoted in the paper you have just read, in the Festinger and Carlsmith experiment the differences between the evaluations of the experiment by subjects in the $20 condition and by those in the $1 condition was significant at the .03 level. What does this imply?

It may be worth stating here a brief summary of cognitive dissonance theory which Festinger has given elsewhere.

> 1 There may exist dissonant or 'non-fitting' relations among cognitive elements.
> 2 The existence of dissonance gives rise to pressures to reduce the dissonance and to avoid increases in dissonance.
> 3 Manifestations of the operation of these pressures include behaviour changes, changes of cognition, and circumspect exposure to new information and new opinions. (Festinger 1957 p 31)

Note that Festinger's idea of consonance refers to *psychological* and not necessarily logical consistency. An illustration of this distinction was provided by Allport's imaginary conversation between Smith and Brown cited in section 7.1. Note also that cognitive dissonance theory has obvious implications for attitude stability and change. As attitudes are interrelated, change in one is likely to create dissonance and so will be resisted for that reason. This is yet another factor underlying the remarkable resilience of central attitudes and beliefs. However, as will be discussed in the next section, one way in which change may be induced is by creating dissonance in such a way that its resolution can be achieved only by the individual concerned modifying his own behaviour or attitudes.

The predictions of Festinger's theory have been tested out in both field and laboratory settings for a wide variety of behaviours and situations. One example which required Festinger and his colleagues to infiltrate the Lake City Believers has already been described in section 3.1. Marian Keech had publicly committed herself to her beliefs. She was surrounded by followers, many of whom had given up jobs and possessions as a result of these beliefs. The failure of her predictions to occur could not fail to arouse dissonance. Producing an elegant re-interpretation that, because of their beliefs, God had saved the world may have helped to alleviate the dissonance experienced but, in itself, was not sufficient to dispel it entirely.

> The dissonance is too important and though they may try to hide it, even from themselves, the believers still know that the prediction was false and all their preparations were in vain. The dissonance cannot be eliminated completely by denying or rationalizing the disconfirmation. There is, however, a way in which the remaining dissonance can be reduced. *If more and more people can be persuaded that the system of belief is correct, then clearly it must after all, be correct.* It is for this reason that we observe the increase in proselytizing following disconfirmation. If the proselytizing proves successful, then by gathering more adherents and effectively surrounding himself with supporters the believer reduces dissonance to the point where he can live with it. (Festinger *et al.* 1958 pp 159–60)

We have seen elsewhere in this unit the potent influence of other people's opinions on our own. Section 5.1 demonstrated that when others disagree with an individual's view, it can create so much dissonance that he may modify his reactions or evaluations so that they are in line with the majority view. We might well expect then that *support* for our views would serve to decrease any dissonance arising from doubts about them.

Mrs Keech behaved in accordance with Festinger's analysis which had been made on the basis of his theory. Where before she had avoided publicity, in the early hours of 21 December she actively sought it for the first time.

> Within minutes after she had read the message explaining the disconfirmation, Mrs Keech received another message instructing her to publicize the explanation. She reached for the telephone and began dialling the number of a newspaper. While she was waiting to be connected, someone asked: 'Marian, is this the first time you have called the newspaper yourself?' Her reply was immediate: 'Oh, yes, this is the first time I have ever called them. I have never had anything to tell them before, but now I feel it is urgent.' The whole group could have echoed her feelings for they all felt a sense of urgency. As soon as Marian had finished her call, the other members took turns telephoning newspapers, wire services, radio stations and national magazines to spread the explanation of the failure of the flood. In their desire to spread the word quickly and resoundingly, the believers now opened for public attention, matters that had been thus far utterly secret. Where only hours earlier they had shunned the newspaper reporters and felt that the attention they were getting in the press was painful, they now became avid seekers of publicity.

(Festinger *et al.* 1958 p 162)

Although interesting, the Keech study represents a single observation for which other explanations may be equally possible. It therefore provides only a weak and inconclusive test of Festinger's hypothesis. In a field test of a rather different kind, Ehrlich *et al.* (1957) noted that people who had purchased a new car were subsequently more likely to look at advertisements for the car they had bought than at those for other makes. Dissonance is likely to be created when choosing a car. The choice of one inevitably means losing the attractive features of the other cars considered and rejected. The purchasers' behaviour was interpreted as being an attempt to reduce this dissonance by seeking confirmation of the positive attributes of the car they had chosen. More precise experimental tests of dissonance theory in situations involving choice, lying and temptation have already been described in Festinger's paper. These represent only a tiny sample of experiments which have confirmed cognitive dissonance theory predictions.

8.2 DISSONANCE AND INTERPERSONAL ATTITUDES

Several studies have shown that attitudes towards other people may be influenced by the need to maintain consonance. In a well-designed experiment which also brings out some of the problems and care needed in experimental research, Aronson and Mills (1959) explored the consequences of having to undergo a difficult initiation procedure in order to a join a group. Their subjects were sixty-three female undergraduates from Stanford University. They were not told that they were participating in an experiment and they presumed that they were volunteering to take part in a series of group discussions about the psychology of sex. Each subject was assigned at random to one of three groups. The first was a 'severe initiation' condition. These subjects were asked to undergo a 'screening test' to ensure that they would not be too embarrassed to participate in the 'discussion' which they were given to understand would follow. The test required them to read aloud in front of the experimenter, twelve obscene words and two vivid descriptions of sexual activity taken from contemporary novels. The 'mild initiation' group also had a screening test but this merely involved

[handwritten margin note:] Buying a car — loss of valued features in rejected cars: confirm the good features of your purchase

59

reading five words with weak sexual connotations (e.g. petting, virgin etc.). The third group was a control condition against which the effects of the two forms of initiation could be compared.

The purpose of this experiment was to see the effect of the initiation procedures on the subjects' evaluations of the discussion group.

Note down your prediction on the basis of cognitive dissonance theory as to which subjects – the severe initiation, mild initiation or control groups – would evaluate the discussion group most highly. Give reasons for your prediction.

In order to compare the evaluations by subjects in the three conditions, it was necessary for each girl to experience the discussion group so that she could give her assessment of it.

SAQ 42

Would it be good experimental procedure to let each girl join a discussion group set up especially for the experiment and then to compare the evaluations made?

SAQ 43

If not, why not?

The experimenters suggested to each subject that, in order to avoid any possibility of embarrassment, she should participate in the first session by means of an intercom. system using headphones and a microphone. They also suggested that if she had not read the book which was to be discussed (which no subject could have done because it did not exist), then she merely listened. Each subject in fact heard a tape recording of a very boring and mumbled discussion among three undergraduate students. In this way the experimenters provided an identical stimulus for each subject which allowed the evaluations made by each group to be compared. All subjects then filled out a series of semantic differential type scales to indicate their assessment of the quality of the discussion which they had heard and the people taking part in it.

No significant difference was found between the evaluations given by the subjects in the control and the mild initiation conditions but significantly more favourable ratings were given by the subjects in the severe initiation group. These results are consistent with the predictions of dissonance theory. To undergo a severe initiation process in order to join a boring group would generate dissonance. One way of avoiding or reducing this dissonance is to see the group as more interesting than it really is.

SAQ 44

Why was a control group necessary?

SAQ 45

Can we assume that all subjects undergoing the severe initiation procedure were more embarrassed than subjects undergoing mild initiation?

Jecker and Landy (1969) confirmed that a similar effect applies in our relations with individuals. They hypothesized that if a person benefited someone, particularly if he disliked that individual, then he would tend to evaluate him more highly in order to reduce the dissonance such a discrepancy would create. Neither the subject nor (in order to avoid any unconscious bias) the person who conducted the experiment knew its true purpose. Subjects were told it was a study of the effects of incentive on a concept formation task; the experimenter that it was to explore the effects of frustration on learning.

Subjects took part individually in a task for which they were rewarded for 'correct' responses. The procedure was rigged so that half the subjects ended up with a small sum of money and the other half with a somewhat larger sum. The experimenter behaved in a uniformly offhand and rather rude way throughout. Subjects were then assigned randomly to one of three groups. To subjects in the first group, the experimenter confessed that his funds were running low and requested them, as a favour, to return to him the money they had earned. The second group were asked by the department secretary to return, for the same reason, their money to the department fund. The third group was a control of whom no favour was requested. All subjects were subsequently asked to rate both experiment and experimenter. The results showed clearly that the subjects who did the experimenter a favour and returned their money to him, evaluated him significantly more favourably than did subjects in the other two groups (this difference being significant at the .01 level). There was a slight tendency for those who had returned to him the larger sum to rate him more highly than those who had given him less money, but this tendency was not statistically significant.

Although the results suggest then that if you do a favour for someone you will rate him more highly, this conclusion requires qualification. It is worth noting that a few subjects refused to return their winnings. These had to be left out of the account and this could possibly have affected the results. Also, subjects in the group who returned their money as a favour to the experimenter had slightly more contact with him. Although this difference was marginal, this may have had some effect on their ratings. Finally, we do not know how far we can generalize from this result. Would it still hold if the favour was of a more substantial kind? These reservations indicate the care necessary in design and the difficulty of drawing precise and generalizable conclusions from research results.

To conclude this section, we will consider the converse prediction. What happens to your evaluation of someone if you treat them badly? Long before Festinger had formulated his theory, Tolstoy had suggested the answer. In the following passage the speaker is a general who held administrative power over political prisoners in St. Petersburg. Tolstoy indicates how his attitude was affected by the office he held.

> 'There's not an innocent one among them. All these people are a bad lot. We know them', (the general) said in a tone admitting of no possibility of doubt. And he really had no doubts – not because it was so but because if it were not so, he would be forced to see himself, not as a venerable hero honourably living out the last days of a good life but as a scoundrel, who had sold, and in his old age continued to sell, his conscience. (Tolstoy 1916 pp 350–1)

Tolstoy's explanation makes good sense in terms of cognitive dissonance theory. But in social science we need, as you will know by now, more than assertion. Support is necessary either of a logical or empirical kind.

In an experiment by Davis and Jones (1960), subjects who were told that they were participating in an experiment to compare how people respond to flattery and to negative evaluations of themselves, were persuaded to read a negative assessment of another person to their face. One group of subjects was given an ostensible 'choice' of which kind of evaluation to read but were told the experimenter would appreciate it if they read the negative one (most subjects acquiesced). In another 'no choice' condition, subjects were just assigned the negative evaluation without comment or discussion. Half the subjects in each group were led to believe that they would meet the target individual again after the experiment. Each subject had already met him in the waiting room prior to the experiment and had presumed that he was a subject like themselves. Of course, he was in reality an accomplice of the experimenter. Each subject was required to read out the prepared negative evaluation to the target person. All subjects were also asked to rate what they really thought of the other man's characteristics both before and after they read the evaluation. The results showed that later evaluations by all subjects were more negative. However, significant shifts occurred only in the case of those subjects who both thought that they would not see their victim again and who could consider that they had some element of choice as to whether they read the flattering or negative account. In the other conditions where there was no choice or where the subject could believe that his negative account could be disclaimed later when he met the victim, the discrepancy between what had been expressed and the subject's genuine evaluation would be likely to be less dissonant.

In an interesting follow-up, Glass (1964) got subjects to administer what they thought were electric shocks to the victim under conditions of choice and where they did not expect to see the victim again as in the experiment described above. He found that the higher the self-esteem of subjects, the more they were likely to derogate the victim. This again is consistent with cognitive dissonance theory. The more an individual believes himself to be a kind and worthy person, the more dissonant is it for him to behave aggressively. The greater dissonance should produce a greater tendency to devalue the victim in order to achieve consonance. Lerner and Simmons (1966) have demonstrated an even more sinister effect that if an individual merely *sees* a person being treated badly, there may be a tendency to devalue him accordingly. The belief that many people hold that the world is a 'just place' is dissonant with seeing a person suffer unless the person suffering can be thought likely to deserve it. The results of the Davis and Jones, and the Glass experiments have interesting implications in relation to compliance. They suggest that, even where an individual

Compliance is discussed in section 5.2

merely plays a part for desired ends and behaves in a particular way or expresses certain attitudes only to please or avoid offending someone, that this may in fact result, provided he had some choice in the matter, in a genuine shift of attitude in a direction consonant with his actions and words. They also indicate an affirmative answer to the question posed in section 5.4 as to whether Milgram's subjects would develop a more negative attitude towards their victims as a result of their actions.

8.3   THE ETHICS OF DECEPTION

The experiments discussed in this section illustrate the elaborate deception often necessary in a laboratory setting to produce the effects which the experimenter wants to study. The ethics of experimental research in social psychology have been the subject of considerable controversy. Experiments like those of Milgram which induce considerable anxiety in subjects taking part, have been in particular subjected to attack. However, in the Milgram experiment described earlier, the anxiety was created largely in those subjects who continued to administer electric shocks. In this case at least, it might be argued that the anxiety could be beneficial in the long term to both subjects and society if it helped the individuals concerned to realize what they were capable of doing. In practically all the experiments which involve deception, subjects are 'debriefed' at the end and told about the deception which they have been subjected to. This in itself can create problems for the experimenters in that it is always possible (and in some cases quite likely!) that debriefed subjects might tell other potential subjects about the real purpose of the experiment and so spoil the results obtained.

8.4   WHAT IS DISSONANCE?

Finally, note that cognitive dissonance, like 'attitude' and 'personality', is a hypothetical construct. Although there are indications that a state of dissonance may produce physiological effects (Zimbardo *et al.* 1966), we cannot see or directly observe it. Essentially it is an explanatory construct helpful in making sense of observed phenomena and predicting the course of events. The factors that contribute to it and the effects it produces are beginning to be delineated by experiments such as those described in this section. However, the problems of generalization, individual differences, and the complexity and variety of social situations still render it difficult to make precise and valid predictions about the behaviour of all people in analogous situations.

9 PERSUASION

One underlying theme running through sections 3 to 8 has been the question – what makes people's attitudes so stable and resistant to change? I have suggested a number of reasons for this. These reasons also provide us with clues as to how it may be possible to change attitudes. A great deal of research has been carried out on this topic which there is no space to discuss in detail here. However, I will give you an idea of some of the basic techniques and principles of persuasion and attitude change as this will also serve to help you review the earlier material of the unit.

9.1 THE 'RATIONAL' APPROACH

Both Unit 7 and section 3 of this unit demonstrated how perception is very much a function of the perceiver. We experience and assimilate material in accordance with our expectations, attitudes and motivation. It is not surprising that a straightforward 'rational' approach which merely presents good reasons why we should change our attitudes or beliefs rarely has much success. A cigarette smoker can doubt the validity of the research demonstrating a link between cancer and smoking. Or he can assure himself that any ill-effects are more than compensated for by the benefits of relaxation that smoking brings. As we saw, Mrs Keech was even able to cope with clear disconfirmation of her belief and still go on happily as before. Evidence and logical reasons by themselves surprisingly rarely produce change in what people feel or believe.

There are exceptions to this, of course. As discussed in section 5.4, education by providing information over time and developing thinking skills, may increase the multiplexity of beliefs held and lead the holder to examine their consistency. This process, in turn, may result in some attitude change. Techniques like some forms of individual and group psychotherapy also act by providing a person with information about his own behaviour and feelings and the way that these are perceived by others which may gradually lead to a restructuring of awareness, and behaviour and attitude change.

See television programme 21

9.2 SOCIAL INFLUENCE

Social pressure is likely to offer more scope as a persuasive technique. The experiments of Asch and Crutchfield showed how group pressure could induce substantial shifts in expressed attitudes and judgements.

SAQ 46

List some of the main factors that determine whether or not a person's attitude will be influenced by group pressure.

Kelman's theory of social influence can be used equally well to explain the process of persuasion as it can to explain attitude formation.

SAQ 47

What are the three forms of social influence described by Kelman and on what kind of relationship between the person influencing and the person influenced does each depend?

The credibility attached to the communicator clearly affects his persuasive power. For example, the same tape-recorded communication advocating more lenient treatment of criminals was found to produce significantly more attitude change when the speaker was introduced as a judge than when it was implied that he had been a criminal (Hovland, Janis and Kelley 1953). Both the credibility and attractiveness of the communicator may be increased if he commences by stating views on which the audience agrees. This has been found an effective means of reducing resistance subsequently to more controversial ideas (Weiss 1957). Other studies have suggested the importance of role characteristics and the kind of person the influencing agent is thought to be. A well-dressed man crossing against the lights on a pedestrian crossing persuaded by his example fourteen per cent of the other pedestrians to follow him but the same man in grubby overalls was followed by only four per cent (Lefkowitz et al. 1955).

9.3 THE 'INSIGHT' TECHNIQUE

SAQ 48

Name the four functions which attitudes serve as described in Katz's paper.

The relationship of personality to prejudice is discussed in section 7

Daniel Katz, whose functional theory of attitudes you encountered in section 6, has devised an interesting method for modifying prejudiced attitudes which are rooted in ego-defensive needs. This is designed to attack the *function* served by such attitudes rather than their content. Prejudiced subjects were given an account of the nature of defence mechanisms and of how prejudice may be generated by personality factors. This account was illustrated by detailed reference to a case study of a person of similar age and background to the subject. A comparison group received a 'rational' communication which argued the need to view their own and other cultural groups in an objective and non-ethnocentric way. Tested six weeks later, a substantial proportion of subjects receiving the insight technique showed an appreciable shift to less prejudiced attitudes. The comparison and a control group receiving no communication of any kind showed little or no change. However, the insight technique produced no effect on the most ego-defensive of the prejudiced subjects. Katz and his co-workers considered that only prolonged individual therapy would be sufficient for these subjects to attain self-insight.

9.4 EMOTIONAL APPEAL

SAQ 49

Distinguish between the cognitive and affective aspects of an attitude.

Although rational communications have been found to be relatively ineffectual, emotionally toned communications tend to have more persuasive impact. If the persuasive communication is designed to get people to behave in a particular way,

64

however, it is important to ensure that the feelings aroused relate to the actual behaviour desired and not to some more general issue. For example, in a study designed to persuade alcoholics to sign up for a treatment programme, McArdle and Fishbein (in press) found that an appeal describing the negative consequences of not signing up for the programme was significantly more effective in getting them to do so than was a more generally oriented appeal about the negative consequences of continuing to drink.

Emotional communications, however, may not be effective if they arouse too much anxiety. In a classic study, Janis and Feschbach (1953) found that a communication which listed the most dire consequences that could result from ineffectual dental hygiene (including kidney disease and blindness which, it was said, could develop as a result of tooth decay!) produced far less effect on tooth brushing behaviour than a more moderately termed appeal. It is quite likely that the more extremely worded communication strained credibility and was also dissonant with the subject's own experience. Some may never have brushed their teeth regularly, and many probably knew one or two other people who did not do so; nevertheless, they had suffered no undue consequences. Another factor may have been that the anxiety created by strong fear-arousing communications led to defensive blocking with the subject being less receptive to its content. McGuire (1966) has also suggested that persuasive effects are likely to be maximal at moderate as opposed to low or high levels of anxiety arousal. As the anxiety level aroused by a stimulus will depend on the initial anxiety level in the subject and his capacity to cope with anxiety-arousing situations, the level of threat optimal for persuasion will vary from subject to subject.

9.5 THE DISSONANCE APPROACH

Public commitment by words or action has been found to be an effective conversion technique by evangelists, weight-watchers and alcoholics trying to 'dry out'. At an evangelical crusade meeting the new converts may be asked to step up onto the platform; at an alcoholics' meeting a member may be required to state publicly his belief in the evils of alcohol and to persuade others to give up drink. Dissonance theory would predict that these procedures are very likely to be an effective method of strengthening newly acquired beliefs and attitudes. As many of the experiments described in section 8 demonstrated, attitudes and evaluations tend to shift in order to maintain consistency with behaviour.

The induction of dissonance has been deliberately used to effect changes in attitudes and behaviour and has been found to be remarkably successful. Wallace (1966) found that subjects who volunteered to support in public debate a view on capital punishment which was opposite to their own, subsequently showed a substantial shift of attitude in the direction consistent with the view for which they had argued. Wallace tried to create maximal dissonance in one group of subjects in the experiment by telling them that the audience had considered their presentation particularly sincere. He assumed that implying that the speaker had sounded as if he believed what he was saying, would create maximal dissonance. Wallace's assumption was supported by a statement made by one of the subjects after the experiment: 'I tend to think of myself as an honest and sincere person. When you told me that the others considered me "a very good actor", I was somewhat baffled . . . actually, a little offended. The more I thought about it, the more I became convinced that what I had said in the debate was what I truly believed' (Wallace 1966 p 311).

Role-playing techniques have been found effective in helping subjects to cut down on cigarette smoking. Alan Elms (1966) found that getting smokers to play the role of a non-smoker and to persuade another subject that he should stop smoking produced some subsequent change in smoking behaviour according to subjects' own reports in response to a questionnaire three weeks after the experiment. Elms also

Role-playing is demonstrated in television programme 21

assessed the fantasy-playing ability of his subjects. He found the correlation between the role-players' fantasy ability and their reported decrease in smoking to be +.69 (significant at the .001 level).

SAQ 50

Can we therefore conclude that the greater the role-player's fantasy ability the more likely is his role-playing to induce attitude change?

Janis and Mann (1965) have found that emotional role-playing is particularly effective. They asked a group of young women who were all heavy smokers to play the role of cancer patients. The experimenter acted as the doctor and several scenes were played through in which the 'patient' was told that she had lung cancer. Attention was focused particularly on the threat of painful illness, hospitalization and early death. Control subjects merely watched and listened to the scenes.

The smoking behaviour of the role-players was studied for the two years following the experiment and compared with that of the control group. Results for both groups are shown in Figure 8. Even though there was some tendency in both groups to

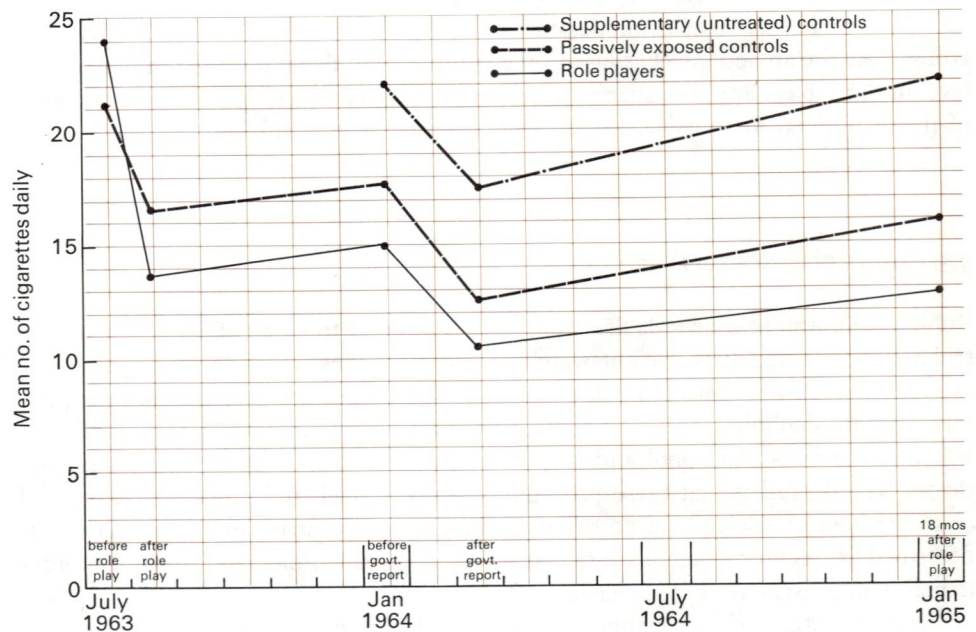

Figure 8   Long-term effects of emotional role-playing on cigarette smoking

Source: Mann and Janis (1968)

gradually revert back to old smoking habits after an initial change, the decrease in the role-players' smoking behaviour in comparison with the control group over the whole period was significant at the .05 level. (During the period in question, the report on smoking and lung cancer by the US Surgeon General was issued and received considerably publicity. As Figure 8 shows, it influenced the results of the experiment. So, in order to compare the report's impact on the two groups of subjects with its effect on other smokers, the smoking behaviour of a third group of untreated subjects not in the experiment was recorded and is also included in the graph. As can be seen, the influence of the report on the smoking behaviour of all three groups appears to be very similar.)

SAQ 51

From the graph in Figure 8, determine the average number of cigarettes smoked per day (to the nearest whole number):

A   by the role-players *immediately before* the role-playing exercise

B   by the control group *immediately before* the role-playing exercise

66

C   by the role-players *one month after* the role-playing exercise

D   by the control group *one month after* the role-playing exercise

E   by the role-players *six months after* the role-playing exercise

F   by the control group *six months after* the role-playing exercise

Also determine the decrease in the average number of cigarettes smoked per day by:

G   the role-players after six months

H   the control group after six months

I   the role-players after eighteen months

J   the control group after eighteen months

10   A NOTE ON PREJUDICE

Two forms of attitude which have an important influence on social behaviour are prejudice and religion. Although both have been touched on indirectly, neither has been treated systematically in the unit so far. In a sense this is not necessary. They are both particular forms of attitudes and beliefs and therefore much of the analysis in the preceding sections applies to them as well. In view of their significance, however, the unit concludes with two brief sections which attempt to relate aspects of the material already covered more specifically to the psychological bases of these two kinds of attitude.

Allport (1954 p 9) defines prejudice as, '. . . an antipathy based upon a faulty and inflexible generalization. It may be felt or expressed. It may be directed towards a group as a whole, or toward an individual because he is a member of that group'.

By this definition, then, not only does prejudice refer to an evaluation which is 'prejudged' or preconceived, but one which is also negative, faulty and inflexible. Judgements of individuals are made on the basis of the stereotype held of the group to which they are thought to belong.

Theory and evidence locating the basis of prejudice in personality dynamics have already been extensively discussed in section 7. But it is important to realize that not all prejudice can be explained solely in these terms. Prejudice, like homosexuality and other distinct forms of human behaviour and experience, may be produced by a variety of causal patterns. Pettigrew (1961) has argued that prejudice may frequently arise from conformity to social norms and situational pressures. He points to the often fragmentary nature of segregation attitudes among American southerners – segregation is accepted in some situations but resisted in others. In West Virginia, for example, according to Minard (1952), black and white miners integrate when working down the pits but segregate almost completely in their social life above ground. Pettigrew cites several studies which show that the F scores of people living in the southern states of the USA where anti-black prejudice is strong, are not significantly higher than those of comparable populations elsewhere. A number of studies (e.g. Roper 1947) have also shown it to be one of the less anti-semitic regions of the USA.

social
norms
—
situational

SAQ 52

What do the observations made in the last two sentences imply?

Pettigrew is not contradicting the findings of the Authoritarian Personality study; he himself (Pettigrew 1959) found a correlation between levels of prejudice and F scores *among* southern subjects. But he is suggesting that situational and normative factors must be considered as well.

The potency of normative and role pressures in inducing some people to aggress against others has been amply testified by studies like those of Milgram which we have considered earlier. Dissonance experiments have also shown that once people are party to discrimination against others or even only observe it, their attitudes and beliefs may shift towards devaluing the group discriminated against. Katz's theory also reminds us that prejudice may serve not only ego-defensive needs but also an instrumental function. Prejudice may provide, for example, the psychological conditions which permit employers or others to exploit target individuals. By his support of prejudice and discrimination, a prejudiced worker also may be more able to reserve for himself jobs and opportunities which offer better conditions and income.

can be instrumental

You might like to see if you can recollect or observe any specific examples of this kind where prejudice serves an instrumental function.

11 A NOTE ON THE PSYCHOLOGICAL BASES OF RELIGIOUS ATTITUDES

Religion comes in many forms from Christianity, Islam and Buddhism to Greek and Roman gods and totemistic systems of tribal groups. To a greater or lesser degree nearly all share certain common features: ritual, some supposed means of supernatural control like prayer, a way of making sense of existence and an ethical code stipulating what is right and wrong. It is these last two aspects, interpretation and evaluation, that we can consider correspond to the cognitive and affective aspects of religious attitudes respectively. The aim of this final section is to consider briefly how the material of the preceding sections can cast light on the psychological bases of these aspects of religious attitudes and beliefs. It is difficult to submit hypotheses in this area to empirical test. The following analysis therefore is inevitably only an interpretation. You must seek to test for yourself its validity in terms of its logic and its consistency with the evidence and argument that has been presented elsewhere in the unit and in the course.

11.1 THE LIMITS OF KNOWLEDGE

Man's capacity for knowledge is inevitably limited. It is limited first by the aspects of the world around him that he has access to. Our senses are capable of perceiving only certain kinds of stimuli. The development of science and technology has frequently produced instruments capable of picking up information which up to that time we were unaware existed. The frontiers of knowledge are being continually pushed forward. We know far more about the nature of the physical world around us and about events in the distant past or in distant space than we did 200 years ago. But it is not unreasonable to assume that there are events in the universe about which man will never know, either because of the limits on the sensitivity of his instruments and senses or because they are physically remote. Secondly, knowledge is limited by the processing power of the human brain. As the young child cannot comprehend conservation or causal relations so also there may be unknown patterns and relationships, ways of understanding and conceptualization, unattainable by the adult mind. Computers may extend our processing, even possibly our conceptualizing capacities but again there will always be limits and the possibility of other unknown ways of conceptualizing and making sense of things differently.

See the discussion on Piaget in Unit 18

Section 1.2 discussed man's capacity for symbolic thought. One of the consequences of this capacity, mentioned there, is the ability to construct conceptions of beings, events and situations which have no referents in the perceivable world. Man can thus transcend the sensory and processing limitations on what he can know, and

68

construct a 'reality' which he can never see or test. As has been argued elsewhere (see Unit 7 section 5, for example) this construction process is a part of all conceptualization and of perception itself. But in these cases construction is constrained to some extent by the characteristics of the stimuli concerned. Where there is no stimulus because the assertions are about events outside sensory awareness, there are few, if any, means for verifying or comparing the validities of 'realities' constructed by different individuals or cultures. Religious beliefs about the nature of existence are usually of this kind. Although belief in God, prayer, heaven, hell and after life may be real, even vivid, experiences in the mind of a believer, there is no effective way of empirically testing their validity. Ethical principles, evaluations of what is right or wrong are also assertions which cannot be proved right or wrong by resort to empirical criteria. It may be possible to determine whether or not a particular course of action is likely to produce a given end but appeal to evidence cannot establish whether the end itself is right or wrong.

See section 2.1 on *verifiability* as a dimension of attitudes.

The fundamental characteristic of religious attitudes then is that they are not testable. It is not possible to decide whether they are right or wrong by direct recourse to observation and experiment. This characteristic is reflected in the proliferation of creeds and ideologies of all varieties. One may contrast the state of natural science. Although controversies and differences of opinion are found there also, there is a great deal of common ground as well and in particular, there are agreed procedures for deciding the respective merits of different positions.

11.2   THE FUNCTIONAL VALUE OF RELIGIOUS ATTITUDES

It is worth considering what functions could be served for an individual by holding beliefs and attitudes towards concepts that are outside the reach of sensory awareness. It is possible to argue that religious attitudes are capable of serving each one of the Katz quadruplet. Religious mythology serves a *knowledge* function in that it provides what Fromm terms a 'frame of orientation'. By dealing with questions of creation, death, the ultimate and infinite, it attempts to provide a total framework for man's understanding. Until recent years, even in our culture, the total framework provided by Christianity dominated man's conceptualization even of the more mundane events which he could himself observe directly. Galileo was forced to recant his assertion that the earth moved round the sun because this was not consistent with the knowledge framework provided by the Church. The concepts and roles offered by a religion may also provide to those who accept them an identity and a definitive set of values. It is interesting that religious interest is often paramount in adolescence: at a time when the search for identity, a frame of reference and personal values is often a primary concern. Religious attitudes may thus serve a *value-expressive* function and offer an individual the means of confirming his self identity. Religious attitudes, in addition, may be relevant to *ego-defensive* processes. The potential that the Christian faith offers for atonement of sins may provide a useful outlet for guilt feelings arising from intra-psychic conflicts. The ways in which the adoption of religious attitudes may offer *instrumental* satisfactions are manifold and will depend on the culture and the individual concerned. Social contact, social approbation and status, power over others, material benefits and a definitive role are all examples of benefits that may, though not of course necessarily, accrue from holding religious beliefs. Perhaps the most important potential satisfaction offered by religion is the possibility of resolving existential dichotomies.

Katz's functional theory of attitudes is discussed in section 6

SAQ 53

What is an existential dichotomy?

Read Fromm in Reader
now, pp 356–9 You have already read in the Reader the first half of the article by Erich Fromm where he uses this term; you should read the remaining pages now.

Elsewhere in the book from which the extract is taken, Fromm argues, rather like Festinger, that 'when confronted by contradictions (the human mind) cannot remain passive. It is set in motion with the aim of resolving the contradiction' (Fromm 1949 p 44). The concepts which form part of religious beliefs often offer ways of resolving existential dichotomies. The idea, for example, that the essence of man is not tangible, that it resides in a spirit or soul which is to a large extent independent of his physical existence means that man no longer dies. The contradiction between life and death is thus annulled. The commitment often demanded by religion to a set of clearly delineated ethical precepts as, for example, the Ten Commandments, cuts down on the possibilities of alternative courses of action and the need for choice. The dichotomy of having potentialities which can never be realized is in this way, at least to some extent, alleviated. The possibility of a relationship with an intangible, all-powerful and all-loving God (at least for Christians) helps resolve the problem of isolation and separation that Fromm argues is also generated by awareness.

This discussion has been concerned only with the function of religious attitudes for the individual. Their functional value in relation to society as a whole is a topic taken up in the following units in this block.

11.3 CHILDHOOD EXPERIENCE AS A SOURCE OF RELIGIOUS BELIEF

As religious beliefs represent assertions about concepts which cannot be perceived, the question arises how they are formulated. This is particularly interesting in view of the fact that the content of the beliefs held by different religions varies.

Freud had no doubt that one of the primary bases of belief in God was the young child's experience of his parents. Several cross-cultural studies of religious beliefs have noted a correlation between traditional child-rearing methods and the idea of god adopted by a society. In cultures where child-rearing methods are permissive and warm, the gods are also likely to be benevolent: where they are harsh and punitive, the gods are more likely to have an evil eye! (see, for example, research by Lambert, Triandis and Wolf 1959). Kardiner (1963) also cites observations of Comanche Indians. Their child-rearing methods tend to be by example rather than by reward and punishment. Their god is generally benevolent. They have no concept of sin, forgiveness, retribution, expiation or hell.

Cross-cultural comparisons, especially of belief systems, are notoriously prone to errors of interpretation. Even if a relationship between the content of a culture's belief and its child-rearing methods could be established, we cannot be sure which is affecting which. The evidence is suggestive only but it is consistent with Freud's idea that childhood experience may provide a source of the content of religious belief.

11.4 FORMATION AND CHANGE OF RELIGIOUS ATTITUDES

As section 5 would lead us to expect, the culture in which an individual is brought up is likely to be one of the primary determinants of the religious attitudes he holds. As the child grows older, however, he becomes capable of greater cognitive complexity and of perceiving logical inconsistency. In a complex culture such as ours, he is also likely to encounter many new ideas. This may lead to dissonance among beliefs assimilated during early experience and those acquired later. This tendency towards change and search for new meaning is particularly characteristic of adolescence. At the same time, lack of confidence and an attempt to establish a coherent self-identity often lead people of this age to seek out a role, person or group with whom they can identify. It might be argued that these are some of the underlying reasons why adolescents form a large proportion of the recruits attracted to the cults, sects and quasi-religious organizations which proliferate in modern western society.

As we have seen in many places in this unit, logic, empirical evidence, and whether or not attitudes can be verified have very little to do with the firmness of the commitment with which they are held. It is interesting in this respect that one psychologist found that subjects were more prepared to commit themselves on the question as to whether there are angels in heaven than on whether there are tigers in India!(Thouless 1935). Once satisfactorily attained, central religious attitudes are likely to be highly resistant to change for reasons that have been discussed in sections 3 to 8 of this unit. The danger for man lies in the power of the unverifiable attitudes of ideologies and religions to override clear and incontrovertible logical and empirical considerations. For example, logic and evidence clearly indicate that some form of population limitation is necessary if man is to survive without the great suffering which would be caused by extensive famine and/or conflict over limited resources. Yet some religious attitudes, which in themselves offer a solution to existential needs, may create concepts and attitudes which make it difficult to accept the most effective methods of birth control. For men to survive, we need to find ways of satisfying existential needs in a way which will not conflict with the requirements of physical survival – we shall need to find ways of satisfying existential and historical dichotomies in harmony.

APPENDIX – WILSON-PATTERSON CONSERVATISM SCALE

This appendix is entirely optional and is not essential reading. It is provided for the benefit of those interested in scoring and interpreting their responses on this scale (given in section 2.3).

Construction

Wilson and Patterson considered it better to use single words than statements as items. They argued that this avoids the risk of misinterpretation and also reduces the likelihood of respondents answering in a particular way merely because they consider it the socially desirable response rather than because that is what they really feel.

Development of the scale began with an attempt to describe the characteristics of the typical extreme conservative. They considered he would be religious in a dogmatic way, have a right-wing political orientation, favour strict rules and punishments, be ethnocentric and intolerant of minority groups, prefer conventional clothes and art etc., be anti-hedonistic in outlook (tend to regard pleasure, particularly sexual, as necessarily bad) be superstitious and resistant to scientific progress.

The constructors then selected a large number of items which they considered would be likely discriminators of these characteristics and subjected them to *item analysis*. For half of the fifty items selected for the final scale, affirmative responses score in the conservative direction and, for the other half, negative responses score in the conservative direction. This rules out any possibility of bias due to acquiescence response set.

The problem of acquiescence response set is the subject of SAQ 34

Scoring

Each 'yes' to an odd-numbered item and each 'no' to an even-numbered item is scored 2. Any response not either a simple 'yes' or 'no' is scored 1. Possible range of scores is therefore 0 to 100.

Interpretation of scores

A score on an attitude scale provides a general indication of the positivity/negativity of the respondent's feelings in relation to the attitude concerned. To give it real

TABLE 5   CONSERVATISM SCORES FOR DIFFERENT GROUPS

Group	N	Mean	Standard deviation
University Students (UK)	50	25.33	13.00
University Students (NZ)	107	32.57	10.36
University Students (USA)	100	42.21	11.31
Housewives (NZ)	44	60.98	12.02
Schoolgirls (State school, UK)	85	36.86	10.19
Schoolgirls (Catholic school UK)	100	51.99	11.30
Professionals and business men (UK)	50	33.82	18.06
Clerical workers (UK)	50	43.52	16.04
Trade apprentices (UK)	187	39.65	8.54
Skilled workers (UK)	50	45.43	12.93
Full-time pop musicians (UK)	76	31.83	10.83

Source: Wilson (1973)

meaning, however, we need to compare it with the scores of other people. The mean (average) scores obtained from several different groups of people are given in Table 5. N indicates the number of people in each group tested. As Huff pointed out in Chapter 3 of *How to lie with statistics*, an average does not provide sufficient information in itself for effective interpretation of any individual score. The knowledge that the average score for a group is 55 does not tell us whether a score of 65 is just above average or one of the highest scores for that group. For this reason *standard deviations* for each group are also provided in Table 5. The standard deviation is an index of the average amount subjects' scores in that group deviate from the mean. As a rough rule, we know that, if the data follows a normal distribution, approximately 34 per cent of the scores will fall between the mean and 1 standard deviation above, and that 34 per cent will fall between the mean and 1 standard deviation below. From the data given, therefore, we can calculate that a score of 38 is well above average for UK university students. It represents the equivalent of the mean (25.33) plus 1 standard deviation (13.00). Therefore, approximately 84 per cent (50 per cent plus 34 per cent) of this student group get scores at or below 38 and only about 16 per cent get scores above that level. The same score, however, would be substantially below average for New Zealand housewives. The mean for this group (see Table 5) is 60.98 and the standard deviation is 12.02. A score equivalent to 1 standard deviation below the mean would therefore be 48.96 (i.e. 60.98–12.02). Approximately 16 per cent (i.e. 50 per cent–34 per cent) of this group get scores at or below this level. A score of 38 would represent a very low score indeed. The least conservative of the New Zealand housewives would therefore probably have similar attitudes to the most conservative of the UK student group.

The relationship of age and sex to C scores (based on data from New Zealanders) is given in Figure 9. It can be seen that conservatism increases sharply with age and that females tend to be slightly more conservative than males. It is not known whether the upward trend of conservatism with age is a result of people becoming more conservative as they get older. The pattern of scores was obtained by sampling people of different ages. The curve may therefore represent differences between the generations as they are now. Wilson emphasizes that both tendencies are likely to be operative.

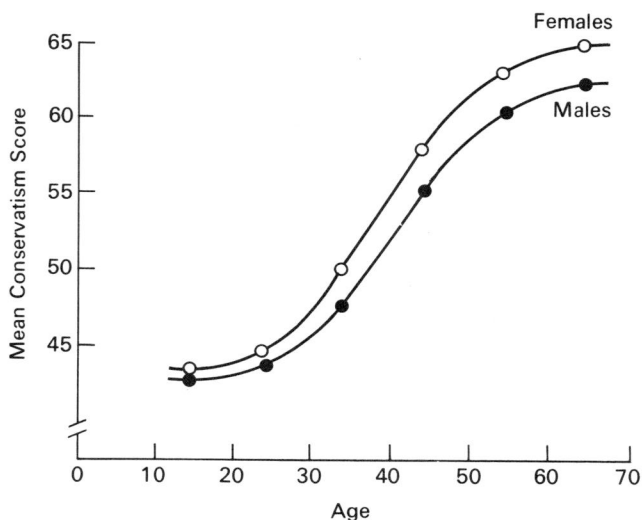

Figure 9 The relationships of C scores to age and sex, based on a sample of 360 New Zealanders

Source: Wilson and Patterson (1968)

FURTHER READING

The following books may be of interest to any students who would like to read further on topics discussed in these units.

On the 'Mrs Keech' study:

FESTINGER, L., RIECKEN, H. and SCHACHTER, S. (1956) *When prophecy fails*, Minneapolis, University of Minnesota Press.

On the Authoritarian Personality study:

BROWN, R. (1965) *Social psychology*, New York, Free Press, Chapter 10.

On the Milgram experiments:

MILGRAM, S. (1974) *Obedience to authority: an experimental view*, London, Tavistock.

On attitudes generally but particularly on attitude change:

ZIMBARDO, P. and EBBESEN, E. (1970) *Influencing attitudes and changing behaviour*, Reading, Massachusetts, Addison-Wesley.

or TRIANDIS, H. C. (1971) *Attitude and attitude change*, New York, Wiley.

SOME IMPORTANT TERMS AND CONCEPTS

Listed below are some of the more important terms and concepts used in this unit. You can check your assimilation of the unit by going down the list. Look up any you are not sure of and refresh your memory.

REFERENCES

ADORNO, R. W. *et al.* (1950) *The authoritarian personality*, New York, Harper and Row.

ALLPORT, G. W. (1954) 'The historical background of modern social psychology', in Lindzey, G. (ed.) *Handbook of social psychology*, Reading, Massachusetts, Addison-Wesley.

ARONSON, E. and MILLS, J. (1959) 'The effect of severity of initiation on liking for a group', *Journal of Abnormal and Social Psychology*, vol 59, pp 177–81.

ASCH, S. E. (1955) 'Opinions and social pressure' in *Scientific American*, vol. 193, pp 31–5. Reprinted in Scientific American (1974 pp 29–33).

ASCH, S. E. (1959) 'Interpersonal influence' in Maccoby, E., Newcomb, T. and Hartley, E. L. (eds.) *Readings in social psychology*, London, Methuen.

BARRON, F. K. (1950) 'Some personality correlates of independence of judgement', *Journal of Consulting Psychology* (1953) vol. 21, pp 287–97.

BETTELHEIM, B. (1943) 'Individual and mass behaviour in extreme situations' in Maccoby, E., Newcomb, T. and Hartley, E. L. (eds.), *Readings in social psychology* (1959), London, Methuen.

BROWN, R. (1965) *Social psychology*, New York, Free Press.

BUTLER, D. and STOKES, D. (1969) *Political change in Britain*, London, Macmillan.

CHRISTIE, R. (1954) 'Authoritarianism re-examined', in Christie, R. and Jahoda, M. (eds.) *Studies in the scope and method of 'The Authoritarian Personality'*, New York, Wiley.

COOMBS, C. H. (1964) *A theory of data*, New York, Wiley.

CROZIER, W. and PINCUS, G. (1926) 'The geotropic conduct of young rats', *Journal of General Physiology*, vol. 10, pp 257–69.

CRUTCHFIELD, R. S. (1955) 'Conformity and character' in Wrightsman (1968).

DAVIS, K. and JONES, E. E. (1960) 'Changes in inter-personal perception as a means of reducing cognitive dissonance', *Journal of Abnormal and Social Psychology*, vol. 61, pp 402–10.

EHRLICH, D., GUTTMANN, I., SCHONBACH, P. and MILLS, J. (1957) 'Post-decision exposure to relevant information', *Journal of Abnormal and Social Psychology*, vol. 54, pp 98–102.

ELMS, A. C. (1966) 'Influence of fantasy ability on attitude change through role-playing', *Journal of Personality and Social Psychology*, vol. 4, pp 36–43.

ELMS, A. C. (1972) *Social psychology and social relevance*, Boston, Little, Brown.

ENGLISH, H. B. and ENGLISH, A. C. (1958) *A comprehensive dictionary of psychological and psychoanalytical terms*, New York, Longman, Green and Co. Inc.

EYSENCK, H. J. (1954) *The psychology of politics*, London, Routledge and Kegan Paul.

EYSENCK, H. J. (1971) 'Social attitudes and social class', *British Journal of Social and Clinical Psychology*, vol. 10, pp 201–12.

FESTINGER, L. (1957) *A theory of cognitive dissonance*, New York, Harper and Row.

FESTINGER, L. (1962) 'Cognitive dissonance' in *Scientific American*, vol. 207, no. 4, pp 93–102. Reprinted in Scientific American (1974 pp 34–40).

FESTINGER, L., RIECKEN, H. W. and SCHACHTER, S. (1956) *When prophecy fails*, Minneapolis, University of Minnesota Press.

FESTINGER, L., RIECKEN, H. W. and SCHACHTER, S. (1958) 'When prophecy fails' in Maccoby, E., Newcomb, T. and Hartley, E. L. (eds.) *Readings in social psychology*, London, Methuen.

FISHBEIN, M. and COOMBS, F. S. (1974) 'Basis for decision: and attitudinal analysis on voting behaviour', *Journal of Applied Social Psychology*, vol. 4, no. 2, pp 95–124.

FROMM, E. (1949) 'Human nature and character' in *Man for himself*, London, Routledge and Kegan Paul, pp 39–50. Reprinted in Potter and Sarre (1974 pp 352–359).

GERARD, H. B. and MATHEWSON, G. (1966) 'The effects of severity of initiation on liking for a group: a replication', *Journal of Experimental and Social Psychology*, vol. 2 pp 278–87.

GILBERT, G. M. (1951) 'Stereotype persistence and change among college students', *Journal of Abnormal and Social Psychology*, vol. 46, pp 245–54.

GLASS, D. C. (1964) 'Changes in liking as a means of reducing cognitive discrepancies between self-esteem and aggression', *Journal of Personality*, vol. 32, pp 531–49.

GOFFMAN, E. (1959) *The presentation of self in everyday life*, New York, Doubleday Anchor.

HASTORF, A. H. and CANTRIL, H. (1954) 'They saw a game: a case study', *Journal of Abnormal and Social Psychology*, vol. 49, pp 129–34.

HEIDER, F. (1958) *The psychology of interpersonal relations*, New York, Wiley.

HOVLAND, C. I., JANIS, I. L. and KELLEY, H. H. (1953) *Communication and persuasion*, Newhaven, Yale University Press.

HUFF, D. (1973) *How to lie with statistics*, Harmondsworth, Penguin (set book).

HYMAN, H. H. and SHEATSLEY, P. B. (1954) ' "The Authoritarian Personality" — a methodological critique', in Christie, R. and Jahoda, M. (eds.) *Studies in the scope and method of 'The Authoritarian Personality'*, New York, Wiley.

INSIGHT REPORT (1974) 'Hidden persuaders in the hostage war', *Sunday Times*, 3 November.

JANIS, I. and FESCHBACH, F. (1953) 'Effects of fear-arousing communications', *Journal of Abnormal and Social Psychology*, vol. 48, pp 78–92.

JANIS, I. and MANN, L. (1965) 'Effectiveness of emotional role-playing in modifying smoking habits and attitudes', *Journal of Experimental Research in Personality*, vol. 1, pp 84–90.

JECKER, J. and LANDY, D. (1969) 'Liking a person as a function of doing him a favour', *Human Relations*, vol. 22, no. 4, pp 371–8.

JONES, E. E. and ANESHANSEL, J. (1956) 'The learning and utilization of contra-valuent material', *Journal of Abnormal and Social Psychology*, vol. 53, pp 27–33.

JONES, E. E. and GERARD, H. B. (1967) *Foundations of social psychology*, New York, Wiley.

JONES, E. E. and KOHLER, R. (1958) 'The effects of plausibility on the learning of controversial statements', *Journal of Abnormal and Social Psychology*, vol. 57, pp 315–20.

KARDINER, A. (1963) *The psychological frontiers of society*, New York, Columbia University Press.

KATZ, D. (1960) 'The functional approach to the study of attitudes' in *Public Opinion Quarterly*, vol. 24, pp 163–77. Reprinted in Potter and Sarre (1974 pp 360–9).

KELMAN, H. V. (1961) 'Three processes of social influence' in *Public Opinion Quarterly*, vol. 25, pp 57–78.

KOHLBERG, L. (1968) 'The child as a moral philosopher', *Psychology Today*, September 11 pp 24–30.

KRECH, D. and CRUTCHFIELD, R. S. (1948) *Theory and problems of social psychology*, New York, McGraw-Hill.

KUTNER, B., WILKINS, C. and YARROW, P. R. (1952) 'Verbal attitudes and overt behaviour involving racial prejudice', *Journal of Abnormal and Social Psychology*, vol. 47, pp 649–52.

LA PIÈRE, R. T. (1934) 'Attitudes versus actions', *Social Forces*, vol. 14, pp 230–7.

LAMBERT, W. W., TRIANDIS, L. M. and WOLF, M. (1959) 'Some correlates of beliefs in the malevolence and benevolence of supernatural beings: a cross societal study', *Journal of Abnormal and Social Psychology*, vol. 38, pp 162–9.

LEFKOWITZ, M., BLAKE, R. and MOUTON, J. (1955) 'Status factors in pedestrian violation of traffic signals', *Journal of Abnormal and Social Psychology*, vol. 51, pp 704–6.

LERNER, M. J. and SIMMONS, C. H. (1966) 'Observer's reaction to the "innocent victim": compassion or rejection?', *Journal of Personality and Social Psychology*, vol. 4, pp 203–10.

MANN, L. and JANIS, I. (1968) 'A follow-up study on the long-term effects of emotional role playing', *Journal of Personality and Social Psychology*, vol. 8, pp 339–42.

MCARDLE, J. and FISHBEIN, M. (in press) 'Positive and negative communications and subsequent attitude and behaviour change in alcoholics'. *Journal of Experimental Social Psychology*.

MCGUIRE, W. J. (1966) 'Attitudes and opinion' in Farnsworth, McNemar and McNemar (eds.) *Annual Review of Psychology*, Palo Alto Annual Reviews.

MILGRAM, S. (1963) 'Behavioural study of obedience' in Wrightsman (1968).

MILGRAM, S. (1974) *Obedience to authority: an experimental view*, London, Tavistock.

MINARD, R. D. (1952) 'Race relations in the Pocahontas coalfield', *Journal of Social Issues*, vol. 8, pp 29–44.

NEWCOMB, P. M. (1959) 'Attitude development as a function of reference groups: the Bennington study', in Maccoby, E., Newcomb, T. and Hartley, E. L. (eds.) *Readings in social psychology*, London, Methuen.

NEWSON, J. and NEWSON, E. (1970) *Four years old in an urban community*, Harmondsworth, Penguin.

ORNE, M. T. (1962) 'On the social psychology of the psychological experiment', *American Psychologist*, vol. 17, no. 11, pp 776–83.

OSGOOD, C. E., SUCI, G. J. and TANNENBAUM, P. H. (1957) *The measurement of meaning*, Urbana, Ill., University of Illinois Press.

OSGOOD, C. and TANNENBAUM, P. (1955) 'The principle of congruity in the prediction of attitude change', *Psychological Review*, vol. 62 pp 42–55.

PETTIGREW, P. F. (1959) 'Regional differences in anti-negro prejudice', *Journal of Abnormal and Social Psychology*, vol. 59, pp 28–36.

PETTIGREW, P. F. (1961) 'Social psychology and desegregation research' in Wrightsman, (1968).

PIAGET, J. (1932) trans. Gabain, M., *The moral judgment of the child*, London, Routledge and Kegan Paul.

POTTER, D. and SARRE, P. (eds.) (1974) *Dimensions of society*, London, University of London Press/The Open University Press (Course Reader).

ROPER, E. (1947) 'United States anti-semites', *Fortune*, vol. 36, pp 5–10.

ROSENBERG, M. J. (1960) 'Cognitive reorganization in response to the hypnotic reversal of attitudinal affect', *Journal of Personality*, vol. 28, pp 29–63.

SANFORD, N. (1956) 'The theory of the authoritarian personality' in McCary, J. L. (ed.) *Psychology of personality : six modern approaches*, New York, Grove Press.

SCIENTIFIC AMERICAN (1974) *Papers on socialization and attitudes*, Reading, Freeman (set text).

SHAW, N. E. and WRIGHT, J. M. (1967) *Scales for the measurement of attitudes*, New York, McGraw-Hill.

STEVENS, S. S. (ed.) (1951) *Handbook of experimental psychology*, New York, Wiley.

THOULESS, R. H. (1935) 'The tendency to certainty in religious belief', *British Journal of Psychology*, vol. 26, pp 16–31.

THURSTONE, L. L. (1927) 'A law of comparative judgement', *Psychological Review*, vol. 34, pp 273–86.

TOLSTOY, L. (1916) trans. Edmonds, R. *Resurrection*, Harmondsworth, Penguin.

WALLACE, J. (1966) 'Role reward and dissonance reduction', *Journal of Personality and Social Psychology*, vol. 3, pp 305–12.

WEISS, W. (1957) 'Opinion congruence with a negative source on an issue as a factor influencing agreement on another issue', *Journal of Abnormal and Social Psychology*, vol. 54, pp 180–6.

WILSON, G. D. (1973) *The psychology of conservatism*, London, Academic Press.

WILSON, G. D. and PATTERSON, J. R. (1968) 'A new measure of conservatism', *British Journal of Social and Clinical Psychology*, vol. 7, pp 264–9.

WRIGHTSMAN, L. S. (ed.) (1968) *Contemporary issues in social psychology*, Belmont, California, Brooks/Cole.

ZIMBARDO, P. (1973) *Proceedings of the American Psychological Association Conference*, Montreal.

ZIMBARDO, P. G., COHEN, A. R., WEISENBERG, M. and FIRESTONE, I. (1966) 'Control of pain motivation by cognitive dissonance', *Science*, vol. 151, pp 217–9.

ACKNOWLEDGEMENTS

Grateful acknowledgement is made to the following sources for material used in these units:

FIGURES

Figure 1 based on W. Crozier and E. Pincus, 'The geotropic conduct of young rats', *Journal of General Physiology*, vol. 10, 1926, The Rockefeller University Press; *Figures 2 and 9* from G. D. Wilson and J. R. Patterson, 'A new measure of conservatism', *British Journal of Social and Clinical Psychology*, vol. 7, 1968; *Figure 3* from E. Jones and R. Kohler, 'Effects of plausibility on the learning of controversial statements', *Journal of Abnormal and Social Psychology*, 57, © 1968 American Psychological Association; *Figure 4* Associated Press; *Figures 5 and 6* Copyright 1965 Stanley Milgram; *Figure 7* Test devised by Henry A. Murray, © 1943 by President and Fellows of Harvard College, © 1971 by Henry A. Murray. Reprinted by permission; *Figure 8* L. Mann and I. Janis, 'A follow-up study of the long-term effects of emotional role playing', *Journal of Personality and Social Psychology*, vol. 8, no. 4, 1968.

TABLES

Table 1 from Thurstone and Chare, *Measurement of Attitudes*, University of Chicago Press; *Table 2* from G. D. Wilson and J. R. Patterson, 'A new measure of conservatism', *British Journal of Social and Clinical Psychology*, vol. 7, 1968; *Table 4* from E. Jones and R. Kohler, 'Effects of plausibility on the learning of controversial statements', *Journal of Abnormal and Social Psychology*, 57, © 1968, American Psychological Association; *Table 5* G. D. Wilson, *The Psychology of Conservatism*, Academic Press, 1973.

ANSWERS TO SELF-ASSESSMENT QUESTIONS

SAQ 1

Unicorn, gryphon, Cyclops, Medusa, innumerable examples of spirits, demons, gods, etc.

SAQ 2

Existential dichotomies are 'contradictions' which stem from the nature of man's experience. They permit of no real solution though men will react to them in different ways. Historical dichotomies or contradictions are not a necessary part of existence. Solutions are possible though it may take some time to find them. Fromm gives the example of 'the contemporary contradiction between an abundance of technical means for material satisfaction and the incapacity to use them exclusively for peace and the welfare of the people'.

SAQ 3

Existential dichotomies arise because of man's self-awareness as a result of 'reason and imagination', i.e. conceptual thinking.

SAQ 4

Any two of: knowing you live and yet that you will die; knowing you have many potentialities that you can never realize; knowing you are an individual and separate and yet dependent on others.

SAQ 5

In constructing a Thurstone scale, judges are asked to rate the degree of positive or negative feeling they consider is expressed by each statement, *not* to indicate their own feelings.

SAQ 6

Valence – i.e. it indicates how the object of the attitude is evaluated. If we assume that the comment is not sarcastic, it clearly expresses a very positive attitude.

SAQ 7

No. It would be too unreliable or inconsistent to be acceptable. The minimally acceptable reliability for an attitude scale would be about $+.8$.

SAQ 8

A Thurstone scale. A Likert scale, in contrast, requires you to indicate the degree to which you agree with each statement.

SAQ 9

The number of ideas and feelings which form part of an attitude held. See section 2.1.

SAQ 10

The *stability* of an attitude refers to its resistance to change, its *centrality* to the degree to which it is an important part of an individual's identity or self concept. The two are likely to go together. See section 2.1.

SAQ 11

In order to select items from the scale which discriminate most effectively between degrees or positivity and negativity on the attitude concerned.

SAQ 12

To *co-vary* means to vary together. Although extraneous factors like subsidies and labour costs will mean that the correlation between the two prices will not be perfect, they are likely to go up (or down) together.

SAQ 13

No. On the evidence given, we cannot necessarily conclude this. We do not know, for example, whether this difference is statistically significant. For other reasons also, see subsequent discussion in the text.

SAQ 14

To eliminate any possibility that the experimenter, even though unconsciously, might treat one group differently from another and thus possibly influence the results.

SAQ 15

Longer statements are more likely to be difficult to learn. If one set contains statements which were significantly longer than the others, then this could influence the result.

SAQ 16

Nine. If you got this wrong or don't understand how it was obtained, read on. On the chart, P stands for pro-segregation subjects, A stands for anti-segregation subjects and N for neutral subjects. > means 'greater than' so P > N means that pro-segregation subjects score higher than do neutral subjects.

.50 means that the odds are 50 in 100 or 1 in 2 that the result is due to chance, .10 that the odds are 10 in 100 or 1 in 10. Neither of these is significant because the possibility that the result was entirely due to chance is too high. .05 (1 in 20), .01 (1 in 100) and .001 (1 in 1000) are significant if we take .05 as our criterion of significance. So the first column of the table indicates that for plausible pro-segregation statements, two comparisons are significant, P > N and P > A. N > A is not significant because it's only at the .10 level. The second column of Table 5 indicates that for implausible pro-segregation statements, again two of the three comparisons are significant; N > P and A > P. A > N is not significant in any way. For the plausible anti-segregation statements also, two comparisons are significant; N > P and A > P. A > N does not reach our criterion level. The last column indicates that for the implausible anti-segregation statements, all comparisons are significant.

SAQ 17

No. On some statements 'antis' are better, on other statements 'pros' are. There is no consistent difference between the groups of the kind that a difference in ability would lead one to expect.

SAQ 18

This is possible. If the 'pros' and 'antis' came into contact more than average with the plausible co-valuent arguments and had had less contact than average with the implausible co-valuent statements, then the results could be due to familiarity effects. We cannot rule out this possibility though it does seem a highly unlikely explanation. Jones and Kohlers' conclusion is more plausible.

SAQ 19

Strictly speaking, seven. Increasing the majority beyond this number does not produce more conformity. In fact the graph suggests that it reduces conformity slightly. But the differences in effect between majorities of any size between three and fifteen are relatively small. Provided there are more than two opponents a substantial conformity effect is likely to be produced.

SAQ 20

Errors due to conformity are reduced to one-fourth of the total produced with a unanimous majority.

SAQ 21

There was an abrupt rise in the conformity behaviour by the subject, reaching almost as high a level as would have resulted from the presence of a unanimous majority throughout.

SAQ 22

To avoid any possibility that knowledge of such information might bias, even if only unconsciously, their assessments.

SAQ 23

It indicates that there is an inverse relationship between IQ and conformity scores: higher conformity scores, to some extent, tend to be associated with lower IQs and *vice versa*.

SAQ 24

(a) No, according to Kelman's theory. (This is generally the case but see the last two paragraphs of section 5.2.)

(b) Yes

(c) Yes

Compliance is distinct from the other two in that it produces change only in *expressed* attitudes and only while the agent has information about what the person influenced is doing. With identification and internalization, the subject really believes in the attitudes adopted.

SAQ 25

(a) No, according to Kelman. (This is generally the case but see again the last two paragraphs on this section – 5.2.)

(b) Probably not

(c) Yes

If the agent ceases to have control over ends which the person influenced desires (compliance) or if the relationship ceases to be satisfactorily self-defining to the person influenced (identification) then the agent's influence will terminate or be diminished. Internalized attitudes are far less dependent on the relationship of agent to subject. They are integrated into the subject's belief and attitude system and will be discarded only if he no longer believes them to be valid or to facilitate his desired goals.

SAQ 26

(a) Control

(b) Attractiveness (in most cases)

(c) Credibility

SAQ 27

(a) Internalization

(b) Identification

(c) Compliance

SAQ 28

No. See subsequent discussion in text.

SAQ 29

Milgram asked this question of a number of people including psychology students. Estimates ranged from 0–3 per cent. For Milgram's actual results, see the subsequent discussion in the text.

SAQ 30

No. While it seems a likely hypothesis to explain his results, it is not conclusively demonstrated by the experiment itself. First, we have no comparison of behaviour under other circumstances when the individuals concerned are playing roles other than that of experimental subject. Secondly, remember that subjects were not selected randomly. They answered an advertisement. Even if we accept that there is a correspondence between being in the situation of experimental subject and propensity to obedience, we still cannot tell whether this correspondence is due to the influence of the role itself or to the characteristics of people who chose to be in that situation (i.e. volunteered to be subjects).

SAQ 31

'Displacement'. Hockett uses this term in a very different way to designate one of the design features of language (see Unit 7, section 3.5).

SAQ 32

(a) Instrumental

(b) Value-expressive

(c) Ego-defensive

(d) Knowledge

Note however that this is a rough assessment only. Many attitudes serve more than one function and it is clearly not possible to judge very precisely on the limited information given here.

SAQ 33

It indicates that this is a very reliable or consistent measure (reliability coefficients are discussed in section 2.4).

SAQ 34

Some people are more likely than others to say yes whatever the question. High scores therefore may merely reflect a tendency to agree and the correlations found between A and F, and E and F scores may be largely due to this. For this reason, most attitude scales are designed so that scores accrue from agreement on some items and disagreement on others, thus any acquiescence effect will cancel itself out. In this context, it is interesting that, as you may remember from section 5.1, Crutchfield found that authoritarian subjects (as measured by the F scale) were more likely to conform to majority consensus.

SAQ 35

The knowledge that interviewers had about their subjects could, even if only unconsciously, bias them to find what they expected to find, especially in view of the fact that they were allowed some latitude in what questions they actually asked. Good research technique usually requires experimenters and assessors to operate 'blind' (see section 3.5 and SAQ 14) and for all subjects to receive identical treatment. But see subsequent discussion in the text.

SAQ 36

A difference of this size between two groups would be likely to occur only as a result of chance, 5 times in 10,000 (i.e. 1 in 2,000 times).

SAQ 37

The prejudiced person projects his repressed impulses onto the targets of his prejudice thus viewing them in negative terms. Prejudice also provides a means of expressing his repressed hostility and, in some cases, a way of vicariously satisfying repressed feelings through concentration on and indulgence in fantasies about the evil ways condemned.

SAQ 38

A

SAQ 39

B

SAQ 40

All subjects had to lie to another person that a boring task was interesting. More dissonance was likely to be created by this in the subjects paid $1 than those who got $20. The recompense the latter received provided some justification for their behaviour. The lower paid subjects 'unconsciously' reduced their greater dissonance by believing that the task was not so bad after all – hence they had not really lied so very much.

SAQ 41

That there are only 3 chances in 100 of this difference occurring by chance. Given the convention of accepting levels below .05 as indicating the effect of experimental manipulation rather than chance, this result is just acceptable as significant.

SAQ 42

No.

SAQ 43

The same group would need to be used each time: otherwise differences in perceived attractiveness might be a function of the composition of the different groups rather than the initiation procedures. Even assuming the experimenters could find a group prepared to go through the same discussion sixty-three times, it would still be impossible to ensure that their performance would be identical each time. For one thing it would be affected differently by the participation of each of the subjects.

SAQ 44

To provide a base line against which the effects of the experimental manipulation could be compared. Without it, there would have been no measure of how the discussion group would be perceived under normal conditions. As subjects were randomly allocated to the three groups and as each was reasonably large (N = 21) we can assume the reactions of a control group would have been similar to those the subjects in the two other conditions would have shown had they not been exposed to the initiation procedures.

SAQ 45

No, not necessarily. There are quite likely to be wide individual differences in susceptibility to embarrassment. However, as subjects were allocated randomly we can assume that *on average* the subjects undergoing severe initiation were more affected than those in the mild initiation condition. Note that the likelihood of such individual differences makes it imperative both to allocate subjects randomly and to use groups of reasonable size. This avoids possible effects arising from bias in the characteristics of the different groups. In a follow-up study Gerard and Mathewson (1966) tried to ensure the probability of greater uniformity of effects within the two groups, by using very strong and very mild electric shocks as severe and mild initiations respectively. They obtained an even more striking result in the predicted direction.

SAQ 46

1   The size and composition of the pressure group
2   Whether or not the group presents a unanimous consensus
3   The individual's personality characteristics
4   The individual's relationship with the group
5   The nature of the attitudes concerned – particularly whether or not they are central.

SAQ 47

Compliance–control; identification–attraction; internalization–credibility

SAQ 48

Adjustment or instrumental: value-expressive: ego-defensive: knowledge functions.

SAQ 49

The affective aspect is positive or negative feelings about the object in question and the cognitive aspect beliefs or ideas about it.

SAQ 50

This may be the case but we cannot be sure from the observed correlation. Note that change in smoking behaviour is measured by means of a questionnaire. Elms took great care to disguise the source of this questionnaire by designating it an area health survey. Nevertheless it is quite possible that subjects with higher fantasy playing ability were more likely to exaggerate the change that had occurred, and this may have been the reason for the correlation.

SAQ 51

A	24	F	18
B	21	G	9
C	14	H	3
D	17	I	11
E	15	J	5

SAQ 52

It is unlikely that anti-black prejudice in this case can be explained solely in terms of authoritarian personality dynamics.

SAQ 53

A 'contradiction' which is generated by man's capacity for symbolic thinking. Examples given in the Fromm paper which was set reading for section 1 are: knowing you live and that you will die; knowing you have many potentialities that you can never realize and knowing you are an individual and separate but dependent on others.

Unit 23
Beliefs and social change: the scientific revolution

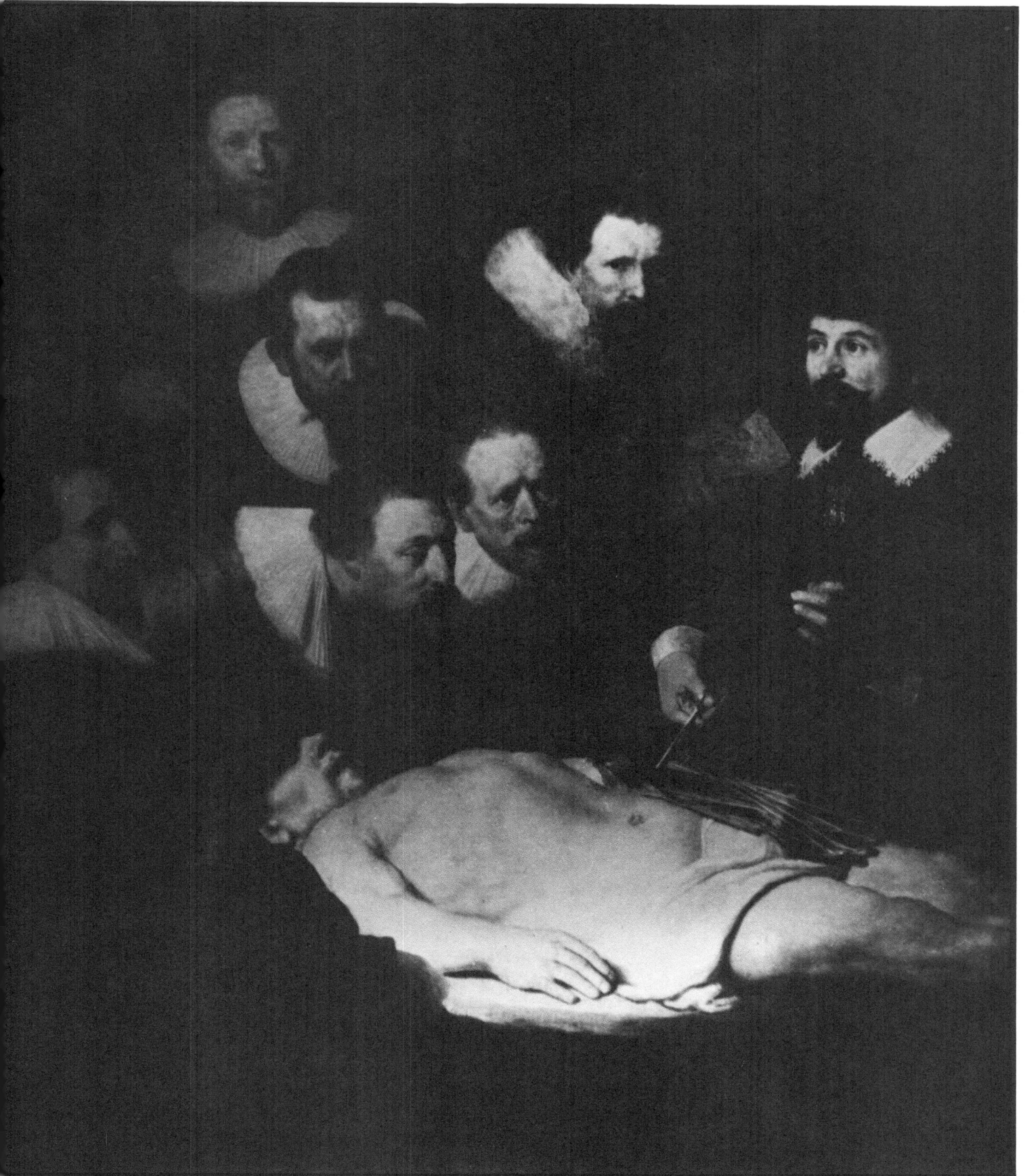

Prepared for the course team by Peter Hamilton

CONTENTS

STUDY OBJECTIVES

1. To demonstrate the interdependence of beliefs, values, knowledge and social structures in contexts of social change.

2. To clarify and explain the conceptual use of the terms: belief, belief-system, attitude, and value, in the repertoire of the social sciences.

3. To illustrate aims 1 and 2 by a case-study, 'Religion and the rise of science'.

4. To show in the case-study how ascetic Protestant religion produced a system of beliefs conducive to modern science.

5. To indicate that even such an 'objective' activity as science is dependent on certain values, beliefs and attitudes.

6. To suggest, quite generally, that knowledge, ideas and beliefs are not free floating, but are closely related to specific types of social organization.

7. To create an understanding of the distinctive contributions of Zilsel and Merton to a sociological understanding of science.

INTRODUCTION

The society that we want to make sense of in this course is a society whose structure, culture and future potentialities have in large part been moulded by the application of scientific knowledge to the solution of practical problems. It is an *industrial* society; a society which would not be possible without a highly developed science and technology impinging on almost all aspects of our lives and social relationships. In this society, science – systematic knowledge of the natural world – is an institutionalized activity. It embodies certain distinct and independent norms of behaviour which characterize the activities and professional relationships of its practitioners, and it is an activity valued by society for its social functions. Science, then, is so important an aspect of our lives that it is essential in a course such as this to examine its social consequences.

Clearly, though, science has not always been so influential in human affairs: it is an activity, and a form of knowledge, with a definable history and stages of development. As an *institutionalized* activity, it has a relatively short history going back only as far as the seventeenth century. Although there was a considerable body of scientific knowledge existing prior to that time, including numerous Greek, Roman, Chinese and Arab scientific discoveries, science never possessed much social favour, nor developed any *autonomy* as an intellectual activity and practice of methodical empirical enquiry. This unit is not concerned, however, with the history of science, for that would be outside the concerns of this course. Rather it is designed as an interesting example of the study of the interrelationships of beliefs, values, attitudes and social structures, with the object of illuminating processes of social change.

Before we begin to look in greater detail at the substance of this unit, it would be as well to raise a few questions concerning the concepts which are employed within the unit. In the two units previous to this one, the concepts of *attitude* and *belief* have been well ventilated, particularly in respect of their use in various theories of personality structure, and in relation to ways of influencing people's behaviour. The use of the concepts of attitude and belief in this unit differs a little, although not radically, from the earlier discussion in Units 21–22.

This unit is primarily concerned with the organization of beliefs and values into systematic groups. That is, we are basically interested in the relationship between certain sorts of social groups on the one hand, and belief-systems and value-systems on the other hand. The unit which follows this one takes up this theme again, and can in many ways be seen as exploring a similar thesis in a slightly different way. The

See Unit 11, section 2.5.4;
also Unit 24, section 2

common element linking the two is the now famous 'Protestant ethic thesis' which was first introduced in Unit 11. Although I do not want to go over its substance at this point, it is worth saying that the object of the thesis is the demonstration of a complex interrelationship between a particular constellation of beliefs, values, and attitudes, and specific forms of social action. What the thesis attempts to demonstrate is that certain religious beliefs about the nature of the world, and about a specific group of people (Calvin's *Elect*) became reorganized into social values and personal attitudes, social roles, norms and institutional patterns which were remarkably effective in stimulating types of social action which we would now call rational, capitalist, economic action (Weber 1904–5). The central issue of the thesis is the power of certain types of belief to create new forms of social action which have both their own internal rationale, and external effects on modes of social organization. In one important sense Weber's thesis is a partial demonstration of cognitive dissonance theory (*cf.* Units 21–22, section 8.1). For the basic source of the rational acquisitive capitalistic action of the ascetic Protestant was, Weber argued, his anxiety about whether he was a member of the Elect or not. Since he could not, in terms of the belief-system of Calvinism, in actual fact know whether he was in such a state of grace, there was a great social and psychological compulsion for the Protestant to assure himself of his salvation by believing that worldly success in a worthy occupation was a sure sign of Election. Thus the cognitive dissonance between the Calvinist beliefs on the one hand and the necessity to believe in personal Election on the other, produced attitudes towards life which powerfully developed economic values and action, and thus created social conditions in which the dissonance could be reduced. In this sense, the central beliefs about Election remained essentially the same, whilst worldly success was reinterpreted to mean – in a certain context – a sign of predestination. Thus the primary concern of the ascetic Calvinist Protestant with his status in relation to God filtered and influenced his perception of the world.

Our concern, in this and the following unit, with a particular aspect of Western culture – the influence of Protestantism – is concentrated on what are termed *belief-systems* and *value-systems*. In Units 21–22, section 1.3, you were given a definition of *belief* as 'an assertion about some aspect of the world or the relation of two such aspects', and that is essentially the same usage as will be employed here. However, it is necessary to make an initial distinction clear, between those beliefs that permit an empirical test of the assertions that they contain, and those beliefs that are so formulated as to be beyond such a test. Examples of the former would include statements like:

1 All birds can fly.

2 The story of the earth's creation in Genesis is true.

3 All sociologists are communists.

4 The earth is flat.

In each of these examples we can identify the beliefs as either *true* or *false*, that is in relation to a fact or set of facts.

The second type of beliefs takes the following form:

1 All men are basically good.

2 Science is the best way to produce true knowledge.

3 I think, therefore I am (Descartes' famous dictum, *cogito ergo sum*).

4 Only the Elect will form part of God's kingdom of Heaven on earth.

5 The order of nature is a reflection of the order of God's mind.

None of these beliefs can be referred directly to some set of facts on the basis of which their validity could be assessed. Rather, they are cast in such a form as to be *untestable* in relation to the empirical world. We may believe in their truth, or their falsity, secure in the knowledge that their validity cannot be tested.

See also Units 21–22,
section 11.1

Now it may be that in any particular belief-system a mixture of both types of belief will be found. A belief-system is an interrelated set of beliefs, values, and attitudes which has some internal consistency and a relatively unified outlook on the world. Religions can usefully be described as belief-systems, but we may also extend use of the term to describe political *ideologies* such as liberalism or communism in their various forms. Science itself may be effectively described as a belief-system, containing as it does certain beliefs about the validity of its methods, about the possibilities of understanding the world, as well as values concerning the proper conduct of scientists and the autonomy of scientific knowledge.

Belief-systems will, then, contain a core of central beliefs. Some of these will be testable beliefs, some not: the core of these central beliefs will most frequently be beliefs of the untestable type – what might be called ultimate values, beliefs stated as fixed and ultimate tenets describing the world as it 'really' is, or should be. Thus, at the heart of Christianity is the belief in the existence of God, a being endowed with the power to create the world itself. Amongst the many organized forms of Christianity this central belief itself may be varied in terms of varying views of God's manifestation on earth – Jesus Christ. But within all variants of what can be called Christianity there remains a certain consistency in the core and central beliefs which constitute the belief-system of the Christian religion.

Science itself constitutes a belief-system in the sense that its existence as a mode of knowledge formation depends to a very important extent on its practitioners agreeing on some basic beliefs about the natural world, and about the validity of methods of understanding that world. Before the Copernican Revolution of the sixteenth century most astronomers believed that the earth was the centre of the Universe, and that the planets, moon, sun and stars revolved around it. This belief in a geocentric universe dated back to the Greek astronomer, Ptolemy of Alexandria (around AD 140) who developed a highly effective mathematical representation of the paths of the planets which was a little more accurate than observations by the naked eye (see Figure 1). Ptolemy's theory was very effective in accounting for movements of the heavens, and it remained current for fifteen hundred years. But it was based on a belief that is, in fact, invalid. People had questioned the belief that the earth is the centre of the universe, even before Ptolemy's time. But the consensus among astronomically inclined scholars, certainly in the West, was that the universe is geocentric, and that consensual belief prevailed for fifteen hundred years, until it was challenged by the rather more accurate observations made possible by Copernicus' and Kepler's theories and the invention of the telescope (see Figure 2). The point is that, although

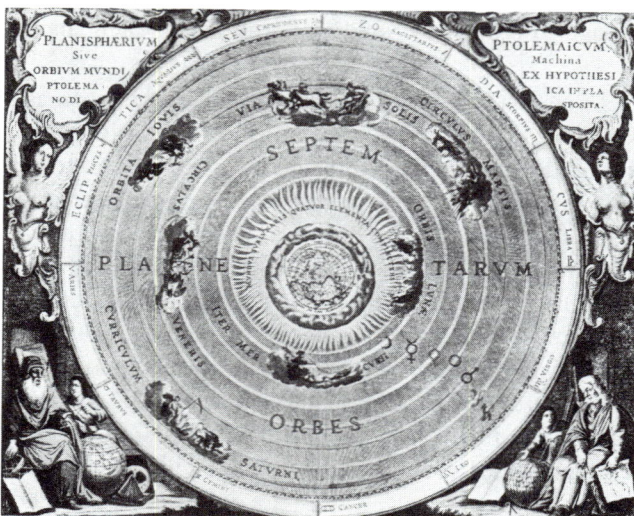

Figure 1   World system according to Ptolemy. This shows the geocentric view of the universe, with earth at its centre

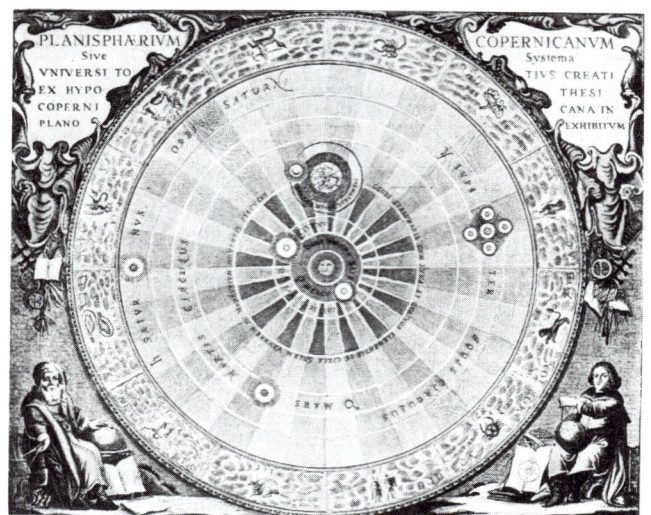

Figure 2   World system according to Copernicus. This heliocentric (sun-centred) conception of the universe replaced the Ptolemaic view

it was based on a false belief, the Ptolemaic system gave very accurate predictions of the movements of the planets. Yet at the same time, because it was based in the belief that the earth lay at the centre of the universe, it also fitted in rather well with other types of beliefs – essentially religious beliefs about the nature of the universe, and especially the belief that the universe was a finite entity, hierarchically ordered in such a way that religious values determined the structure of being, 'rising from the dark, heavy and imperfect earth to the higher and higher perfection of the stars and heavenly spheres' (Koyré 1957 p 2).

Resistance to changes in the philosophical and religious beliefs lying behind conceptions of the universe were quite as important as the scientific nature of the changes. For what was involved was the replacement of a view of the universe as finite, fixed and immutable (a view corresponding very closely to the account of the universe provided in Genesis) by a view which stressed the infinity of the universe – a very radical and far reaching step in man's conception of his own role within the natural order (Koyré 1957).

The concept of *value-system* is rather closely connected to that of belief-system. By a value-system we mean a system of norms, morals, and evaluations of social practices, ranked in terms of certain standards having continuity, cohesion and organization. A value-system, such as that informing the criminal law of this country, may well be closely connected both to specific beliefs and to certain types of belief-system. It provides the essential mode of ranking the value of specific practices and social activities, in relation to one another and to values in other institutional spheres.

Let us now begin to look at the problems to which the unit is addressed.

The Agricultural and Industrial Revolutions were perhaps the most significant and far reaching group of *social* changes that have ever occurred in human society, greater even than those of the neolithic revolution in their implications for the development of human society. Their repercussions are still with us in a very tangible form, and will continue to be so for a very long time. Yet the changes that have occurred have meant that human life is rather more secure and pleasant now – at least for those in industrialized societies – than it was two hundred and more years ago before this vast social transformation had begun. Life is no longer, as Thomas Hobbes put it 'nasty, brutish, and short'. We in the industrialized western world have the advantages of medicine, of a reasonably secure food supply (*pace* neo-Malthusian prophets of ecodoom), of extensive and efficient methods of communication, of near-universal literacy, and in some countries, political democracy.

Malthus: see Unit 5, section 1

For most of these changes, and indeed for many of the mechanical innovations that figure so prominently in the Industrial Revolution we have to look to the application of scientific knowledge to practical problems as the key to their understanding.

It is common to think of science as a *purely* intellectual activity, rather than as a distinctive sphere of social behaviour. After all, science is a form of knowledge that is in most cases in written form, and thus available, in principle, for any literate and numerate person to learn, teach from, or forget. Also scientists are engaged in creating knowledge by discovering 'laws of nature' that are not open to change by human agency. The structure of their knowledge has to reflect the structure of natural events. Because science has as its subject matter 'nature', and employs systems of thought to study that subject matter, it is often seen as a process of the development of ideas. Indeed there is a discipline (essentially in the humanities area) called the *history of ideas* which, amongst many other things, treats the history of science as a largely intellectual process mostly untrammelled by considerations of such 'material' factors as social structures, political situations or economic processes. A history of ideas approach to the development of science would stress the intellectual methods employed to explain the structure of the natural world. The development of theories and discoveries would be explained as a consequence of the finding of discrepancies between theories and the natural events they were supposed to be explaining, or of the developing awareness of logical problems within the theories themselves.

In part, this is an effective approach. The nature of science as an institutionalized activity involves scientists in working on problems which are determined by the body of theory, experimental and mathematical techniques of their scientific speciality, rather than on problems presented by the external society: '. . . compared with other professional and creative pursuits, the practitioners of a natural science are effectively insulated from the cultural milieu in which they live their extra-professional lives' (Kuhn 1968 p 81). But the 'intrinsic' approach to the history of science, made effective by the relative insulation of natural sciences from cultural constraints, begins to fall down when we look at the emergence of specific scientific specialities, the grouping of sciences together and the timing of scientific evolution. In view of these issues, an approach which includes external factors is very necessary in explaining changes which cannot be explained by the intrinsic approach.

Within this unit a rather different view of scientific development is being offered; or to be more precise, such a *conceptual* analysis of science is not considered to be the main object. We are more interested in the social variables that facilitated the development of science, and in the societal context in which science first came to have a relatively autonomous existence, considered as a legitimate activity by society; and which contained practitioners whose main role was to be 'scientists', who took their main societal status from that role and from their location within a *community* of scientists. By the term *scientific community* we are referring to the integrated organization of scientists into a community sharing certain norms of behaviour which determine how they should behave in any given scientific situation. The scientific community has certain characteristics which we will explore later. But, like any community, its members have to be socialized into its structure of values and norms. The consequence of that socialization process – largely what we would term professional education – is a certain pattern to the progress of scientific development. I will be referring to this pattern more explicitly later in the unit.

I will not be referring in any but a fairly general way to the development of science after the seventeenth century, but simply dealing with the social processes of development up to that time. The Zilsel and Merton articles (to be found in the Course Reader, *Dimensions of society*, Potter and Sarre 1974) included in this week's work are essential to a social scientific understanding of the development of science. The article by Zilsel, 'The sociological roots of science' (1942) provides some of the historical background to the particular situation we will be looking at – the *institutionalization* of science in seventeenth century England.

The article by Merton (1970a) is a chapter from his book *Science, technology and society in seventeenth-century England* and is the central material out of which your understanding of this unit should be constructed. Merton first published this study in 1938, and although the book is still a significant contribution to what has now come to be called the sociology of science, it is fair to say that its central thesis has been extensively criticized, both by sociologists and historians of science. Nevertheless, the material presented by Merton in defence of his thesis is very persuasive, and you will have to make up your own mind whether the critics of the 'Merton thesis' provide a sufficient challenge to its core elements to justify its rejection.

Why should we be looking at the developments of science three hundred and more years ago in a course designed to 'make sense of society', you might reasonably ask. There are in fact several important reasons why we wish to look at this situation.

Firstly, the social sciences are interested in *social change*, in the processes by which values, beliefs, habits, behaviour and action are altered in such a way as to give a new configuration to what we call society. The development of science, from a highly proscribed area of knowledge in the medieval period to the 'scientific revolution' of the seventeenth century, indicates a whole series of social changes which altered the social valuation of scientific activity and gave scientific knowledge a new status. That status emphasized the growing independence of science from control by religions or secular authority and its growing relationship with technology and practical affairs such as accountancy and commerce. There was a scientific revolution not because of any purely intellectual advances or inventions, but because social conditions – particularly in England – were extremely favourable to the emergence of an empirical, experimental science with a high social status. This social change in the cultural evaluation of science was crucial to the development of industrial technology, and it is significant that such an outcome was fully intended by the scientific community of seventeenth century England.

The new attitude towards science, then, was one manifestation of a more general reorientation of social and cultural attitudes which can be viewed as part of the beginnings of the Industrial Revolution itself. For that reason, an historical study such as the one contained in this unit, is an important part of any social scientific understanding of modern society. For we are not dabbling in history for its own sake, but to understand some specific processes of social change which altered the belief-systems of our own society in ways which are still important to us.

The second, and connected, justification for the study of the 'scientific revolution' is a *methodological* one. That is, an historical case-study is one of the methods by which the social sciences develop their understanding and explanations of social phenomena. So, in presenting this unit we are demonstrating not simply the relationships of a belief-system with particular social changes, but indicating and explaining how the historical case-study method may be used. The social sciences are not merely concerned with the here and now, and they do not – or at least should not – operate without the benefit of an historical dimension in their perspectives. For to know anything about conditions 'now' requires in most cases an understanding of how they once were and why they changed or remained static. Similarly, our understanding of the past is open – though with some technical and methodological problems attendant – to enhancement by sociological, psychological, economic and other analyses. The only way to apply theories and concepts of the social sciences to phenomena that one cannot study by interview or directly observe (except in a somewhat decayed and inert state!) is to use the same materials that the historian employs – in the main written records and contemporary artefacts. It is sources such as these that form the basis of the present unit.

1   THE PROBLEM

As was pointed out earlier, this unit is not simply about science and its patterns of development. It is rather more about the interrelationship of beliefs, attitudes, and social change. Science has been picked because its 'rise' is interesting: contrary to what we might believe, science developed rapidly at a particular stage in its history not just because of theoretical (or, as we might say, *intrinsic*) advances, but also because of the stimulation provided by certain social and cultural, *extrinsic*, factors. Any explanation of the processes by which a 'scientistic' belief system has come to be current in modern industrial societies would have to take account of the reasons why science came to have a *social value* and a distinct *status* in the first place.

Although it should be clear by now that this unit is about the *social* basis of scientific development, and about the beliefs and values conducive to that development, a certain qualifying note should be injected. The argument presented here is not the rather simplistic one that social changes produced, or determined the nature of, intellectual changes. That sort of crude sociology of knowledge in which theoretical advances, alterations in the structure of knowledge and its usage, are held to be dependent solely on social structural factors, is not to be purveyed here. We are interested, rather, in a somewhat more subtle relationship between beliefs, values, knowledge and social organizations. For although a great deal of theoretical knowledge about the physical world existed prior to the seventeenth century, and despite there being many advances in technology before that time – mapmaking, building, foundry work, ship building, navigation, printing, mining, the manufacture of guns, gunpowder, lenses etc. – there was little attempt to connect the speculative theories of the high status scholarly scientists with the experimental techniques and empirical knowledge of the low status 'technologists', the craftsmen, seafarers, businessmen, artisans and artists. The 'rise' of science consists precisely in the unification of scholarly reason with techniques of experimentation and empirical observation, in the bringing together of activities hitherto divided by differences of social status. We are concerned with the agency that effected such a unification; and one of the principal elements of that agency in England was a religious ethic – Puritanism. Puritanism, in many ways the epitome of the ascetic Protestantism which so concerned Max Weber, stressed both the religious value of studying nature in a rational and purposive manner, and the importance of carrying out such a study in a practical and experimental way, rather than treating it in a purely contemplative manner.

Connected to the emergence of a religious ethic which valued scientific knowledge and scientific experimentation was a series of changes in the nature of society. Essentially, these changes may be described as the formation of a 'middle class' composed of merchants, craftsmen, artisans, and the like, who were possessed of a practical outlook on life and who wanted to improve their social and economic position within society.

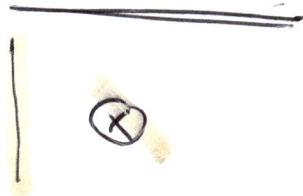

Figure 3   William Gilbert, first English scientist to unite technological knowledge with methods of rational thought

Figure 4   Galileo Galilei, the great Italian scientist whose achievements did much to create modern science

Before reading the next section of this unit you should read the article by Edgar Zilsel 'The sociological roots of science' in the Reader and answer the SAQs set out below.

Now read Zilsel in Reader, pp 370–83

SAQ 1

Zilsel identifies three social groups which, he argues, were crucial to the development of science up to the seventeenth century. Who were these groups and what were their principal characteristics?

Answers to SAQs for Unit 23 are on pages 120–1

SAQ 2

What four 'sociological conditions' of the period 1300–1600 does Zilsel isolate as facilitating the rise of science?

SAQ 3

Why should Zilsel pick out Gilbert, Galileo and Bacon as significant figures in the development of science? Provide a brief answer concentrating on the intellectual and social changes that these men exemplified.

Although Zilsel's article is a concise statement of a wide range of changes, it does rather overemphasize the importance of economic factors in the development of scientific thinking to the exclusion of social and cultural transformations. However, the article does suggest a broad view of the changes taking place in Western society in the transition from feudal to early capitalist – or *mercantilist* (*cf.* Units 11 and 12) – society. Zilsel rightly concentrates on the social esteem or status of those engaged in scientific and technological activities. Modern science, he suggests, is not possible whilst rational thought and empirical knowledge are separated. The clue to an understanding of the 'scientific revolution' lies in the processes which brought the two together and gave the conjoined activities an institutionalized status within society. It is to that theme that we now turn.

2 THE INSTITUTIONALIZATION OF SCIENCE AND THE SCIENTIFIC ROLE

Although we now speak about an *international community* of scientists – partly because of the universal nature of scientific method and the general acceptance of its attendant belief-system – it is important to note that in its historical development science has had many centres of activity. Discounting the classical period of the Greek and Roman civilizations, this centre has exhibited periodical shifts. Up to the mid-seventeenth century the centre was Italy, from then until the late eighteenth century it was England, followed by France until the middle of the nineteenth century when it shifted again to Germany, remaining there until the 1920s. Since that time the United States has held pre-eminence, with Britain in a secondary position (Ben-David

TABLE I

Comparison of Investment in Science and Scientific Output in Selected Countries

	Year	R & D Expenditure (millions of dollars)	R & D Expenditure, Per Cent of Total Spent on Basis and Applied Research (not including Development)	Qualified R & D Personnel Year Number		Nobel Prizes 1951–1966	Percentage of World Production of Papers in: Chemistry (1960)	Physics (1961)
Britain	1964/65	2,155	38.6	1964/65	59,415	18	16 (Commonwealth)	14
France	1963	1,299	51.2	1963	32,382	4	5	6
Germany	1964	1,436	—	1964	33,382	7	9	6
Japan	1963	892	—	1963	114,839	1	9	8
U.S.A.	1963/64	21,323	34.5	1963/64	474,900	44	28	30
U.S.S.R.	1962	41,300 millions of old roubles		1962	416,000—lowest estimate 487,000—highest estimate	7	20	16

Source: OECD, *The overall level and structure of research and development efforts in OECD member countries*, Paris, 1967, p. 14, Table 2, p. 59, Table 3; Joseph Ben-David, *Fundamental Research and the universities*, OECD, Paris, 1968, p. 26; Wallace R. Brode, 'The growth of science and a national science program', *American Scientist* (Spring-March 1962), 50:18; D. J. de Solla Price, 'The distribution of scientific papers by country and subject – a science policy analysis', Yale University.

1971 p 15). It is possible to isolate minor centres which have been significant in a particular area or group of sciences. But the main centres of activity have tended to monopolize and dominate the development of science during the period of their leadership.

These shifts do not seem to be closely connected to economic factors such as economic growth or overall wealth. At the time when Spain and Portugal were the major seafaring and trading nations of the western world, and could thus be expected to have a major interest in astronomy and its navigational uses, it was landlocked Germany which produced the crucial astronomical advances of Copernicus and Kepler. Even now, as Table 1 shows, there is not as close a connection between investment in science, and scientific output measured in terms of Nobel Laureates, as might be expected. As the table indicates, although the USA expends roughly ten times the amount of scientific research as Great Britain, American scientists accounted for less than three times the number of Nobel prizes, as compared to British scientists, during the period 1951–1966. Rather, these shifts appear to be more closely associated with social factors such as the social evaluation of the role of the scientist, and the presence of institutional and organizational factors which stimulate scientific talent and allow it to flourish in an atmosphere where it receives socially important rewards.

2.1 THE SOCIAL ROLE OF THE SCIENTIST

The first location in which science was accorded high social esteem, and in which the social role of the scientist was institutionalized for the first time, was seventeenth century England.

Figure 5 Gresham College, London. Set up in 1580, it was one of the first homes and centres of the new scientific studies in England

You will remember the discussion of 'social roles' in Unit 19. In that unit, in section 1.2, we described *role* as 'a bundle of expectations and obligations to act in specific ways in certain settings'. For science to become an established part of society, a form of knowledge with traditions and a social organization with some stability and recognized value, required the emergence of the role of scientist as an accepted and legitimate 'bundle' of expectations and obligations. Mere interest in an area of study cannot establish, of itself, a scientific tradition:

> . . . the existence of people interested in the regularity of heavenly phenomena, or in the characteristics of plants or animals, or any other question defined today as scientific could not in itself give rise to a scientific tradition. Where these interests were not considered as integral parts of any role, there emerged

hardly any tradition at all. Traditions developed only where such knowledge was considered as part of different roles: astronomy as part of the priestly role; knowledge of plants as something appropriate to farmers; and that of animals as useful for hunters or herdsmen. But there was no tendency to subsume such knowledge under abstract laws or often not even under any laws, since they were not considered intellectual concerns but technical information.

The emergence of a new role takes place within a more comprehensive social setting . . . its very emergence implies a change of social values. In the case of the scientific role, that change in values meant the acceptance of the search for truth through logic and experiment as a worthwhile intellectual pursuit. This modified philosophical and religious authority, raised the dignity of technological knowledge, created new conceptions and norms concerning intellectual freedom in general, and eventually had far-reaching effects on practically all the traditional social arrangements . . . the emergence of the scientific role was connected to changes in the normative patterns (*institutions*) regulating cultural activity, and also (subsequently and indirectly) to other kinds of social activity.

(Ben-David 1971 p 17)

In understanding how modern science developed, then, we have to look at *two* interrelated factors: the conditions under which the social role of the scientist was established, and the characteristic elements of that role.

The context in which the scientific role was developed and established was one of considerable scientific advance. In particular, 'the scientific revolution' (as it has been called) which occurred in England during the seventeenth century, and which is most often associated with the name of Newton, was itself an example of the creation of what is now called a scientific *paradigm*.

This concept, first developed by the historian of science, Thomas S. Kuhn, is applied to innovations of scientific theory – like, for example, Newton's classical mechanics or Einstein's relativity theory – which come to exert a major influence on the development of a mature science. A *paradigm* determines what will be considered 'normal' science by scientists, that is 'research firmly based in one or more past scientific achievements . . . that some particular scientific community acknowledges for a time as supplying the foundation for its further practice' (Kuhn 1962 p 10). In looking at the institutionalization of science in seventeenth century England we are concerned both with the establishment of the scientific role *and* the parallel emergence of a paradigm. Kuhn has persuasively argued that paradigms involve the development of a normal science which operates along traditionalized dimensions, and which constrains professional scientists to work on problems that the paradigm defines as significant and worthy of solution. My discussion of the development of the scientific role involves a consideration of the related intellectual and social factors which created both the first effective paradigm of physical science, and the first institutionalization of science as a valued social activity. I shall return to a further consideration of the concept of scientific paradigm in the conclusion of this unit.

2.2 FACTORS IN THE EMERGENCE OF THE SCIENTIFIC ROLE

The explanation of the emergence of an autonomous, institutionalized scientific role developed in this unit is conducted in two parts. At this stage we will be looking at developments before the seventeenth century which prepared the ground for the role of scientist by changes in other intellectual roles and by certain changes in the social structures of western societies. In the next section we will be looking in detail at the *value-complex* or value-system of Puritan England and the social support which the religious ethic of Puritanism gave to science.

In most *traditional* societies, learning and education are justified primarily as a basis for some practical activity – religious, legal, medical or governmental. In such

pre – 17th century . . .

100

contexts they tend to have an amateur status, and a very rudimentary organization: knowledge is rarely seen as a commodity subject to economic pressures, nor is it frequently systematized. Famous masters attract pupils from far and wide to sit at their feet, to be 'taught' only when the sage or guru has time to spare from his principal activities.

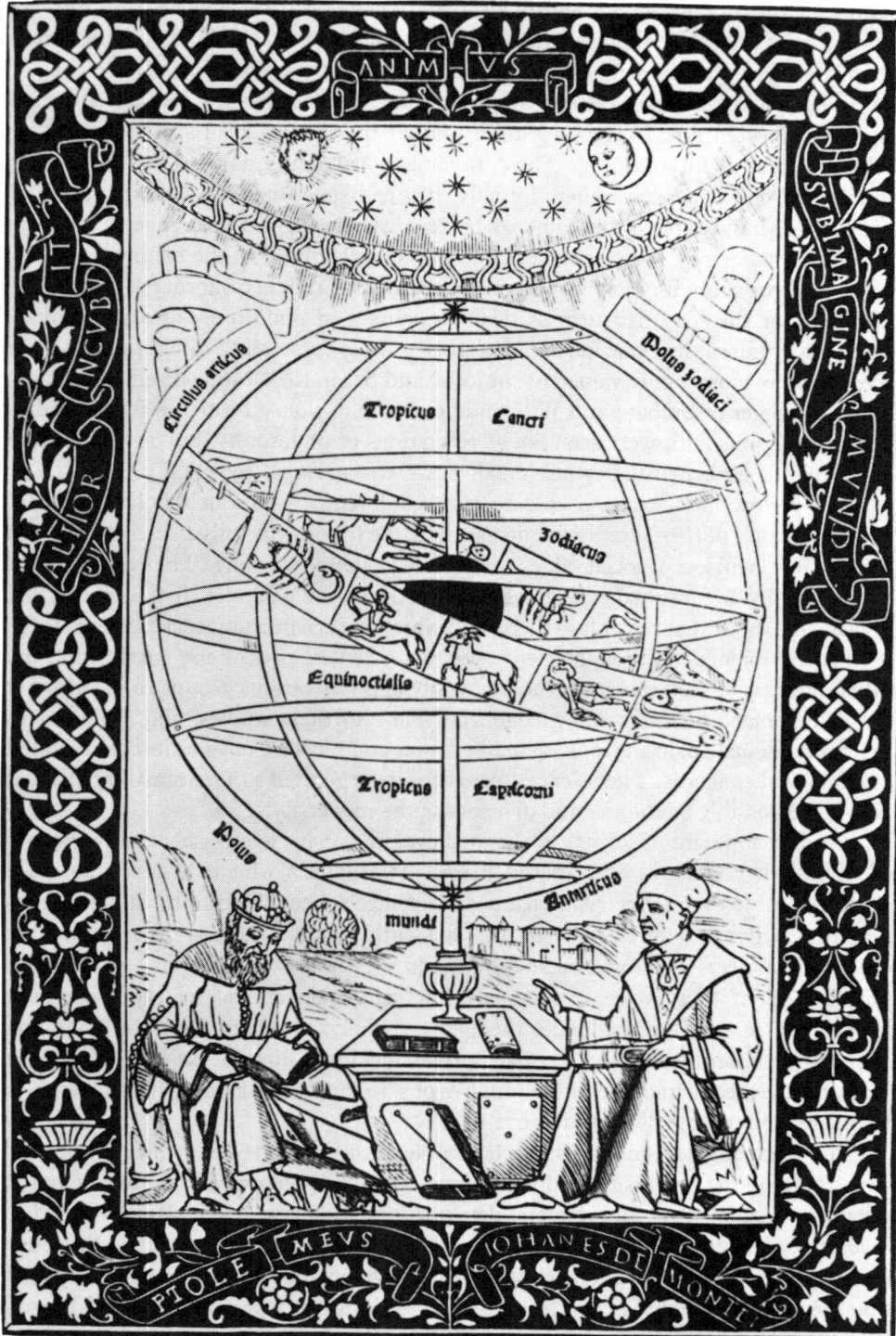

Figure 6 An armillary sphere, designed to show mechanically the movement of the planets and stars in relation to the earth. A mechanical representation of the geocentric universe

This situation largely characterized the early history of the European universities from the mid-thirteenth century and to begin with conditions were little different from those in other traditional societies. But the European universities were situated in towns, and because the towns were mostly secular corporations outside the authority of the state there was a tendency for friction between 'town and gown', a conflict not helped by the absolute authority of the church over all matters spiritual and educational. Ultimately the university populations were regulated by being made into corporations of scholars authorized by the church and recognized by the government. This situation produced a certain independence for scholars from both church and state, and it also developed the university as an educational institution in its own right, rather than simply a convenient location for a famous master. An indication of the nature of this organizational and institutional change can be gauged from the fact that by 1300 the University of Paris had 6000 students, many of whom were attracted to the university for the studies it offered, rather than to particular masters.

In such a context the role of teacher–scholar began to have a distinct and high status, connected now to teaching ability rather than to practical services in law or religious affairs, for example. These organizational developments had significant intellectual consequences. Where initially they had specialized in particular areas of knowledge, universities soon came to be seen as offering a wide range of subjects unified by *philosophy*, which thus became the central subject of the medieval university – and probably its most important department. Students wanting to study law, medicine, or theology had to pass through courses in philosophy as a preparatory step. Also, philosophy came more and more to possess a systematic differentiation from theology (the most highly valued of subjects) and began to be rationalized by philosophers like Siger of Brabant and William of Ockham in such a form that its contradictions of religious faith were seen not as refutations of philosophy, but as proof of the existence of a higher truth beyond human reason (Ben-David 1971 p 48).

The philosophers came to be a large and influential group of scholars and academics because of these developments, at the same time as the universities themselves became powerful loci of social values about knowledge and learning. The establishment of philosophy in the medieval university was only one example of the intellectual division of labour that took place there, and which in turn introduced a greater role for the natural sciences. Although science was not a central part of any curriculum, the differentiation of studies within the university allowed various groups to incorporate the rudimentary scientific knowledge available into their studies, and pursue it in their spare time. Logicians took up mathematics and physics, physicians concentrated on biological concerns. The sciences were thus incorporated as a marginal intellectual area made possible by the size and diversity of the university.

The development of science in the medieval university was closely tied to the fate of philosophy, since it was, in the main, philosophers who cultivated the main scientific subjects: geometry, dynamics, and mechanics. Philosophy suffered geographical shifts of interest, but by the sixteenth century there were a number of chairs in subjects like mathematics, astronomy, natural philosophy, Aristotelian physics. All of these were of relatively low status, dependent on the incumbent having degrees in law, medicine, theology or philosophy. But they did have one important consequence: the regular, professional teaching of science. (Table 2 indicates the steady increase in the number of science chairs at European universities between 1400–1700) (Ben-David 1971 p 52).

16th century

The Renaissance, the rebirth of classical learning, and the emergence of humanistic studies in the universities from the sixteenth century depressed the social value of science. Advancement and esteem depended on being a good classical scholar. Scientists had little autonomy in an area seen as irrevocably peripheral, and useless for personal advancement. Their role was to serve universities whose primary social function was to supply lawyers, civil servants, clerics and physicians: and for such professions it was more important to know the classics than to learn science. Consequently, the universities could not be an adequate social base for science, which could not be given sufficient social value because of its inapplicability to either general or professional studies (Ben-David 1971 pp 45–55).

During the Italian Renaissance some further elements of a rudimentary scientific role – begun in the medieval university – were created in the links between artists and scientifically inclined scholars. Although these links were of relatively short duration

TABLE 2

Number of Salaried Chairs at Selected Universities by Fields, 1400–1700

	1400	1450	1500	1550	1600	1650	1700
Bologna							
Science	3[a]	—	2[b]	2	2	2	2
Medicine	11	2	3	3	5	5	3
Other	33	9	15	16	20	22	23
Paris (Sorbonne) and Collège de France)							
Science	—	—	—	2[c]	2	2	2
Medicine	—	—	—	2	3	3	3
Other	—	—	—	8	12	18	20
Oxford							
Science	—	—	—	—	—	3[d]	3
Medicine	—	—	—	1	1	2	2
Other	—	—	—	15	15	20	20
Leipzig							
Science	—	—	—	—	2[e]	2	2
Medicine	—	2	2	3	4	4	6
Other	—	—	—	—	17	17	23

[a] Astrology; natural philosophy; physics. [b] Arithmetic and geometry; astronomy. [c] Mathematics. [d] Natural philosophy; geometry; astronomy. [e] Arithmetic and astrology; physics and natural philosophy.

Source: Sorbelli and I. Simeoni, *Storia della Università di Bologna* (Università di Bologna, 1944); A. Lefranc, *Histoire du Collège de France*, (Hachette, 1893); J. Bonnerot, *La Sorbonne*, (Paris, Presses Universitaires, 1927); C. E. Mallet, *A history of the University of Oxford*, (New York, Longman, 1924); H. Helbig, *Universität Leipzig* (Frankfurt a.M.: Weidlich, 1961).

they did inaugurate a new status for those engaged in some aspects of empirical work and technological advance. These links were based on common technical interests: the artists (amongst whose numbers were included architects and engineers) had the practical knowledge which would help the scholars to understand the classical manuscripts that were their object of study. At the same time the artist-engineers were brought into contact with classical treatises on perspective, architecture, mechanics, etc. which their lack of knowledge of Latin and Greek would otherwise have prevented them from using. Subjects such as Greek geometry appeared more meaningful in relation to practical problems of architectural design, visual perspective, or gunlaying.

In the courts of the great Renaissance princes this artistic location of scientific knowledge altered the status position of the 'scientific' scholar and made him and his associate artists and engineers of comparable prestige to more traditionally established intellectuals. But the relationship was a transient one. Eventually the artist-engineers had learnt enough from the scholars and their association ended. The consequence of this was that by the sixteenth century science in Italy remained tied to the interests of an exclusive, scholarly group primarily based in the nobility, and with almost no connection with other social groups or more mundane and practical concerns.

By contrast, science fared rather differently in northern Europe, a society which was characterized by a rather more dynamic class structure in which a new active middle class, which was searching for social mobility and possessed of an ascetic Protestantism peculiarly adapted both to economic enterprise and scientific thinking, was emerging. Whereas in Italy science was essentially an upper class entertainment which appeared both morally and religiously dangerous, in northern Europe science was supported and justified by claims as to its utility in technology and production, and it became very closely connected to an emerging conception of *progress*.

The particular interests of the new middle class in trade and profit, commerce and business, motivated a special emphasis on practical application of scientific and technological knowledge. In England and Holland in the sixteenth century a network grew up around the scientific interests of a number of men whose principal contributions were to navigation, mining, lens grinding, instrument making and other practical concerns. For many of these men sea trade, or their connections with it, was their live-

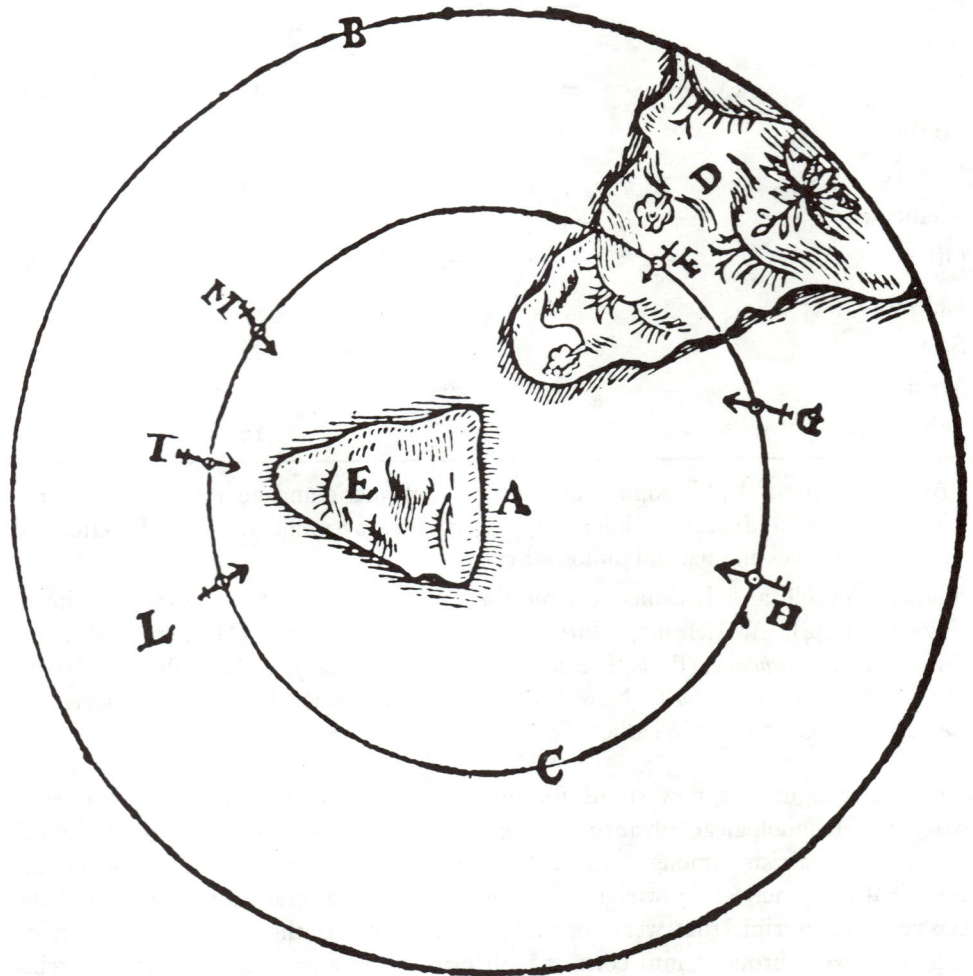

Figure 7   A diagram from Gilbert's De Magnete, *the first modern scientific work on magnetism and electricity*

lihood. Trade was bursting the boundaries of a traditional society, and the identification of scientific interests with the economic aspirations of the middle classes was to connect it to the mainspring of social change, especially in England. The emergence of this new, urban middle class, humble though its origins were, formed a better base for the institutionalization of science than did the rather rigid system of social strata in sixteenth century Italy. In the countries of northern and western Europe the great expansion of trade and commercial activity was eroding the limits of traditional society. The development of science was made more possible in such a social context, since it could be promoted by social groups whose expanding fortunes were created out of the discovery of new places, trade routes, markets, and new kinds of goods. In such a context – as opposed to the situation in Italy – there was a much greater readiness to accept that science had a better claim to represent a more valid way to truth than did traditional, scholastic, philosophy. And in the northern part of Europe, particularly in the Protestant countries, such a view of science also implied an active attitude towards its propagation. The development of science, then, depended on the activity of the minority who believed in it, fighting for its general recognition in the public arena, and forming associations directed toward its advancement.

Because of the nature of Protestantism in countries such as England it became possible for religion to legitimate both the search for scientific knowledge *and* the economic values of the new middle class. Ultimately, in some sections of Protestantism it was possible for science to be seen as an integral part of religious belief, in the sense that exploration of nature was a glorification of God's handiwork. This was a rather different state of affairs than that obtaining in many Catholic and a few other Protestant countries, in which science was seen often as a *challenge* to religious authority. Indeed some Protestant communities which were socially or politically enclosed and tightly knit tended to oppose science as a potential challenge to revelation and religious authority: such was certainly the case in Geneva and Scotland, where science tended to receive much less value and esteem than in the Netherlands and England, and paradoxically enough, less even than in Catholic France, Italy, and some parts of central Europe.

The unification of science and religion was most effective in countries where Protestantism, especially in its Calvinist forms, could not form tightly bounded religious communities. The closely knit communities tended to be small and relatively

Figure 8   Isaac Newton. His work in physics and optics provided the first major paradigm in these sciences

105

undifferentiated; consequently they usually lacked any intellectual group apart from the clergy, who in such a situation were highly sensitive to any suggestion of heresy. The large Catholic countries, by contrast, had a tradition of learning, a distinctive and differentiated intellectual class and some degree of specialization in non-religious intellectual interests. Science could develop – though fairly slowly – in some Catholic countries whereas it could be held back by strict Protestant communities. Simple differences in religious ethics, or in theological ideas, are not themselves enough to explain England's 'scientific revolution'. However, some specific social conditions did allow science to form a significant aspect of the cultural system of English society, and permit the establishment of a scientific role, and the institutionalization of science as an activity with high social value. The explanation of these changes then, has to take into account the interaction of Calvinist Protestantism with the English social structure of the seventeenth century. It was this interaction which gave the boost to science that we now recognize as most crucial in its 'modern' development.

Let us now go on to look in more detail at the interaction of Calvinist Protestantism – what has been called the Puritan ethic – with social structural factors in seventeenth century England.

3 PURITANISM AND THE INSTITUTIONALIZATION OF SCIENCE IN SEVENTEENTH CENTURY ENGLAND

In discussing the emergence of a scientific role, we have mentioned the social requirements for institutionalization: the development of a distinctive social role or set of social roles which are related in a specific way to a particular activity and which are recognized as possessing a certain social value by the rest of society. (You might like to refer back to the discussion of *social role* and *institutionalization* in Unit 19, section 1.2 if you feel concerned at the use of these concepts.)

Institutionalization also implies that the activity concerned will develop *norms* – standards of behaviour and action – suited to the realization of its aims and to its relative independence from other *institutions* – as, e.g. the family, politics, economic organization, etc. – and requires that, at the same time, these other institutional areas will adapt their norms to it. Consequently, the institutionalization of science required not only the existence of people prepared to think of themselves primarily as *scientists*, but more importantly the adaptation of general cultural values and the reorientation of other social institutions and social groups to the values and beliefs embodied in science.

This necessary adaptation and reorientation was made possible in England principally by two factors:

1   The changing class structure and the relative fluidity of social structure.

2   The characteristics of 'Puritan', Calvinist Protestantism and its social organization.

From the mid-sixteenth century the emergent middle class began to associate themselves with two interconnected sets of beliefs, or *belief-systems*. The first was the religious ethic of ascetic Protestantism. In Unit 11 this ethic was outlined in relation to Max Weber's thesis about the connection between Calvinism and the development of capitalism, and it is dealt with in more detail in Unit 24. It will be sufficient to say here that the driving force of the Calvinist – and in England the principal Calvinist religious groupings were known as the *Puritans* – was a deep psychological anxiety about their *certitudo salutis* – or how they could be certain of their *salvation*. Although theologically the membership of the *Elect*, who would be saved and thus reside in Heaven, was known only to God, the anxieties of Calvinists about their predestination tended to create an ethic which identified a state of Grace with material success in a 'calling' or worthy occupation (Weber 1904–5).

Thus the Puritan ethic stressed the necessity of hard work in a *useful* occupation

See Unit 24, section 2.2

as the most effective way of glorifying God and, as a result, of becoming more sure of salvation. When the pursuit of scientific knowledge came to be seen as a worthy occupation, the religious ethic tended to provide both a justification and a motive for scientific activity.

The second belief-system associated with the new middle class was connected to many Protestant ideas and sought a reorientation of educational and intellectual values. Basically connected to the experimentalism and empiricism of the Renaissance artisans – as you will remember from the discussion by Zilsel and from earlier sections of this unit – these values were developed by Protestant scholars such as Francis Bacon (1561–1626), Comenius (1592–1670), and Samuel Hartlib (died ? 1670) into an *utopian world view* of great attraction to the new middle class. This *world view* contained several elements – the notion of universal education, scientific and technological co-operation towards the eventual conquest of nature and the unification of science, experiment, and experience. Bacon, in particular, stressed the importance of co-operation amongst craftsmen and scholars, which he thought would result in various advances for society, especially in relation to the improvement of men's living conditions. As part and parcel of these ideas, Bacon stressed the necessity for science to be based on the assiduous and encyclopaedic collection of facts, and the careful review of existing knowledge.

Figure 9 Jan Amos Comenius. One of the authors of the utopian world view of scientific and technological cooperation so important to Protestant scientists

In the changing social structure of England between the mid-sixteenth century and the latter part of the seventeenth century (a period including, we must not forget, two revolutions and a civil war) these two belief-systems interacted with the economic and political interests of the middle classes to create a *problem solving approach* to both human and scientific affairs, an attempt to create a new civilization based in part on scientific method and scientific knowledge, and legitimated by Protestantism.

Protestantism made such a situation possible partly because its leaders sympathized with the attack on traditional sources of authority, and partly because it possessed no universally constituted religious authority like the Papacy. Consequently there was some variation and freedom of interpretation of the Bible for the individual believer: 'a Protestant who felt that God's will and the discoveries of science were in harmony could speak in good conscience, provided that he lived in an environment where church authority was unstable or weak' (Ben-David 1971 p 69).

In England, because the Puritans could not form a closed religious community they did not seek to enforce conformity in doctrine and practice. Indeed this situation was more likely to result in the adoption by Protestant governments of science and of elements of the scientific utopia: during the Commonwealth period the government came very near to accepting the utopia as a basis for its official education policy.

Figure 10   Theodore Haak. One of the members of the 'invisible college', who was instrumental in the formation of the Royal Society

Science, paradoxically enough, also influenced the relative cohesion of Protestantism in England, unifying it against the dissension caused by political and theological dispute. Science could provide one theme or policy that all Protestants could agree on because it did not contain the seeds of dispute over matters of religious belief or practice.

3.1   THE MERTON THESIS

The chapter from Merton's book about science in seventeenth century England (Merton 1970a) deals with some of the principal religious motives for scientific development in that period. In that sense it aptly summarizes the *Merton thesis*:

> . . . the thesis of this study (is) that the Puritan ethic, as an ideal-typical expression of the value-attitudes basic to ascetic Protestantism generally, so canalized the interests of seventeenth century Englishmen as to constitute one

important *element* in the cultivation of science. The deep rooted religious *interests* of the day demanded in their forceful implications the systematic, rational, and empirical study of Nature for the glorification of God in his works and for the control of the corrupt world (Merton 1957 pp 574–5).

(The concept of the 'ideal-type' as employed in the first sentence of this quotation needs some explaining. In both this unit and Unit 24, 'Beliefs and social strata', the concept of 'ideal-type' is used as a methodological device, that is as a way of understanding or explaining social phenomena. The 'ideal-type' was first used in sociology by the German sociologist Max Weber as a way of getting at the essential characteristics of a system of social relationships or an ethical system of social norms, such as *capitalism* or the *Protestant ethic*. By 'ideal-type' Weber meant an abstract characterization of related phenomena, the attempt to provide an initial picture of these phenomena which could serve as the preliminary to creating hypotheses about them. The ideal-type has no basis in reality, but rather is a 'one sided accentuation of one or more points of view' and the synthesis of a range of individual phenomena into an 'analytical construct' (Rogers 1969 p 17).)

Figure 11   Robert K. Merton, author of Science, technology and society in seventeenth-century England *(1970)*

Perhaps a word of caution is necessary before you read the Merton chapter. Bear in mind that it is one chapter of a book that deals with many aspects of the institutionalization of science in seventeenth century England. In particular Merton is *not* trying to argue – as many of his critics seem to think – that Puritanism was either the sole or most important *cause* of scientific development, or of the scientific revolution itself. His is perhaps a more subtle argument. It is that the Puritan ethic was instrumental in creating a societal *value-complex* (e.g. belief-system or cultural system) in which the various other motivating elements of science could be integrated with scientific knowledge itself in order to give science a social value which established it as an important and esteemed activity, and coordinated that activity with the main institutional areas of society.

Now read Merton in Reader, pp 384–404

Now read the Merton chapter (pp 384–404 in the Reader) and complete the following SAQs.

SAQ 4

In talking about the 'rising class of bourgeoisie' how does Merton describe the ways in which they manifested their 'increasing power'?

SAQ 5

How, and from what sources does Merton discern the 'chief motive forces of the new science'?

SAQ 6

In describing the Puritan evaluation of science, Merton showed that Puritanism imparted a three point utility to science. Which *three* factors does he isolate:

A   Science enlarged man's control of nature

B   Science was intellectually worthwhile

C   Science questioned religious belief

D   Science was a practical proof of the scientist's state of grace

E   Science glorified God

F   Science helped in creating religious ritual

G   Science influenced social thought?

SAQ 7

Which *two* 'highly prized values' of science were particularly appropriate to the Puritan culture of the mid-seventeenth century:

A   Belief in the possibility of mathematical representation of the natural world

B   Empiricism

C   Utopianism

D   Radicalism

E   Utilitarianism

F   Intellectual cooperation?

3.2   SOME THOUGHTS ON THE MERTON THESIS

Although the argument referred to here as the Merton thesis has some importance as a sociological study of the interrelationships between science and religion, it should be stressed that it is a part – and only a small part – of a very extensive litera-ture on the 'Protestant' motives for science dating back to the 1880s (Kemsley 1973).

However, the Merton study has attracted a great deal of criticism concerning the *sociological* thesis that it contains. As was pointed out at the beginning of this unit, essentially two positions on the development of science seem to be possible –

a *history of ideas* approach concentrating on *intrinsic* intellectual factors, and an *institutional* approach which stresses the significance of social and organizational *extrinsic* factors. (Intrinsic and extrinsic, that is, to the substance of scientific knowledge itself.) Both approaches do tend – as of course they must – to accept certain premisses of the other's argument, and naturally it would be foolish to ignore the intellectual changes that formed the basis of modern science in any analysis of its social development. (One very good example of the intrinsic approach is Koyré, 1957, which concentrates almost exclusively on the philosophical and logical evolution of *cosmological* theories, i.e. theories of the structure of the universe.)

The sociological and extrinsic theory of scientific development has been extended to the analysis of general historical themes, and in particular to the explanation of the causes of the English Civil War. In his book, *Intellectual origins of the English Revolution*, the historian Christopher Hill argued that science, along with Puritanism and the rise of the new middle class, was one of the primary causes of the changes in political attitudes and behaviour culminating in the civil war, the attempts to abolish the bishops and the House of Lords, and the execution of Charles I (Hill 1965a). This argument, based in part on the sociological thesis of Merton and others about the connections between Puritanism, science and the new middle classes, has generated a considerable literature which it would be inappropriate to examine here. (Principal sources are: Kearney 1964; Hill 1964; Whitteridge 1964; Hill 1965b; Kearney 1965; Rabb 1965; Hooykas 1972). It would be fair to say that many of the critics of the Hill thesis base their criticisms on alleged deficiencies of the Merton study, and other works connected to that study. (Stimson 1935 1939 1948; Jones 1936; Mason 1953: with Merton these are the main proponents of the thesis that the Puritan ethic was instrumental in scientific development. Principal critiques of this thesis are to be found in: Rabb 1962; Hall 1963; Kemsley 1973.)

Figure 12   One of Newton's early telescopes, the fruit of his pioneering work in optics

In most cases no dispute is entered concerning the more general thesis that *Protestants* were very much more active in both science and the production of scientific discoveries than *Catholics* in both the period of 'scientific revolution' and subsequently. Rather, the principal attack levelled at Merton concerns his employment of the term 'Puritan' to refer to a number of religious denominations with a 'core of common values which was accepted by all' (Merton 1970b p 57). By describing such groups as the Anglicans, Calvinists, Presbyterians, Independents, Anabaptists, Quakers, and Millenarians as subscribing to a 'substantially identical nucleus of religious and ethical convictions', Merton suggested that they all fell under the heading of *Puritanism* in the social implications of the ethic that they followed. (The term Puritan has a precise ecclesiastical meaning, referring to the reform of the church of England in a Presbyterian manner; Merton was not concerned with this aspect at all.) Basing his examination of this 'Puritanism' on Max Weber's analysis of the Protestant ethic, Merton found that its central core of values was *Calvinist* and that this stressed persistent hard work as a means of salvation and as 'establishing the conviction of a state of grace' (Merton 1970b p 57). The central characteristic of the criticisms of this use of 'Puritanism' is that it is too wide and loose a conceptualization, and that it does not take sufficient account of historical changes in the theology of the various groups lumped under the general heading. Merton's analysis of the relationship between 'Puritanism' – or more properly its *ethic* – and science, and his contention that the Puritan ethic was a *motive* for scientific development are both predicated on the assumption that the most common social values, or *value-system*, of mid-seventeenth century England came to include important elements of the Puritan ethic. Because the Puritan ethic itself, as a belief-system, was consonant with the aims and values of emergent science as a belief-system, its incorporation into the value-system of English society created an environment in which science

Figure 13 Thomas Sprat, *who wrote an important history of the Royal Society as an apologia for the new science*

Figure 14 Frontispiece of Sprat's History of the Royal Society of London *(1667). Shows (1) Bust of Charles II (2) Sir Francis Bacon (3) Viscount Brouncker*

and scientists could flourish, since they had achieved a relatively secure level of social esteem. The profession of scientist for the first time achieved a societal legitimacy which encouraged talented individuals in their scientific practice. Because the Puritan ethic stressed utilitarianism, empiricism, the glorification of God in his works by the 'useful' study of his handiwork, nature, religion became both a sanction and a justification for science. In that sense, the Puritan ethic was both motive and reward for engaging in scientific work, since during the period there was little practical difference between religious and social values. This is borne out by an examination of the religious inclinations of seventeenth century English scientists. Thus, when we look at the composition of the Royal Society, seven out of the ten men who began meeting at Oxford in secret in the 1640s – the so-called 'invisible college' – were of Puritan inclinations. After the Royal Society was formally inaugurated in 1654, and given a Royal Charter in 1662, a list of its members for 1663 shows that 62 per cent of the initial membership of the society were clearly Puritan. And indeed by the late 1660s the Royal Society was being attacked for its Puritan origins, in a Restoration atmosphere in which the 'taint' of Puritanism invested science with a radical tinge! Indeed Sprat's *History of the Royal Society* (Sprat 1667) was intended as an *apologia* for the society which stressed how fitting science could be for the nobleman, and how it could be connected to the religious concerns of the established church. In the new political atmosphere it had become necessary to stress the 'safeness' of scientific thought, and to present it as supporting religious authority by enhancing the active contemplation of nature in all its aspects.

The utilitarian and empiricist slant of the Puritan motivation of science was strongly present in the work of nearly all seventeenth century English scientists. In the case of the Royal Society many of its stated objectives were connected to practical concerns. Society members had a great interest in problems of sea travel, and these interests were themselves a complementary motive for science. Technical problems such as finding longitude at sea were important in the development of logarithms, mathematics, and astronomy: the discovery of the satellites of Jupiter, and Newton's Lunar theory were both prompted by the longitude problem. Flamsteed's tidal theory was devised because of the need for accurate tide times in tabular form, essential both to the Royal Navy and to navigators generally.

Another concern of society members was with the 'planting and propagation of trees', suggested by the Navy's interest in the diminishing size of forest preserves, and its continuing need of wood for ships. This led on to other interests of direct importance both to the Navy and to maritime traders, to concern with hydrostatics, hydrodynamics, and mechanics generally: Hooke's law on the tension of springs emerged at the same time as he was working on problems associated with the building of ships from various types of wood and the use in them of different types of cord.

It is quite possible to see in the development of science during this period a concern with projects designed to give technological assistance to business. In particular, such research was frequently formulated in order to help extend possible markets both inland and overseas – the extension of markets being (as you will remember from Units 11 and 12) one of the primary requirements of a growing capitalism. As a statistical support of this argument Merton analysed the minutes of Royal Society meetings over four representative years – 1661, 1662, 1686, 1687 – and classified the items discussed as to their relationship to socio-economic requirements of the period. Over the whole period looked at by Merton, only 41.3 per cent of the total number of investigations and experiments were *pure research*, unrelated to socio-economic demands. And Merton argues that: 'On the grounds afforded by this study it seems justifiable to assert that the range of problems investigated by the seventeenth-century English scientists was appreciably influenced by the socio-economic structure of the period' (Merton 1957 p 627).

The institutionalization of the scientific role involved scientists in becoming an 'autonomous, distinct, and respected intellectual community' (Ben-David 1971 p 74). One of the primary factors in the establishment of such a community was agreement among scientists on scientific method. The importance of the 'scientific utopia' in this agreement on scientific method cannot be overstressed. It was precisely the acceptance, from the 1640s onwards, of the tenets of Baconianism that made such an agreement possible. Bacon had stressed induction, experiment, and the necessity of constant reference of experimental statements to data and evidence. Although in themselves the collection of data and experiment, without prior reference to theory, cannot guarantee scientific results, nevertheless the research strategies Bacon proposed helped to give the scientific community autonomy. For the experimental method allowed agreement on methods whilst preventing the creation of a closed philosophy based on science. Scientists could follow different interests and pursue different theories, yet at the same time feel like members of a community because they all used a common language – verification of facts by controlled experiment (Ben-David 1971 p 74). Such a 'universal language' meant that scientific dispute could not disrupt the cohesive nature of the community. A consensus was not necessary on areas of knowledge but only on the methods and techniques which the scientist should employ to extend knowledge of the natural world.

The institutionalization of science created certain intellectual and social norms, as part and parcel of the activity of science:

1   The necessity of exact and empirical research as the method leading to the discovery of significant new knowledge.
2   That scientific knowledge is distinct and independent of other modes of acquiring or defining knowledge, such as traditional authority, abstract speculation, or religious revelation.
3   A set of social norms which control and orientate scientific activity towards certain general goals. These can be summarized as:
(a) *universalism*: all knowledge claims are subject to purely impersonal criteria which are pre-established and open to all, without reference to personal or social factors.
(b) the *obligation* to make knowledge *communally* available, by the recognized method of publication of discoveries for public use and criticism. Scientific knowledge is not the personal property of the scientist. (In practice this norm may be challenged by business interests, e.g. in the legal protection of inventions by patent.)
(c) proper *acknowledgement* of the contributions of others to scientific knowledge – there are relatively few examples of fraud in science, since scientific claims to priority in research are immediately open to professional scrutiny. Esteem is only awarded on the basis of real achievements, verified independently by other community members.
(d) *organized scepticism*, involving suspension of judgement until empirical proof is available, and the constant attempt to refute existing theories and experimental findings.

It was the development of such norms that gave science the distinctive independence from other institutional spheres that characterized its establishment as an integral part of western industrial society. The establishment of such norms and the consequent institutionalization of science were basic goals of the Royal Society. Importantly, its members did not see themselves and their work as part of a great new system of speculative philosophy, but instead saw science as a more important enterprise with greater dignity.

Although the French *Académie des Sciences* was established in 1663 it is arguable that only in England at this time were general institutional norms adapted to the requirements of autonomous science: relatively free speech, some religious and political tolerance, and a degree of flexibility in culture and society which would allow of their change by science and technology.

Scientific ideas began, in the late 1660s, to be influential in other intellectual spheres and to suggest the resolution of other types of problem by scientific methods. Both economic and political philosophy, and the practical aspects of economics and politics were seen as analogous to self-regulating mechanical systems, rather than as orders based on some supreme authority. The structure of political society could be thought of in the same way as the structure of matter: individuals held together like atoms by the conflicting forces of church, state, lords, monarch. Economics, similarly, was capable of being thought of as the regulation of certain quantities such as supply and demand, their equilibrium as forces represented by price (Letwin 1965).

On the continent, by contrast, science was still held to be potentially subversive: a philosophy which had to be prevented from influencing political, social and economic thought. Science had become an accepted part of English society and culture, and it was possible and not very dangerous to try to apply the new experimental approach to practically any part of private or public life. Science had begun the long climb to its present position of pre-eminence in the scale of cultural values, a preeminence which is only now gradually being eroded by the beginnings of a feeling that science and technology will not be able to provide indefinitely for material progress.

4   REMARKS ON THE SOCIAL STRUCTURE OF SCIENCE

In this short concluding section of the unit, it will be useful to suggest some implications of the view of science taken in it.

In essence, we have concentrated on an institutional or socio-cultural view of science, trying to establish how social structures and belief-systems have interacted to produce a distinctive set of social values and social roles connected to science. This has implied a particular conception of scientific development, ignoring the discoveries and contributions of men like Galileo, Harvey, Newton, Napier, Boyle, Hooke etc, in favour of the influence of beliefs about the social and religious values of scientific knowledge. We have tried to make clear that this concentration on institutional, social and cultural factors does not involve the presumption that intellectual development was unimportant and that only the 'material conditions' mattered. Rather, the emphasis has been on social factors because the unit forms part of a social science course, and because we can show that social factors are as important as intellectual factors in creating the necessary conditions for scientific advance. Indeed in one sense the unit is concerned with showing how even such an apparently 'objective' activity as science is controlled and formed out of certain values, beliefs and attitudes which would commonly be called subjective in their basic orientation. Lastly, the emphasis on social factors is justified by the fact that when we talk about science we cannot describe it as if it one day 'fell from the skies' fully formed: rather, we have to understand how science itself has established characteristic elements of social organization adapted to its practitioners' conceptions of, and values about, their scientific activities. Science, in that sense, has a history which contains both social and intellectual developments. A *full* account of the rise of science – which of course this unit has not attempted – would take both social and intellectual factors into account and examine their interrelationships.

Indeed a *full* account constructed in such a way would probably offer a substantially different view of science to that which would be gauged from the average science textbook. Textbooks tend to employ a rather unhistorical view of science. The overall impression that they tend to give of scientific development is of a piecemeal process of accretion and accumulation of discoveries and bodies of experimental data. Textbooks give a rather unilinear view of science, and in that sense they mirror

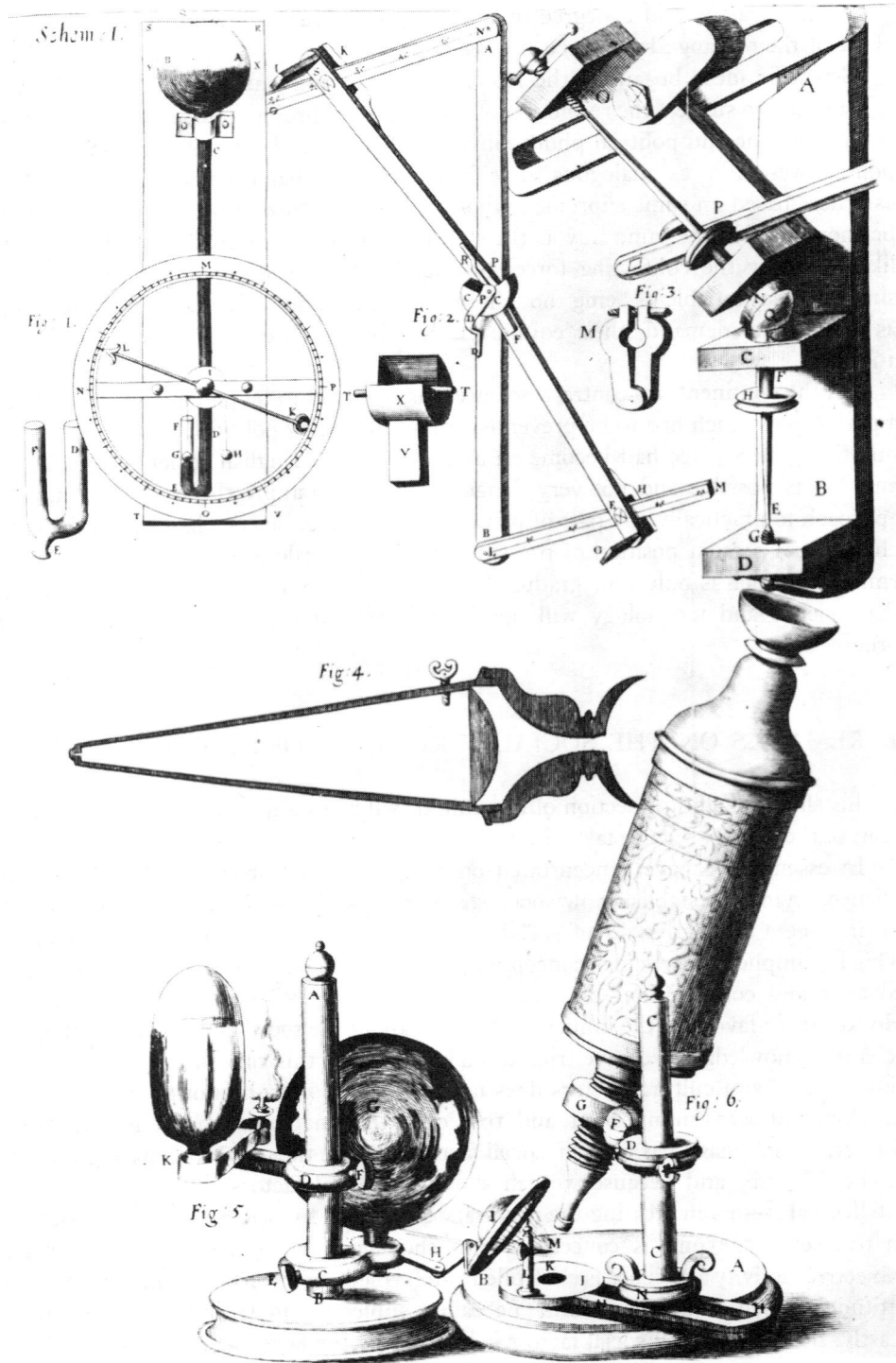

Figure 15   Details of a microscope invented by Newton

the conception that scientists themselves have of science, which is rooted in their education and in the traditions of scientific research. Science has in fact developed in a much less uniform and more controversial way than most standard textbooks would allow, revered as they often are as authoritative statements of the scope and content of science. The realization that textbook science – to which in a sense we are all subject in our conceptions of science – focuses on a rather restricted idea of scientific normality, has led to a concern with the social structure of science itself, and to the influence that that social structure has on scientific development. For, if we are to take the textbook impression of science as given, then the past history of science looks very strange indeed: viewing that history leads to some disturbing discoveries, and the impression develops that:

. . . once current views of nature (as, e.g., Aristotelian dynamics, phlogistic chemistry, geocentric cosmology) were, as a whole, neither less scientific nor more the product of human idiosyncrasy than those current today. If these out-of-date beliefs are to be called myths, then myths can be produced by the same sorts of methods and held for the same sorts of reasons that now lead to scientific knowledge. If, on the other hand, they are to be called science, then science has included bodies of belief quite incompatible with the ones we hold today. (Kuhn 1962 p 2)

What becomes increasingly clear is that the social organization of science itself involves certain preconceptions and beliefs which determine the progression of scientific research. The professional education of scientists, it has been argued, initiates them into a pre-existing tradition of research and professional work, or *normal science*, as was indicated earlier (section 2). In that sense the scientist's education provides him with a convenient, and traditionally established, selection of 'conceptual boxes': he is expected to devote time and effort to forcing nature, through his experiments, into those 'boxes'. The scientific community, then, develops a tradition of 'normal research' which is usually based on a particular theory or group of theories – a *paradigm* for scientific research. This *paradigm,* constructed out of a recognized scientific achievement (as, e.g. Newton's physical laws; Einstein's relativity theory) determines the form and substance of research for a community of scientists, sometimes for several generations. *Scientific revolutions*, such as the one we have been looking at in this unit, occur when the paradigm no longer supplies *normal research* with interesting or significant puzzles to solve by experimentation and theoretical elaboration. The *revolution* consists in the scientific community's 'rejection of one time-honoured scientific theory in favour of another incompatible with it '(Kuhn 1962 p 6). In a sense, because it alters the nature of the research tradition, the *scientific revolution* also changes the rules on which scientific reputations have been built. In fact, a scientific revolution accomplishes a structural change in the scientific community as well as a theoretical change in the way it looks at its objects of study.

> That is why a new theory, however special its range of application, is seldom or never just an increment to what is already known. Its assimilation requires the reconstruction of prior theory and the re-evaluation of prior fact, an intrinsically revolutionary process that is seldom completed by a single man and never overnight. (Kuhn 1962 p 9)

In the example discussed in this unit, the *scientific revolution* of the seventeenth century, we can discern the formation of a paradigm and a tradition of normal research in the processes of institutionalization of science and development of the scientific role. In this particular case the major scientific innovations were in physics, exemplified by Newton's achievements in optics, in cosmology and in dynamics. Physical problems, in the main, united a group who had previously been primarily interested in the study of nature and transformed them into a profession and a community, institutionalized officially as the Royal Society. Prior to this stage, physical science was in very much of a *pre-paradigm* state where different 'schools' competed in their explanations of phenomena. There was no agreement on basic data; all facts seemed relevant or plausible, and it was difficult to organize the data in terms of its significance, since that could only be provided by an effective theory.

The institutionalization of science, then, is at least as closely related to changes in the intellectual structure of scientific knowledge, as it is to social and cultural factors. But it is quite crucial to point out that intellectual agreement implies consensus over intellectual methods and a tradition of research, accompanied by the development of a specific role and the creation of a scientific community with certain norms and a characteristic social structure.

Science does not exist outside of, or independently of, society. Its organization and even intellectual development are closely moulded by irreducibly social factors: this unit has attempted to demonstrate that point.

REFERENCES

BEN-DAVID, J. (1971) *The scientist's role in society: a comparative study*, New Jersey, Prentice-Hall.

HALL, A. (1963) 'Merton revisited, or science and society in the seventeenth century', *History of Science*, vol. 2, pp 1–16.

HILL, C. (1964) 'Puritanism, capitalism and the scientific revolution', *Past and Present*, no. 29, pp 88–98.

HILL, C. (1965a) *Intellectual origins of the English revolution*, London, Panther.

HILL, C. (1965b) 'William Harvey (no parliamentarian, no heretic) and the idea of monarchy', *Past and Present*, no. 31, pp 97–103.

HOOYKAS, R. (1972) *Religion and the rise of modern science*, Edinburgh, Scottish Academic Press.

JONES, R. F. (1936) *Ancients and moderns*, St Louis, Washington University Studies.

KEARNEY, H. F. (1964) 'Puritanism, capitalism and the scientific revolution', *Past and Present*, no. 28, pp 88–101.

KEARNEY, H. F. (1965) 'Puritanism and science: problems of definition', *Past and Present*, no. 31, pp 104–10.

KEMSLEY, D. S. (1973) 'Religious influences in the rise of modern science', in Russell, C. A. (ed.) *Science and religious belief*, London, University of London Press, pp 74–102.

KOYRÉ, A. (1957) *From the closed world to the infinite universe*, Baltimore, The Johns Hopkins Press.

KUHN, T. S. (1962) *The structure of scientific revolutions*, Chicago, University of Chicago Press.

KUHN, T. S. (1968) 'The history of science', in *International encyclopaedia of the social sciences*, London, Macmillan.

LETWIN, W. (1965) *The origins of scientific economics*, London, Methuen.

MASON, S. F. (1953) 'The scientific revolution and the Protestant reformation', *Annals of Science*, vol. 9.

MERTON, R. K. (1957) *Social theory and social structure*, New York, Free Press.

MERTON, R. K. (1970a) 'Motive forces of the new science', in *Science, technology and society in seventeenth-century England*, New York, Harper and Row, pp 80–110. Reprinted in Potter and Sarre (1974) pp 384–403.

MERTON, R. K. (1970b) *Science, technology and society in seventeenth-century England*, New York, Harper and Row.

POTTER, D. and SARRE, P. (eds.) (1974) *Dimensions of society*, London, University of London Press/The Open University Press (Course Reader).

RABB, T. K. (1962) 'Puritanism and the rise of experimental science in England', *Journal of World History*, vol. 7, pp 46–67.

RABB, T. K. (1965) 'Religion and the rise of modern science', *Past and Present*, no. 31, pp 111–26.

ROGERS, F. E. (1969) *Max Weber's ideal type theory*, New York, Philosophical Library Inc.

SPRAT, T. (1667) *History of the Royal Society of London*, London. Reprinted 1959, London, Routledge and Kegan Paul.

STIMSON, D. (1935) 'Puritanism and the new philosophy in seventeenth-century England', *Bulletin of the history of medicine*, vol. III, pp 321–4.

STIMSON, D. (1939) 'Amateurs of science in seventeenth-century England', *Isis*, nos. 31 and 32.

STIMSON, D. (1948) *Scientists and amateurs: a history of the Royal Society*, New York.

STORER, N. (1966) *The social system of science*, New York, Holt, Rinehart and Winston.

THORNER, I. (1952) 'Ascetic Protestantism and the development of science and technology', *American Journal of Sociology*, vol. 58, pp 25–33.

WEBER, M. (1904–5) *The Protestant ethic and the spirit of capitalism*. Published 1930, London, Allen and Unwin.

WHITTERIDGE, G. (1964) 'William Harvey: a royalist and no parliamentarian', *Past and Present*, no. 30.

ZILSEL, E. (1942) 'The sociological roots of science', *American Journal of Sociology*, XLVII, January, pp 544–60. Reprinted in Potter and Sarre (1974) pp 370–83.

RECOMMENDED READING

BEN-DAVID, J. (1971) *The scientist's role in society: a comparative study*, New Jersey, Prentice-Hall.

BOAS, M. (1970) *The scientific renaissance*, London, Fontana.

HAMILTON, P. (1974) *Knowledge and social structure*, London, Routledge and Kegan Paul.

KUHN, T. S. (1962) *The structure of scientific revolutions*, Chicago, University of Chicago Press.

LAKATOS, I. and MUSGROVE, A. (1970) *Criticism and the growth of knowledge*, Cambridge, Cambridge University Press.

MERTON, R. K. (1973) *The sociology of science*, Chicago, University of Chicago Press.

WHITLEY, R. (ed.) (1973) *Social processes of scientific development*, London, Routledge and Kegan Paul.

ACKNOWLEDGEMENTS

Grateful acknowledgement is made to the following sources for material used in this unit:

FIGURES
Figure 1 Fred Stein; *Figures 2, 8 and 12* Science Museum, London; *Figures 3–6* Mary Evans Picture Library; *Figures 7, 10 and 11* Mansell Collection; *Figure 9* British Library; *Figure 13* Science Museum, London. Crown copyright; *Figures 14 and 15* Ronan Picture Library.

TABLES
Tables 1 and 2 from J. Ben-David, *The scientist's role in society*, Prentice-Hall Inc, Englewood Cliffs, New Jersey, 1971.

ANSWERS TO SELF-ASSESSMENT QUESTIONS

SAQ 1

The three groups which Zilsel identified were:

A   *university scholars;* based in the universities, a high status group who concerned themselves with scholastic methods of rational argument. In relation to scientific knowledge they tended to avoid concern with physical laws, experimentation and observation in favour of explanations couched in terms of the 'ends' and 'meanings' of natural phenomena.

B   *humanists;* mostly secretaries of great lords and government officials, this group developed a form of secular learning which stressed knowledge of the Greek and Roman classics. In relation to knowledge of the natural world, they were more interested in the style or form of such knowledge than its content. As with the university scholars they rejected the vernacular and wrote mostly in Latin. They also rejected and despised any form of manual labour.

C   *artists; artisans and craftsmen;* a group with much lower social esteem than the *scholars* and *humanists*, they were mainly concerned with the plastic arts and technology. In the main, though some had connections with the *scholars* and *humanists*, they were engaged in the extension of empirical knowledge related to their particular occupations and lacked the intellectual training necessary to placing that knowledge in a systematic framework. Importantly, they wrote many technical works in the vernacular for use by their colleagues, and they tended to work in cooperation with each other.

SAQ 2

The four 'sociological conditions' were:

A   in the transition from a feudal to an early capitalist socio-economic system there occurred a change in the 'bearers of culture', from knights and clerics to townspeople.

B   a significant rise in the rate of technological innovation for manufacture and warfare. This developed 'causal' thought at the expense of 'magical' thought.

C   the communalism of the feudal period was replaced by an emphasis on individualism and criticism of traditional authority, connected to the extension of economic competition.

D   a movement from a society ruled by an emphasis on traditional and customary values and obligations towards one based on rationalism. The economic rationalism of early capitalism was closely related to the development of rational scientific methods.

SAQ 3

I would answer this question as follows:

Gilbert, Galileo, and Bacon are examples of a new social type of intellectual worker. In each case they had broken down social and intellectual barriers dividing the *liberal* and *mechanical* arts. Gilbert was an academic scholar who wrote, in 1600, a book based on his contacts with the artisan class, and on experiments and empirical observations.

Galileo's scientific achievements were based on practical problems of his day, and he too had links with the artisan class. Much of his later scientific work was written in the vernacular and thus could be of use to people other than scholars and humanists.

Bacon was an important propagandist for scientific method. His ideas on scientific cooperation were influential in the foundation of scientific learned societies such as the *Royal Society* and the *Académie française*.

Each of these men exemplified the convergence of the interests of upper class and lower class social groups in a common arena—scientific knowledge.

SAQ 4

Merton identified three ways in which the 'rising bourgeoisie' showed their increasing power:
A   positive espousal of science and technology
B   because of their growing economic and social significance as a group, a great belief in *progress*.
C   an increasing hostility towards the traditional class system which restricted their access to political control.

SAQ 5

Merton takes the writings of important scientists of the period and examines them for any reference to religious motivations for science. In particular he looks at the writings of Boyle, Ray, Willughby, Wilkins, Oughtred, Barrow, Grew, Wallis, Newton and others.

SAQ 6

A
D
E

SAQ 7

B
E

Unit 24
Beliefs and social strata

Prepared for the course team by Kenneth Thompson and Vincent Worth

CONTENTS

INTRODUCTION

You start off this week's work with something of an advantage in that you have already been introduced to a number of key ideas in the unit. Section 3 of Unit 23 discussed the interrelation between beliefs and action in terms of the effect of the Protestant ethic on the development of science, and in this unit we spend part of the time considering the effects of the same beliefs on the rise of capitalism. Again, last week's television and radio programmes examined relationships between nineteenth century Methodism and political ideologies and structures, a further theme taken up in this week's work.

The last unit showed us how science as an institution has related to the social context in which it developed in recent centuries and reminded us, if we needed reminding, that scientific knowledge significantly shapes the kinds of lives we lead in today's industrial world. The relatively high standard of living we enjoy is due, in large measure, to the increase in the efficiency of productive processes that technology has generated. More recently, we have become aware of the costs of living in technological societies – oil crises, pollution, and so on – so that we perhaps feel that survival depends on our collective re-assertion of control over a world that applied science has largely created.

By contrast, we may tend to think of religious beliefs as of concern only to people's private lives, as having some importance perhaps on ritual family occasions like birth and death, but possessing little relevance to the central institutions of modern societies – the economy and the polity – which seem to function outside any legitimating religious framework. But the significance that many people continue to attach to their own and others' religious beliefs and practice, the development of many of our social institutions within a religious tradition, and the importance of religion in helping us to understand other times and other cultures, all these clearly justify the study of religious beliefs in any attempt to make sense of society.

At the end of the double unit on attitudes that began the present block, the author considered the psychological bases of religious attitudes and suggested that religion functions for the *individual* in giving him an identity and a set of moral rules by which to evaluate behaviour. In this unit, we broaden the perspective by relating religious attitudes and beliefs to their *social* contexts and, through examining empirical examples, try to trace out some of the ways in which social scientists have sought to reveal and explain connections between the beliefs of social groups and their actions. In order to achieve this aim, we shall consider three studies of the relationships between the religious beliefs of certain groups and the effects of these on their political and economic actions in periods of rapid social change. We shall pay particular attention to the ways in which the belief system of a group may induce it to initiate social change or to seek some form of adjustment to it. The kinds of social change we shall be examining are those usually subsumed by the terms 'industrialization' and 'modernization'. We shall also briefly consider the importance of religious organizations in mediating beliefs and their social consequences.

See Unit 21–22, section 11.2

STUDY OBJECTIVES

After studying this unit you should be able to:

1   Understand the kinds of theories that social scientists use to deal with the relationships between the beliefs and actions of groups initiating or responding to social change.

2   Appreciate the types of methodological problems involved in evaluating such theories.

3   Use and assess evidence relevant to the hypothesis that beliefs may operate as independent variables in the processes of structural change.

4   Appreciate the need to see religions as social organizations as much as systems of ideas, attitudes and values.

5   Achieve the detachment necessary to deal with religious beliefs as constituents of a social science explanation.

6   Develop further your ability to integrate written, spoken and visual material.

STUDY GUIDE

Your work on this unit has been designed to follow a particular sequence with several different sources to draw from. You may not be able to follow the sequence exactly as set out below, but you should be aware of the relationship between the different components.

1   Read the introduction and sections 1 and 2 in the correspondence text, pp 127–36.

2   Read section 3 in the correspondence text and Michael Hill, 'The Halévy thesis' in the Reader, *Dimensions of society* (Potter and Sarre 1974) pp 405–23. Television programme 23 is also about Methodism and the working class and is based on research by Robert Moore, published in his *Pitmen, preachers and politics*. Radio programme 23 provides further discussion of the Halévy thesis. As you study section 3, review the notes you made on these programmes.

3   Read section 4 in the correspondence text, including the article on cargo cults by Peter Worsley. This week's television programme 24 features extracts from David Attenborough's film of the John Frum cargo cult with commentary by Peter Worsley. Radio programme 24 contains a sociological discussion of cargo cults. To conclude this part of your work, read Yonina Talmon's 'Millenarian movements' in the Reader, pp 424–41 and the comments in the correspondence text.

4   Read section 5 in the correspondence text which includes some comments on and asks you to read 'Religion in Sparkbrook', Chapter VII of Rex and Moore, *Race, community, and conflict* (1967) pp 173–90.

5   Read the final sections of the correspondence text on methodology and conclusions.

Progress through the week's material will as usual be facilitated by careful attention to the Self-assessment Questions.

1   RELIGIOUS BELIEFS, SOCIAL STRATA AND SOCIAL CHANGE

See Unit 21–22, section 11

In the unit on attitudes the author delineated what he considered to be certain common features of religion – ritual, a way of making sense of existence, and so on – but he had to qualify this definition by relating these features to *nearly* all religions. Sociologists experience the same kind of difficulty in trying to define religion in a way that encompasses all known empirical examples.

If you asked a number of people to explain what they understand by religion their definitions would probably range from the all-inclusive to the narrowly specific. One type of definition might include everything that men consider to be the highest good but for a researcher such a definition would entail investigation of virtually all social behaviour. A narrower definition might refer simply to belief in God, but we should find this empirically inadequate since it would exclude an important belief system like Buddhism. One way of understanding religion was discussed in Unit 19 where we were considering the relationship between our small, routine worlds and the larger institutional structures that encompass these and give them meaning. Although our everyday worlds are self-evidently real and meaningful, they require further and frequent legitimation, especially in times of upset and crisis, and it is religion that can provide overarching structures of meaning that pattern and integrate other

See Unit 19, section 2.2

beliefs (Berger and Luckmann 1963). By claiming to explain the nature of man, his origins and ultimate destiny, religion transforms everyday events by setting them in a more comprehensive framework of meaning.

A wide range of possible ways of defining religion exists, therefore, and it would be a useful exercise for you to try to formulate your own definition, alone or as a group activity, though you may wish to wait until you have completed the week's work. You will probably find that you need to make the distinction, easily glossed over, between religious beliefs as aspects of culture and consciousness on the one side, and religious practice as part of social structure on the other.

Social structure was defined in Unit 19 as 'persistent patterns of social relationships' and, in this sense, those who interact on the basis of shared religious beliefs form a social structure. But people relate to each other in many different roles and one of the most important underlying influences on interaction is the pattern of inequality that characterizes a community or a society. By social inequality we mean the unequal distribution of valued resources, material or symbolic. Those who share a similar rank we can think of as *strata*, as layers in a system of social stratification like caste or social class systems, though we should remember that these terms refer as much to the social relationships consequent on inequality as to the distribution itself. (We have already met these terms earlier in the course, in Units 16a and b and 19, and they will be elaborated further in Unit 28.)

Social structure and social stratification: see Unit 28

Religious beliefs relate to social strata in various ways. Religion can, for example, act as an integrative mechanism, as a form of social control, in giving a feeling of rightness or legitimation to a particular distribution of power which might otherwise cause social division and conflict. Both the doctrine known as the 'divine right of kings' and the beliefs underlying the traditional Indian caste system have operated in this way. Religion has also functioned as a channel of social mobility, or as a means of transcending the harsh reality of deprivation. Discovering links between religious practice and the life-styles of different social strata has been a frequent task of social science research into religion, and in Chapter VII of Rex and Moore, *Race, community, and conflict* (1967) pp 173–90, you will be able to read about the relationship between religion and class cultures in a modern industrial society.

Social strata

Because we are socialized from childhood to accept and operate the institutions of an industrialized society, we seldom consider the difficulties involved in making the necessary transition from the thought forms and institutions of pre-industrialized society to those characterizing the modern world. However, there have been a number of studies of this problem by social scientists and historians, and some of these studies have become the subject of perennial debates because of the fundamental questions they raise about social science methodology.

Pre-industrial societies have usually been found to possess a general belief system which gives meaning and moral justification to the established social order by reference to some supernatural or sacred power which creates or sustains it. In other words, there is a religious sanction behind the social order. In such a situation, the problem of transition to a modern industrial society can also be posed as a question concerning the kinds of changes which might be required in people's most fundamental beliefs if they are to initiate, or at least accommodate, changes which challenge their taken for granted social worlds and their sense of social order.

Pre-industrial societies

The relationship between what people believe and how they behave has already been considered as a psychological phenomenon in the first part of the present block. The shared beliefs of groups and strata have been of continuing interest to sociologists, especially in trying to relate such beliefs to the processes of social change. This relationship has been posed as a particularly crucial one by Marx, for example, who argues that the revolutionary change leading to the classless society depends on the prior development of class consciousness, a set of beliefs about one's true social interests. We have seen, in Unit 23, how beliefs about the supernatural world influenced the development of beliefs about the natural world. And in much of the rest

Marx.

Class consciousness: see Unit 16, section 4

129

of this unit, we shall examine the general problem of relating religious beliefs to social strata and social change by considering three approaches by social scientists to the interpretation of historical events and some of the controversies which these attempts have generated:

1 The Weber thesis on Protestantism and the rise of capitalism, particularly in seventeenth century England. You have already read a brief account of this in Unit 11 (pp 25–6) and a further restatement of the 'Protestant ethic' in Unit 23.

2 The Halévy thesis on Methodism and the English working class in the eighteenth and nineteenth centuries. Again, you know something of this from last week's television and radio programmes.

3 Attempts to explain the startling eruption and spread of 'cargo cults' (defined in section 4) among the native populations of the islands of Melanesia in the twentieth century.

At the beginning of each section, we shall suggest the main points to look for which are relevant to understanding our general problem area. And in each of these studies about the relationship between the beliefs of various groups and their attitudes to social change, there are also three issues to be kept in mind:

(a) The effects of beliefs in making sense of and giving meaning to social order.

(b) The legitimation, or sense of rightness, that beliefs give to the social order or to changes in the social order.

(c) The creation of religious motivations to act in ways that have an impact on politico-economic development.

SAQ 1

We referred above to 'the difficulties in making the necessary transition from the thought forms and institutions of pre-industrialized societies'. If you encountered a culture in which fathers sell their daughters in marriage, would you consider such behaviour cruel, mercenary, irrational, or immoral? As part of your answer, look back at the definition of ethnocentrism given in Units 21–22, section 7.1 and ask yourself if you have been biased by ethnocentrism.

Answers to SAQs for Unit 24 are on pp 152–6

---

2 RELIGION AND CAPITALISM: THE WEBER THESIS

We turn now to the first study – Weber's work on the link between Calvinism and the rise of capitalism, *The Protestant ethic and the spirit of capitalism*, published in 1904–5 as part of an intended series of comparative studies in the sociology of religion. Max Weber (1864–1920) was a German sociologist whose contribution to the development of modern sociology was most important and extensive.

Weber's study is discussed at some length in this unit because of its significant contribution to our ideas about the beliefs–social change relationship; because of the nature of the controversies it has generated; and because it raises a number of important methodological issues. Additionally, since you are familiar with Weber's general argument, the present treatment will help you to follow the argument more closely.

First, to restate the argument in general terms: the Weber thesis illustrates the theme that the direction and rate of politico-economic development in a country depends to a large extent on 'mental' factors – beliefs and perceived interests – especially in those who constitute a socially aspiring group who are potential innovators. There needs to be present in their minds a set of values or aspirations to the realization of which economic development is deemed to be advantageous. Furthermore, there should also be present beliefs and habits which prize change and presuppose its possibility, which are conducive to the formation of physical and personal capital

130

(technical and vocational expertise, for example) and which favour scientific knowledge and bring esteem to the innovators.

2.1 WEBER'S APPROACH

The central theoretical problem of *The Protestant ethic and the spirit of capitalism* was whether men's conceptions of the cosmic universe, and their related religious interests, could influence their actions and social relationships, particularly in the field of economic action. In addressing this problem, Weber claimed that an adequate explanation should take account of a *subjective* dimension – men's beliefs and perceptions of the world – as well as of the *objective* social structures within which these subjective factors operate. This approach is expressed in the concept of *action*: Weber attempted to interpret action by understanding men's motives from a subjective point of view – the sociologist putting himself in the actor's place. He considered that subjective interpretation need not result in a totally individualistic set of interpretations because there are *typical* patterns of meaning that the sociologist can abstract.

Social action: see Unit 19, section 1

Weber formulated these patterns of meaning as ideal types – the *ethic* of a set of religious beliefs and the *spirit* of an economic system. But he was also aware that the consequences of men's beliefs and actions are often very different from what those involved intended or expected. (You perhaps recall from the introduction to Block 1 that if individual consumers all decided to save more out of their incomes with the *intention* of increasing their future prosperity, the resultant but *unintended* fall in demand for consumer goods would lead to a loss in their income.) In *The Protestant ethic and the spirit of capitalism* Weber showed that the Puritan, although his primary intention was to serve God, also helped to create the necessary conditions for the development of capitalism. Modern capitalism in its beginnings required a certain kind of personality. This personality type resulted from belief in a set of ideas which *unwittingly* resulted in the development of those personality traits useful in capitalist enterprise. In other words, Weber considered ideas and belief could act as *independent variables* in processes of social change.

Ideal types: see Unit 23, section 3.1

Independent and dependent variables: see Unit 18, section 1

2.2 THE PROTESTANT ETHIC THESIS

The main steps in Weber's argument are as follows:

1 Weber began his study by indicating the characteristics which distinguished modern capitalism as an ideal type. Modern Western capitalism, a system of profit-making enterprises based on market relations, constituted a set of institutions dependent on the availability of a formally free, wage-earning class separated from ownership of the means of production. (Weber would probably not disagree with Benham's depiction of these institutional forms as 'private property, freedom of enterprise, and freedom of choice by consumers' (Reader p 206).) But Weber was more interested in the spirit, the ethos that informed the type of organization involved in capitalist enterprise. Above all, it was its characteristic *rationality* that distinguished modern capitalism for Weber, an ethos of rational activity that emphasized order, discipline and hierarchical organization.

See Benham in Reader, pp 206–12

There have always existed motivations to wealth and indeed to greed but these, Weber argues, are clearly different from the orientation to economic activity that he calls capitalism which '*may* even be identical with the restraint, or at least a rational tempering, of this irrational impulse (of greed). . . . Capitalism is identical with the pursuit of profit, and forever *renewed* profit, by means of continuous, rational, capitalistic enterprise' (Weber 1962 p 493). The spirit of capitalism could only develop and bring people to act in certain ways, if it were able to break through established and constraining modes of thought. These constraints included 'spiritual' obstacles (ethical ideas derived from magical or religious beliefs) like the strong

131

moral proscription on usury in the Middle Ages, or the attitude to work that Weber called 'traditionalism', an unwillingness to work harder than is necessary to earn sufficient income for living.

Optional reading: Reader, pp 491–8

It would help you at this stage to read quickly through Weber, 'The development of modern Western civilisation' in the Reader, pp 491–8, which is an edited version of Weber's own Introduction to his study. However, since this extract will form part of the set reading for Block 10, do not worry if shortage of time prevents you from reading it now.

2 Weber then suggested that evidence for the connection between economic orientations and a more fundamental set of beliefs might be found in statistics that correlate religious allegiance and occupation:

> A glance at the occupational statistics of any country of mixed religious composition brings to light with remarkable frequency a situation which has several times provoked discussion in the Catholic press and literature, and in Catholic congresses in Germany, namely, the fact that business leaders and owners of capital, as well as the higher grades of skilled labour, and even more the higher technically and commercially trained personnel of modern enterprises, are overwhelmingly Protestant. (Weber 1930 p 35)

Statistical correlation: see Unit 3, section 2.2

Weber did not, however, use statistical correlation as a proof but rather as a guide to further lines of enquiry. He considered that a more important method was to demonstrate the existence of a correspondence or congruence between Protestantism and capitalism at the level of ideas and attitudes – the *spirit* of capitalism and the *ethic* of the ascetic branches of Protestantism. Ascetic Protestants were those whose 'distinctive goal always remains the alert, methodical control of (their) own pattern of life and behaviour' (Weber 1965 p 168).

He described the congruence between the two systems of value attitudes as an 'elective affinity' and believed he had established the existence of a causal relationship between them because he claimed to have shown that the Protestant ethic had preceded the development of the spirit of capitalism. Weber did not claim that the Protestant ethic was the *sole* cause of capitalism, but he did believe it had been *a* causal factor. Technological innovation, changes in financial, commercial and legal institutions, and political centralization were all clearly involved, but institutional and material factors were insufficient alone. A subjective factor was also required in order to provide an adequate causal explanation.

3 The essence of Weber's argument about the part played by ideas in the historical process was that they generated and confirmed particular psychic traits and thereby produced a particular type of personality. Once selected, socialized and sustained by organizations, such as ascetic Protestant sects, this personality type acted out certain patterns of behaviour. Although these patterns originated in religious beliefs, they led to an unintended outcome – the growth of a characteristic outlook on work and wealth from which in turn the institutions of capitalism developed.

Sect organization: see section 5

Weber specified the 'elective affinity' between the two sets of beliefs by tracing the way in which the ascetic Protestant ethic evolved from the Calvinist doctrine of predestination. According to this doctrine, men's eternal salvation or damnation is predetermined by God and nothing can alter God's will which is ultimately unknowable. Man stands alone before his maker. In contrast to the Catholic Church, Calvinism had no priesthood to mediate between God and men and no sacramental conferral of grace by which salvation could be assured (though most sects did and do have ministers – or 'preaching elders' – and sacraments in which grace is invoked, but not conferred). Calvinism thus created in the adherent a severe state of anxiety, an insistent concern with knowing whether he were saved. But how was he to know this? What signs of God's favour and of membership of the elect were available?

The only sure sign of election, the ascetic Protestant would argue, was the possession of true faith. But how could this be recognized? True faith was displayed in a

It is hard to believe that such "success" was the epitome of Calvinism — that the new entrepreneurs were working furiously in a state of anxiety about avoiding Hell-fire.

way of life that gave the highest glory to God, a life in which the Commandments were rigorously observed and in which worldly achievement, particularly in one's vocation, corresponded to the will of God and manifested his glory. Success in one's calling, therefore, signified true faith and consequently gave a certainty, as far as this was possible, of membership of the elect and salvation. But success had to be striven for by continuous and systematic self-control, hard work, thrift and austerity, the hallmarks of the ascetic, individualistic way of life in which every activity, including the conduct of business, was guided by reason, rather than by tradition or sentiment.

Now business success normally results in an increase in wealth and in the enjoyments that wealth can bring. But the ascetic Protestant regarded himself rather as a steward of worldly goods than as an owner with the right to use them for his own pleasure. Thus the ascetic attitude to vocational success brought about a single-minded commitment to work, to high productivity, but a rejection of the affluent life-style that success would have made possible. But if success in business enterprise were to continue to manifest and increase God's glory, then the fruits of success had to be used in the most effective way – the rational, systematic reinvestment of profits.

Even when the religious motivation towards the acquisition and reinvestment of wealth eventually declined, when Calvinism had been absorbed and diluted in the

---

W O R K S

of the late

Doctor Benjamin Franklin

Consisting of

HIS LIFE WRITTEN BY HIMSELF,

together with

Efsays, Humorous, Moral & Literary,

Chiefly in the Manner of

THE SPECTATOR.

ADVICE TO A YOUNG TRADESMAN.

WRITTEN ANNO 1748.

REMEMBER that *time* is money. He that can earn ten fhillings a day by his labour, and goes abroad, or fits idle one half of that day, though he fpends but fixpence during his diverfion or idlenefs, ought not to reckon *that* the only expence; he has really fpent, or rather thrown away, five fhillings befides.

Remember that money is of a prolific generating nature. Money can beget money, and its offspring can beget more, and fo on. Five fhillings turned is fix; turned again, it is feven and three-pence; and fo on till it becomes an hundred pounds. The more there

is of it, the more it produces every turning, fo that the profits rife quicker and quicker.

Beware of thinking all your own that you poffefs, and of living accordingly. It is a miftake that many people who have credit fall into. To prevent this, keep an exact account, for fome time, both of your expences and your income. If you take the pains at firft to mention particulars, it will have this good effect; you will difcover how wonderfully fmall trifling expences mount up to large fums, and will difcern what might have been, and may for the future be faved, without occafioning any great inconvenience.

In fhort, the way to wealth, if you defire it, is as plain as the way to market. It depends chiefly on two words, *induftry* and *frugality*; that is, wafte neither *time* nor *money*, but make the beft ufe of both. Without induftry and frugality nothing will do, and with them every thing. He that gets all he can honeftly, and faves all he gets (neceffary expences excepted), will certainly become *rich*—if that Being who governs the world, to whom all fhould look for a bleffing on their honeft endeavours, doth not, in his wife providence, otherwife determine.

An OLD TRADESMAN.

Figure 1 By 1748, thrift and careful money management represent important social values in themselves, subject to no more than a general religious sanction

133

process of 'secularization' there still remained an ethical element of ascetic devotion to impersonal tasks for their own sake – self-discipline, hard work, dedication to one's calling, and mastery of one's world. The examples of the pure spirit of capitalism that Weber drew from the writings of Benjamin Franklin, one of the most prominent eighteenth century Americans, gave evidence of this.

4 In addition to demonstrating the relationship between Protestantism and capitalism by showing how the ethic of the first was congruent with that of the second, Weber tried to support his argument in a later series of comparative studies. In these, instead of asking directly what specific factors accounted for the appearance of capitalism in modern Western societies, he asked why anything like it had failed to appear in any of the other great civilizations of the world. His general conclusion was that although material conditions were quite favourable for capitalistic development in China, India and Judea at certain periods, the 'economic ethic' of the dominant religion in each culture was unfavourable for such a change. Confucianism in China involved adjustment to the world rather than the Puritan mastery of it. Classic Hinduism in India tended to maintain and reinforce traditionalism through the doctrine of *karma*, a belief in rebirth into a higher caste if one's present caste duties were faithfully performed.

Weber could, therefore, draw the conclusion that particular economic conditions do not inevitably lead to the rise of capitalism. Another condition – one that relates to values and beliefs – is necessary. This in turn generates a particular motivation, a willingness to break the bonds of tradition, and a set of attitudes favourable to change and congruent with it.

[handwritten margin note: broken by the religionists to effect society, and of which others took advantage — themselves not necessarily religious!!]

SAQ 2

Which of the following, according to Weber, characterize the spirit of capitalism:

A   unlimited greed for material goods
B   the pursuit of profit
C   rationality
D   moral decline
E   capital investment?

SAQ 3

What, briefly, is the substance of Weber's Protestant ethic thesis?

SAQ 4

What corroborating evidence, that you have met previously in D101, would you use to support Weber's interpretation of the impact of Protestant beliefs on other spheres of life (besides economic behaviour)?

Weber's account of the effect of the Protestant ethic on economic developments has proved to be very fruitful for later sociological theory and research. His study provided an exemplary analysis of the way in which a change in the value-system of a society, or group, could facilitate a process of structural differentiation (increasing specialization and autonomy of institutions). As Weber set out to show, a particular form of Protestantism removed close normative control from man's economic activities and yet at the same time provided values and motivations which were conducive to the success of those economic activities. Among modern sociologists who study the problems of modernization in developing countries, there seems some agreement with Weber that there is a point in the process at which it is crucial that certain values which sanction innovation come to the fore. (See also end of section 2.3.2.)

134

We have encouraged you to be critical about what you read in the correspondence texts and set reading and it would be worthwhile jotting down in the margin any criticisms that have so far occurred to you. Remember that criticism is not a negative activity concerned simply and solely with discovering weaknesses and faults (though this kind of criticism is of course important in the self-correcting nature of scientific knowledge); a critical approach also acknowledges and learns from fresh, stimulating ideas that reading and thinking generate. Give further thought to any marginal comments you have made and raise them if necessary with your tutor/counsellor. We are concluding this section of the correspondence text by considering briefly some criticisms of Weber's thesis and some later reinterpretations.

2.3.1 *The causal link between Protestantism and capitalism*

The first main type of criticism of Weber's thesis has questioned the historical grounds of the alleged direct causal connection between the Protestant ethic and the development of capitalism. It has been pointed out that the first Calvinist communities were conservative and restrictive towards economic activities because of their predilection for the regulation of all aspects of life, and these communities were also less developed economically than some areas of early capitalism in pre-Reformation Catholic Europe (see Fischoff 1971 pp 418–30).

A similar kind of criticism has denied that there was any direct causal link and that any tendency for Protestants to be more involved in various aspects of economic, scientific or modern political activities was due to structural situations – such as the minority position of Protestants in some countries. In probably the most well-known study, after Weber's, Tawney (1926) argued that the Calvinist attitude to work and wealth was brought about not by theological influences and their psychological consequences, but by economic and political pressures arising from the objective social position of the Calvinists. Weber himself had argued, however, that other minorities, such as Catholics in Germany, had shown no evidence of similar innovatory behaviour: 'Thus the principal explanation of the difference must be sought in the permanent, intrinsic character of their religious beliefs, and not only in their temporary external historico-political situations' (Weber 1930 p 40).

A different form of criticism challenges Weber's thesis on psychological grounds, in particular his interpretation of the specific mechanism through which Calvinist belief provided motivation for economic activities, i.e. that the Calvinist doctrine of predestination gave rise to great anxiety among believers and so urged them to undertake in a compulsive way, this-worldly activities to prove their status among the elect. (See Eisenstadt 1969 pp 297–317 for an account of these and other criticisms.)

2.3.2 *Some broader implications of Weber's thesis*

In recent times, reappraisals of Weber's thesis have revealed its potentially wide scope for comparative analysis, i.e. comparing institutional forms in different societies and at different times. The effect of this re-examination has been to shift the course of the argument from the question of the allegedly direct causal relation between Protestantism and capitalism to that of the *transformative* capacities of Protestantism (or similar ideologies). By 'transformative capacity' is meant their *capacity to legitimize, in religious, or secular ideological terms, the development of new social institutions and individual motivations* (Eisenstadt 1969 p 306).

Weber viewed new religions as possible agents of cultural breakthrough. In *The Protestant ethic and the spirit of capitalism*, he was mainly concerned with analysing the religious belief-system of Calvinism in order to reveal the mechanism which gave it the capacity first to transform central social institutions and secondly to transform or develop roles and the motivation to perform roles, especially the role of entrepreneur. In later studies Weber examined different social strata in order to determine

[handwritten margin note:] Believers who regard work as duty — other matters such as sport / recreation they might regard as worldly and thus eschew. cf Plymouth Brethren

their propensities to support new religious movements. He suggested that it was the relatively 'alienated' groups which were the most susceptible to the appeal of prophetic movements and which would break through the established (institutionalized) order. In particular it was members of relatively deprived groups outside the main prestige structure of their society who were most likely to support such movements. Thus he claimed that Puritans in England tended to be rank and file yeoman farmers, craftsmen and small merchants, who were not centrally situated in the main prestige structure, and yet were not economically oppressed.

Relative deprivation: see section 4

A radical breakthrough was likely to occur when relatively deprived groups sought to reconstitute the established system of beliefs and norms in order to remove the discrepancy between the expectations institutionalized by that order and their actual experience. The search for grounds of meaning which could remove the discrepancy between institutionalized expectations and actual experiences led to more generalized and fundamental rationalizations. In the case of Calvinism, this rationalization took the form of emphasizing the transcendence of God and the ultimate sovereignty of God's will.

This type of analysis has been applied to studies of the development of societies outside Europe and America (Bendix 1966; Bellah 1957 1971). The common argument that runs through these acknowledges the significance of economic and political institutions in the process of development, but emphasizes the important part played by religious values (or their equivalent) in stimulating economic growth, whether the values are those of Calvinist entrepreneurs in Europe, of the Samurai class in nineteenth century Japan, or of Communist administrators in Russia and China.

Furthermore, it has been argued that Weber's main theoretical contribution lay not in the assertion of a causal connection between Protestantism and capitalism, but in proposing the mediating agencies (the intervening variables) to explain this causal connection. As we have seen, this connection appears to be cultural or psychological in character. But a case can also be made for seeing the connection in structural/organizational terms. In other words, Weber's thesis was not only about the connection between religious values and economic development, but also about the crucial part played by the social organization of the *sect* in linking Protestant theology and the rise of the capitalist spirit (and behaviour).

In order for the capitalist spirit to develop, it had to break through the traditionalist world with its traditional ethic institutionalized in social structure, and buttressed by sanctions. For any new ethic to take hold 'as a way of life common to groups of men' it had to be institutionalized in a social structure which taught the new ethic to members, selected them on the basis of whether they lived up to it, and required them continuously to prove they possessed it (Berger 1971 p 492). In section 5, we shall take up again the question of the ways in which religious beliefs are socially organized.

SAQ 5

How would you define Weber's primary interest in religious beliefs?

SAQ 6

What is meant by the term 'transformative capacity'?

SAQ 7

In what sense did Weber show that religious beliefs can act as an independent variable in processes of social change?

SAQ 8

How does *The Protestant ethic and the spirit of capitalism* illustrate Weber's approach to social research?

The second study we have chosen to illustrate the overall theme of this unit parallels Weber's analysis in a number of ways. Halévy's thesis on Methodism and the English working class is used here to examine the part played by beliefs in facilitating an adjustment to social change by the labour force.

Elie Halévy (1870–1937) was a French historian among whose published works was a history of England in the nineteenth century. What particularly interested him was why England, in the earlier part of the century, was a relatively harmonious society. According to a Marxian interpretation of history, Halévy argued, England as the first society to turn to a capitalistic mode of production should have been the first to experience revolution as a result of the 'internal contradictions' of capitalism and yet, in comparison with other European societies, England was the most free from revolution. Halévy claimed that the answer to this apparent paradox lay in the influence of religion, that the absence of revolution was an unanticipated consequence of the Methodist revival. Just as Weber had shown the effects of religious beliefs on economic activity, so Halévy drew attention to their political consequences.

The Methodist revival, begun in the eighteenth century by John and Charles Wesley, represented an attempt from within the Church of England to evangelize those who had been lost to the Church during the accelerating urbanization of past decades. In spite of the intention of its founders, Methodism was unable to stay within the Church of England and became one of the non-conformist religious groups that had evolved from earlier forms of 'dissent'.

Halévy contrasted this development with the situation in a country like France where, in the eighteenth century, religion had been identified with the state so that radicals who wanted to overthrow the state were inevitably led to attack religion. In England, on the other hand, Methodism was rejected by the Church of England and became associated with the non-conformist tradition. Non-conformity, by transmitting a particular moral code, acted as a form of social control and influenced its more radical converts to think in terms of reform rather than revolution.

We must now turn from the contemplation of the benefits with which we are favoured, to the consideration of a State of Society which has existed, and we fear still exists, in some of the Northern Counties. We look at the principles which have given birth to this state of things, with the utmost horror; principles which are alike destructive to the happiness of the Poor, and of the Rich. And although we are well assured that our Societies are uncontaminated with that spirit of insubordination, violence, and cruelty, which has caused so much distress and misery, yet we cannot but dread the operation of its insidious and infectious nature, and the speciousness with which it aims to seduce the credulous and simple. We, therefore, as faithful Ministers, cannot refrain from sounding a solemn alarm, lest any of our dear people should be drawn away by the dissimulation of evil-disposed men. We proclaim loudly and earnestly, " Fear the Lord and the King: and meddle not with them that are given to change. Avoid them. Come not near them. Say of them, O my Soul, come not thou into their Secret : unto their assembly, mine honour, be not thou united." Destruction and Misery are in their Ways : and the Way of Peace have they not known. O Brethren, what would be our grief and distress, if, after all our labours, *publickly and from House to House*, and after having in the face of the World vouched for your loyal, your peaceable and honest deportment, we should be deceived in any one of you. We can scarcely think this ; but forgive our godly jealousy, and justify our expectations, and ye shall be the Crown of our rejoicing when these times of delusion shall have passed away. We know well, and feel for, the situation of the poor, their want of employment, and the dearness of provisions; but murmuring and discontent will not alleviate their sufferings : they will rather aggravate them. Be ye therefore patient. Let the richer Brethren assist those who are poor, and let all hope and trust in Him, who hath said, I will never leave thee nor forsake thee; and in due time you shall reap if you faint not.

But Methodism was more than a form of social control. In containing revolution it also socialized its members into appropriate work disciplines and provided working class leadership among those who learned the skills of organization and persuasion in the training that Methodism provided, At the same time, Methodism taught self-discipline, proscribed violence, and emphasized orderly change. As a recent writer has suggested: 'Methodism . . . became the first working class movement, the

Figure 2 From 'Address of the Preachers assembled at Sixty-ninth Annual Conference', Leeds, 1812 (printed version p 2)

During the last year, as you are doubtless aware, considerable agitations of a political nature have occurred, in various parts of this country. Some evil-minded men, disciples of infidelity, have taken advantage of the distresses of the poor, to foment and increase those agitations, by the circulation of seditious and blasphemous publications, under ensnaring titles, and in cheap forms. The danger was seen; our people were admonished; and they heard the voice of pastoral affection and caution. In this time of trial, the Methodist Connexion has been steady to the principles of the Bible, so zealously maintained and exemplified by our venerable Founder;—and has given new proof of attachment to the person and family of our beloved Monarch, of obedience to the laws, of gratitude for unexampled civil and religious privileges, and of zeal for the support of our unrivalled constitution. We rejoice, Brethren, to know, that these are also your sentiments, and that you are resolved with us to " fear the Lord and the King," and to " meddle not with them that are given to change."

Instructed by the Holy Scriptures, which, as an undoubted Revelation from GOD, we receive as the only rule of our faith and practice, to " Honour the King " as well as to " Fear GOD," we abhor and detest all principles of disloyalty; and, as far as our influence may extend among those of YOUR MAJESTY's subjects who are the objects of our Pastoral Instruction, we shall continue, by our constant teaching, advice, and example, to discountenance sedition and disorder in all their forms, and strongly to enforce subjection to the Laws, and to all Civil Authorities constituted by the State: And no longer than we thus prove ourselves worthy, shall we expect the protecting shade of the Laws to be extended over us. Hitherto, however, we have had the unspeakable satisfaction to witness a strict adherence to these duties among our Societies, notwithstanding the unexampled pressure of distress in the nation, and in the manufacturing districts in particular, in which they have largely shared, but which they have endured with exemplary patience and submission.

Note to Figures 2, 3 and 4: The Halévy thesis exemplified in early nineteenth century sources. These extracts from the official minutes of addresses given at Methodist annual conferences emphasize the duty of members to avoid radicalism and sedition, to honour the king and to obey the laws.

first mass movement, to be structured according to rational principles, and consequently the first stable mass movement to persist over time' (Wilson 1966 p 27).

In essence, then, the Halévy thesis suggests that Methodism inculcated appropriate work disciplines in the new industrial working class and that its individualistic spiritual discipline channelled off any collectivistic revolutionary potential. In Weberian terms, a positive *affinity* existed between elements of a religious belief-system and the requirements of a particular form of politico-economic development – industrial capitalism.

Like Weber's study, the Halévy thesis has generated a wide critical response and some of the issues that have been raised in the debate are discussed in Michael Hill, 'The Halévy thesis', reprinted in the Reader. The article contains a good deal of historical detail. You do *not* need to memorize this. Read through fairly quickly and try to link what you read with any notes you made from last week's television and radio programmes. Look out for the main points of the debate and then try to answer the Self-assessment Questions below.

Now read Hill in Reader, pp 405–23

SAQ 9

What, according to Hill, are the main propositions of the Halévy thesis? In what ways has the thesis been criticized or elaborated? Try to answer as briefly as possible.

SAQ 10

What are the major similarities between the Weber thesis and the Halévy thesis?

Check out this

They are taught to be *industrious.* **An active and la-borious life is conducive to health, cheerfulness, and longevity. When man was in a state of primitive inno-cency, " The Lord God took the man, and put him into the garden of Eden, to dress it, and to keep it." After the fall, when man was driven out of Paradise, he and all his sons were doomed to labour as a punishment. But the punishment was designed, in reality, and in the issue, to be a blessing. It is the privilege and the happiness of man to be employed, though to weariness and fatigue. But there is in fallen man such an unwillingness to labour, such an inclination to sloth and inactivity, that we have reason to be thankful, that, if the bulk of mankind will not work, neither shall they eat. Hence the business of the world, its manufactures, its trade, its commerce, the arts and sciences are carried on with spirit and effect, the major part of the population of the earth is compara-tively healthy and happy, and in our own country, we are greatly indebted to laborious poverty for our national in-dependence, grandeur and glory.**

Figure 5   From John Stephens's sermon, The Mutual Relations Claims, and Duties of the Rich and the Poor *(Manchester 1819)*

Note to Figure 5 : John Stephens, in a sermon delivered in Manchester in 1819 and subsequently printed, explains the lessons and advantages that the poor can derive from their state of poverty. His message reinforces the idea of work-discipline emphasized in contemporary Methodist speeches and writings.

4   RELIGION AND COLONIALISM: CARGO CULTS

From thinking about seventeenth century Protestants and eighteenth and nineteenth century Methodists, we now move to a twentieth century example of relationship between religious beliefs and social action in particular social strata, this time out-side Europe in the area known as Melanesia, a long chain of large and small islands to the north and east of Australia. You can check their location on the map accom-panying Worsley's article on page 140. The example we have chosen is that of *cargo cults* and in studying this phenomenon we hope that you will further develop the important skill of learning from and integrating several sources – the correspondence text, set reading, and radio and television. The order in which you use the different sources will depend on your own study-habits. You may, for example, begin with Talmon or leave this until the end of the section, though we have assumed the latter.

The term *cult* is used by sociologists to refer to a form of religious expression, usually spontaneous and relatively transient, in the sense that the cult lacks the organizational structure of religious movements like Puritanism or Methodism and therefore their sense of 'permanence'. Cargo cults derive their particular name from the belief, which they all share, in the imminent coming of a new age (a millenium, to use the Christian term) when the ancestors will send cargoes of material goods. These goods will include the desirable manufactured commodities possessed in such apparent profusion by the white residents and wartime visitors.

4.1   'PROGRESS AND CULTS IN MELANESIA'

Peter Worsley's (1962) article supplements his television commentary on David Attenborough's film and his radio discussion. In this article, Worsley provides a descriptive account of cargo cults, suggests how Melanesians draw on their traditional categories of thought (interspersed with some accretions from Christian missionary teaching) and then attempts a more general but brief explanation of cargo cults.

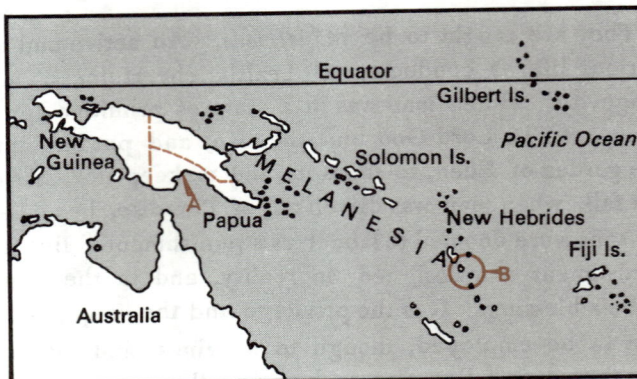

A. Location of the Vailala Madness, 1919-31
B. Location of John Frum Movement, 1938-58

Figure 6   Map of Melanesia

Readers of the *New Yorker* will remember a recent vivid account of Japanese stragglers left stranded on remote islands of the South Pacific after World War II. One of these unfortunate men, finally forced out of hiding in the bush by desperation, screwed up his resolution and entered a New Guinea village. He was surprised to find that, far from being greeted with fear or suspicion, he was hailed as a messiah. Before long, he found himself the centre of an active religious cult, and began to enjoy the role. Clearly, to the villagers, this pale-skinned being from the unknown was a returned spirit of their dead ancestors.

We do not know what happened to this particular Japanese, but we do know that the cult which sprang up around him was by no means unique. In fact, dozens of similar religious movements have sprung up right across Melanesia, that island world to the north and east of Australia.

Indeed, the first records of such 'prophets' and strange new religious beliefs occur in the very earliest European records: as long ago as 1867. And as the Australians, Germans, Dutch and French step by step divided the region between them, one cult after another was reported from every part of Melanesia. To the average white man, the movements seemed so irrational that they could not be regarded as 'normal' in any sense. Hence one of the most famous movements was termed the 'Vailala Madness'. But were they madness? Let us look at the typical history and beliefs of a so-called 'Cargo Cult'.

(1) The basic pattern is remarkably consistent. Following a dream, a man announces that the rule of the white man is shortly coming to an end. The ancestral spirits of the dead are about to return from the Land of the Dead, by ship or aeroplane, bringing with them all the goods of the white man which the native islanders so urgently desire, but which they are too poor to buy. Why are they poor?

(2) In Melanesian thinking, white men have plenty of money and goods, and Melanesians very little, because the whites possess some special knowledge – some Secret – which gives them access to and control over wealth; not only money, but also tinned food, mirrors, machines, clothing, flash-lamps, etc., all of which somehow, mysteriously, appear – literally out of the blue – in ships and planes. All these goods, called 'cargo' in the local pidgin English language, are then handed over to the whites in return for pieces of paper (cheques, bills of lading, receipts, etc.).

(3) Now in traditional Melanesian thought, it is clearly recognized that without carrying out certain human activities, one cannot expect to obtain results. If you do not work hard in your garden, planting, tilling, weeding, etc., you cannot expect magical results. But, equally, unpredictable events do happen: crop diseases, hurricanes, wild animals, can all ruin the results of months of hard labour. To the Melanesian, such unwelcome visitations are not necessarily accepted as accidental. For them, the world is an integrated moral whole. Accidents do happen; but a man who behaves anti-socially can expect mystical, not merely man-made retribution. His crops may suffer, his children sicken. Human activity, magical precautions, spiritual harmony between man and man, between man and the rest of the world of which he is part – all these are essential to the ongoing of the world.

(4) But white men do not work. They must, therefore, be in control of abnormal powers. They only contribute the purely spiritual components in what is normally

140

an integrated whole. Clearly, they possess special and abnormal knowledge which enables them to avoid the necessity of actual labour. Far from seeing the whites as a group who owe their power to material and technological superiority, then, the opposite holds: their power is peculiarly a spiritual power. Whites erroneously believe that Melanesians are dominated by magico-religious notions, that they cannot think 'scientifically'; Melanesians believe whites to possess fantastic, superhuman power. One can actually see white men handling the magical devices – pieces of paper, pens, pencils, radio sets – which embody this power. So Melanesian cult-believers start making their own imitations: 'radio sets' made of wood, 'aerials' made of creepers. And they imitate European ways: flowers placed in bottles on tables become important symbols. In a tragically extreme case, canoes of cult enthusiasts, incensed by Japanese brutality, and armed only with wooden 'rifles' which they expected to turn into real weapons at the crucial moment, sailed out to attack Japanese vessels. The wooden rifles failed to turn into metal; and protective magic water failed to save the believers from being shot down in scores by machine guns.

This faith, then, is very real and compelling. It is a faith that inevitably brings them up against the white man, who clearly uses his power only for his own benefit, and keeps the islander poor. Since white men do no work, it obviously cannot be they who produce the goods they so meanly 'corner'. Melanesians work, but these goods are not produced in Melanesia (where there is virtually no factory industry at all). The goods come from some unknown land beyond the horizon. Obviously it cannot be the whites who make them there. The unknown land must be the Land of the Dead, where the ancestors of the Melanesians make the 'cargo'. If justice reigned, the living Melanesians would get the goods made by their ancestors, and consigned to their descendants in the islands. But here the white man's spiritual power, and his knavery, enter the picture. The goods made by dead Melanesians, and dispatched to living ones, are diverted by the whites, who use their secret powers to have the 'cargo' delivered to themselves. If the Melanesian could only learn this Secret of the Cargo, everything would come to him as the ancestors intended.

In these so-called Cargo cults, the attempt to acquire material things through the acquisition of secret spiritual powers is central to cult belief. But the experience of the white man's social order in recent decades has also decisively strengthened, and apparently confirmed, the basic beliefs of the cults.

Firstly, the missionaries have brought the white man's secret Book, the Bible, to the islanders. In it, the end of the world and the inversion of the existing order is announced. The mighty shall be humbled, the meek exalted: a millenial reign of God's justice will begin, in which there will be abundance for all. But the white men cunningly tear out of the Bible the key pages containing the Secret, and withhold them from their coloured subjects.

Since the white man came, life in the islands has been unpredictable. There have been long periods of comparative quiet punctuated by sudden bursts of chaotic and violent change. Governments, seemingly all powerful for a while, prove ephemeral: the Germans were expelled in 1914, to be replaced by the Australians. Then came the Japanese, only to be ejected in their turn by a wondrously wealthy, unknown people (some of whom were black) called Americans, who poured 'cargo' into the area and as mysteriously disappeared.

Economically, too, the white man brought wealth and forced labour, prosperity and depression, as world prices for gold, rubber, and copra swung wildly from year to year. It was a meaningless, arbitrary world in which anything could happen. Sons no longer paid traditional respect to their elders; men of authority were ignored by governments and upstarts installed in high positions; the older beliefs were attacked by missionaries and teachers. White officials appeared once or twice a year in your village, held medical inspections, tried a few cases according to their strange standards of justice (they denied that witchcraft existed, yet punished those who practised it), forced the villagers – sometimes at gun-point – to dig latrines (for which they appeared to have a special affection), and then disappeared for another year. Thousands of young men were taken to the plantations of the coast, and some never came back. The whole social order was shattered, twisted, turned on its head. If such things had happened, why should not the end of the white man's rule occur as suddenly as it had begun? Even the end of the world could happen too.

Hence the extraordinary emotionality of these movements. Whole districts are swept by outbursts of hysteria, in which people are afflicted by compulsive dancing, praying, head-shaking, possession; in which prophets 'speak with tongues', and deities appear in human form. For the Melanesian is attempting to grapple with change on a scale that few other societies have encountered. He is endeavouring not merely to make rational sense out of what seems to be a lunatic white world, but to find himself in the process. He knows that the past has gone, that he has to come to terms with a confusing new world. In the Cargo cults, then, he is concerned not just with his relationship to things, but with the creation of himself, in Kenelm Burridge's graphic phrase, as a 'new man'.

In his attempts to understand the white world, to orient himself within it, he uses tools of understanding which are derived from his traditional religious and philosophical concepts. Ideas taken from Christianity are also combined with indigenous religious belief. Given these assumptions, his thinking is by no means irrational. As we have seen, it is a highly logical attempt to make sense out of a world of which he has only very partial knowledge.

Underlying the whole is tremendous frustration and envy deriving from the colonial situation. The movements, accordingly, tended to become increasingly militant during the inter-war and wartime years; they were a serious embarrassment to Dutch, Australian, and Japanese administrations alike. Government officials found whole villages facing starvation because the people had abandoned their gardens, killed off their livestock, and thrown their money into the sea. What need would there be for these few paltry possessions in the new, rich life shortly to begin?

The new, rich life never does come, but the belief in the coming of the cargo dies very slowly, because the basic situation which gives rise to these frustrations and aspirations remains only slightly changed. 'UN Finds New Guinea Cult a Bar to Progress', reported the *New York Times* on July 6 this year, almost 100 years after the first 'prophet' was reported in an obscure Dutch mission journal.

Recently, Cargo cult adherents have developed a new notion: that the Americans are coming back, with great supplies of goods on the World War II scale. In what appears to us fantastic idiom, the adherents of the cults are perhaps only expressing in extreme form the widespread belief that the US is an inexhaustible reservoir and fount of all desirable things. These things can easily be dispensed to the rest of the world, and, moreover, should be, for the whites, after years of dominance, owe the backward countries a moral debt.

At the same time, a New Guinea Parliament is being prepared. Three thousand natives are to be trained for taking-over at independence. Nothing could more graphically underline the immensity of the problem faced by these particularly backward emergent countries, which have had to compress into a few decades, even a few years, developments which took hundreds of years in other lands.

Increasingly, as development proceeds, the peoples of Melanesia are likely to find secular and orthodox political forms of expression of their aspirations. All over the world, millenarian movements have flourished in peasant and 'stateless' societies where they provide a unifying belief and organized formal institutional arrangements amongst people who lacked these, and who have developed new common interests.

In more complex societies, too, millenarian cults have provided vehicles of expression for those who find themselves in opposition to established orthodoxy; Buddhists in China; Muslim reformers in the Arab world; Jews in the ancient world, and – in our own history – as recently as the Ranters of the English Civil War. And minor movements prophesying the end of the world, still persist.

But secularization has thrust the millenarian sects into the backwaters of the modern world. Though today, perhaps, we no longer smile in *quite* the same way at people carrying placards announcing the imminent end of the world, our response to even the most appalling of world problems is eminently a secular one.

In the backward part of the globe, too, the trend everywhere has been away from millenarism to nationalist political movements. There is no reason to doubt that this will happen increasingly in Melanesia also, but the modernization of that region will take a long time, and full-blown Cargo cults, or strands of Cargo thinking, are likely to be with us, therefore, for a good time to come. (Worsley 1962 pp 16–17)

SAQ 11

What is a cargo cult?

SAQ 12

Who was John Frum?

SAQ 13

Are the beliefs of cargo cults irrational?

Figure 7   Stills from Attenborough film

4.2   CARGO CULTS, MILLENARISM AND SOCIAL SCIENCE

The process of abstracting particular features from distinctive phenomena like cargo cults and comparing these features with those of similar social phenomena, in this case millenarian movements, represents a characteristic mode of operation by social scientists. At the end of his article, Worsley attempts to make sense of the cults by fitting them with the more general category of belief and action, *millenarism* though you should note that he also claims (in radio programme 24) that to understand why Melanesian cults take their particular form, it is necessary to 'understand the movements in terms of what they mean to the people engaged in them'. Can one generalize, then, about situational factors that predispose certain groups to develop millenarian beliefs, whatever shape the action expressing these beliefs takes?

By considering the common features of a wide range of millenarian movements, Talmon does provide us with a taxonomy of predisposing factors in the first part of the Reader extract. Read through the introduction and the first section, 'Conditions of development', and then answer the following Self-assessment Questions:

Now read Talmon in Reader, pp 424–34, line 14

SAQ 14

Which of the following are contributory factors to the emergence of millenarian movements:

✓ A   multiple deprivation

✓ C   relative deprivation

✓ E   rapid social change

✓ B   sudden crises

✓ D   cultural disintegration

✓ F   social isolation?

SAQ 15

Which of the following statements are false:

A   Millenarian movements are always recruited from the lowest social strata.

B   The leaders of millenarian movements are often of middle-class origin.

C   Most millenarian movements have arisen within the Judaeo-Christian tradition?

SAQ 16

Why are cargo cults classified as millenarian movements?

At the beginning of the Talmon extract 'deprivation' is discussed, a concept particularly relevant to our understanding of cargo cults as a type of millenarian movement. Multiple deprivation, i.e. disadvantage in terms of 'poverty, low status and lack of power' represents an important baseline from which millenarian movements may grow, but of more significance is what Talmon (Reader p 425) calls 'not so much . . . the lack of means to supply traditional wants, but rather . . . the emergence of a set of new expectations'. In other words, when Melanesians could compare their own

143

Reference group: see
Unit 19, section 1.3

social situation with that of their fellow-islanders only, their aspirations remained relatively limited. But with the appearance of powerful colonizers and others with desirable 'cargo', the *reference groups* that Melanesians used for purposes of comparison shifted: new aspirations were generated although no institutional means of achieving these were apparent. Melanesians thus experienced *relative deprivation*, an awareness of discrepancy between a conception of the good life as represented by white cargo-users and a conception of life as it really is. One might hypothesize that some Open University students were motivated to apply for admission by their awareness of relative deprivation. When higher education was experienced by few people, then one's reference groups were unlikely to have been graduates. With the expansion of and greater demand for higher education, relative (educational) deprivation was likely to increase, but for many people the institutional means to realize their educational aspirations remained unavailable until the Open University admitted its first students. (We shall not try to develop a cargo cult–Open University analogy, but you may like to follow this line yourself.)

Relative deprivation tends to characterize periods of rapid social change when normal, institutionalized expectations are disrupted. Talmon adduces evidence to suggest that 'millenarism occurs mainly in periods of transition' of this kind. Cargo cults, in this sense, can be understood as *transitional ideologies*, sets of beliefs that 'explain' the present and help to bridge the gap between the old and new cultures in a period of transition, that link awakened expectations and the inadequate institutional means for satisfying those expectations. They provide at one and the same time a moral explanation and an anticipated remedy for inequality.

When we discussed the Weber and Halévy theses, the distinction was drawn between the intended consequences of beliefs and action—salvation—and their unintended consequences. In a similar way, Worsley suggests that, as well as expressing a particular world-view, cargo cults act as a means of creating bonds of solidarity and of shared interests among those previously lacking common institutional relationships. By locating cargo cults in the general category of millenarian movements in both peasant and more complex societies, Worsley also suggests that cargo cults may be seen as movements expressing an incipient political awareness.

Now read the remainder of
Talmon in Reader,
pp 434–41

Worsley clearly stands on the 'positive functions' side of the argument that Talmon discusses in the section entitled 'functional analysis'. Read the remainder of the extract and answer the following questions.

SAQ 17

What do you understand by negative and positive interpretations of millenarism?

SAQ 18

What are the positive functions of millenarian cults, according to Talmon?

Finally in this section, a suggested activity to help you review what you have so far read in the unit.

At the end of section 1, we asked you to bear in mind three issues concerning the effect of beliefs in making sense of the social order, in justifying or legitimating that order, and in creating religious motivations that have an impact on politico-economic development.
How would you illustrate each of these in what you have read on the Protestant ethic, Methodism and cargo cults?

You may be in a situation where you have to attempt this alone, but it would be much more effectively undertaken in a group where you can exchange and argue about ideas.

5 THE SOCIAL ORGANIZATION OF RELIGIOUS BELIEFS

In Unit 23, the difference between a 'history of ideas' approach to scientific know-ledge and that of the social scientist was discussed. The latter's interest lies less in the validity of, or changes in, beliefs about the natural world than in the interplay of these beliefs with the societal context in which they appear, change, and become institutionalized in a community of scientific practitioners. Similarly, in our consideration of religious beliefs in this unit, we are not primarily interested in beliefs in themselves, in the sense of their truth-value, but in their social location and consequences, and therefore in the social arrangements by which beliefs are shared and translated into action.

If beliefs are to be given social expression and to attract converts, some means has to be created to transmit and sustain these ideas, to develop loyalty and commitment, to safeguard the purity of beliefs and to control members' behaviour. In other words, shared beliefs must operate on an organized basis, and at several points in the correspondence text you have so far read, the significance of the social organization of religious beliefs has been highlighted. For example, it was argued at the end of section 2 that Weber's contribution to our areas of interest lay particularly in his explaining the mediating factors between Protestantism and capitalism, cultural factors in the realm of ideas and motivations, but equally structural factors in the social organization of the Protestant sect. Forming organizational links between the Church of England and traditional 'dissent' was, according to the Halévy thesis, an important function of Methodism. Again, cargo cults perform a mediating function in making available organizational arrangements which can evolve into secular and political structures. Religious beliefs emerge, are consolidated, expressed and maintained in social groups—Puritanism, Methodism, the Church of England and so on—each with distinctive organizational forms. The particular form of organization created in order to institutionalize a belief-system and to translate it into a pattern of behaviour is, therefore, a crucial intervening variable between beliefs and actions.

In order to facilitate analysis and to generate theory, social scientists may try to simplify the complexity of empirical reality by creating typologies from a range of similar phenomena. In the case of religious organizations, one relatively simple typology distinguishes between church, sect, denomination and cult as ideal types, and further sub-classifications have been made of these broad types though it is not necessary to go into these sub-types in this unit.

The *church* is the most inclusive of these types. Like the Roman Catholic Church, it makes claim to social inclusiveness by its mission to convert the whole world. It tends to come to terms with the secular world though claiming spiritual jurisdiction over it. The church precedes the individual who is usually born into it by infant baptism. Its characteristic internal organization is hierarchical. The *sect*, by contrast, opposes some aspect of the established order. The empirical range of types of sects is wide but they are usually composed of a small, exclusive, dispossessed group which is hostile or at least indifferent to the world, though some sects may attempt a fundamental reformation of the world. Membership of sects is voluntary, but total commitment is demanded. Internally, sects display little organization beyond the local group; and even within this structure role distinctions are not sharply drawn. *Denominations* tend to evolve from those sects which have admitted new members: for example, the children of original members, who have not necessarily shared the conversion experience of their parents. This-worldly achievement that may follow from sect members' self-imposed discipline can also bring about a shift from sect to denominational form. While denominations remain separated from the state, they come to terms and co-exist with it. Authority roles with some degree of democratic participation characterize the internal organization of denominations. The *cult* represents a form of spontaneous, religious expression. Cults are usually open, voluntary loosely organized and centre on a single belief. As you have seen in the Melanesian example, cults tend to flourish in conditions of rapid social change.

In spite of structural differences, the three main types – church, sect, denomination – have similar functions of socialization and control. In terms of their individual members, religious organizations transmit values, beliefs and appropriate behavioural norms: they confer a particular identity and sustain this identity in the social group of adherents, thereby inducing commitment; they provide a social base by which beliefs and action are legitimated and reinforced, and they act as a form of control through rules that sanction conformity.

5.1 RELIGIOUS ORGANIZATIONS IN SPARKBROOK

Now read Rex and Moore, pp 173–90

Perhaps before reading section 5 you had some general ideas about the functions of and differences between religious organizations in the light of what you had read so far in this unit and some of the concepts you have met in other parts of the course – socialization and community, for example. Chapter VII of Rex and Moore (1967) (which was not part of Unit 20 set reading) illustrates some of these differences and some of the functions that religious organizations perform. Additionally, it brings our study of religious beliefs to (almost) the present day and locates them in British society. As you read the extract, note particularly the characteristics of the organizations discussed, and ideas that enable us to relate religious beliefs to particular social strata. Some Self-assessment Questions follow to help you to test your response and systematize your ideas.

SAQ 19

What, according to the authors, are the functions of the churches in Sparkbrook? (Note that *initially* the authors use the term 'churches' in the generic, everyday sense of the word rather than in the specific sense of 'church' as an organizational type.)

SAQ 20

What distinction did Niebuhr draw between types of religion, and how, in general terms, is his distinction manifested in Sparkbrook?

SAQ 21

Do you agree with the authors' proposition that 'English and West Indian religious groups (tend) to maintain not ethnically different cultures but class cultures that in general also set them apart from one another'?

6 A NOTE ON METHODOLOGY

The studies of religious beliefs and actions that we have examined raise many problems of interpretation and explanation for social scientists. In one sense, the distant and perhaps exotic nature of some of the belief systems we have studied throws them into sharper focus against known and familiar ways of thinking and makes their distinctive features more visible. On the other hand, the very 'strangeness' of such beliefs creates an acute problem of understanding, of getting inside the minds of people living in societies with cultural forms very different from our own. Why not, then, simply admit the unfamiliarity of certain sets of beliefs and turn our attention to observable actions and the interconnections between actions and their social consequences? Do not the physical sciences, by observing and formulating theories about the relationships between objective natural phenomena, provide us with a model of how *real* science should be conducted?

The latter question was discussed in Unit 19 when a distinction was drawn between the nature of the phenomena that natural and social scientists study. We also discovered in SAQ 1 what happens if we observe and interpret a custom like wife-purchase in terms of our own thought categories. We cannot in fact observe and understand *action* (in contrast to 'behaviour'), given the Weberian definition of action. It is not enough to observe the objective structure of behaviour: our understanding and explanation of Puritan wealth-accumulation, of building images of John Frum, or of working hard must draw on the subjective dimensions of these forms of social action. Weber (1947 p 88) expressed the methodological principle involved here when he claimed that sociology was a science 'which attempts the interpretive understanding of social action in order thereby to arrive at a causal explanation of its course and effects'. For Weber, then, the subjective dimensions of meaning and intention are the causes of social action even though social action can itself bring about unintended consequences. To show a causal connection between Protestantism and capitalism, as we have seen, Weber needed to demonstrate that certain ascetic Protestants saw the world in a particular way and acted towards it; an unintended consequence of their actions was the creation of an ethos in which capitalism could flourish. Similarly, Methodist beliefs about how one should live one's life caused certain individuals to act in ways that in the longer term resulted in their upward social mobility.

Natural and social sciences: see Unit 19, section 5; also Block 9

Let us look at the implications of a strategy following from the methodological claims made so far, that only by taking into account subjective and objective dimensions of social action can the social scientist be said to have provided an adequate causal explanation.

1   It is not possible for the social scientist, as an ordinary human being, to empty his mind of presuppositions – values, attitudes, beliefs that enable him to make sense of his own world. Yet he seeks to provide an interpretation of the beliefs, interests, motivations and action of people perhaps far removed in place and time, a process in which he is constantly in danger of inserting his own categories of thought and experience. This danger is well exemplified in the David Attenborough sequences that form part of this week's television programme. Attenborough was not, of course, commenting on cargo cults as a social scientist; nevertheless, his account illustrates the kind of problems that we all face in making sense of society, especially a society that is unfamiliar to us. Attenborough's ethnocentricity, for example, shows through clearly in his labelling cargo cults as a form of 'rather frightening religion' and the leader of the Tanna cult, Nambus, as 'either a rogue or a madman.'

2   The social scientist, then, has to try to discard, or at the least to be aware of, ethnocentric assumptions. He has to cultivate detachment, but at the same time to empathize with his subjects, i.e. to see life through their eyes, to understand their *typical* world-view. Understanding others' world views as an essential part of research is discussed by Peter Worsley in radio programme 24. Both Weber and Halévy faced the particular problem of reconstructing world-views long after the event. You may like to spend a few minutes thinking of the difficulties of empathizing with those whose world view was dominated by the anxiety generated by a belief in predestination or by a conviction that the delivery of cargo was imminent.

3   If the social scientist is to meet the problem of understanding his subjects' world views, he has somehow to come to terms with the language that structures their thought. Earlier parts of the course, Units 7 and 19, were at pains to point to the importance of the study of language in understanding social phenomena, and some of the material discussed in the present unit exemplifies both the significance of and the problems inherent in studying other people's language. Let us look at an illustration. In one way or another, the studies have been concerned with the economic implications of particular forms of social action in which the notion of 'work' has been of central importance. We hope that you can analyse 'the meaning of work' in industrial societies after your study of Units 1 and 16, but in a commonsense way

you may still feel that everyone knows what work *means*. But does the concept of work have a common trans-situational meaning?

Peter Worsley's comments in radio programme 24 when he describes Melanesian crop-growing, illustrate the problem of language and meaning. Seeds are planted, the fields weeded, and so on. In addition certain magical spells have to be performed. The phrase 'in addition' suggests two separate activities – work, followed by a religious ritual to ensure that the crop will grow. Yet the Melanesians use a single word, usually translated by Westerners as 'work' to describe both using digging sticks in the fields *and* ritual spell performance. Even this language difference poses fewer problems for the social scientist than the Melanesian linguistic conflation of technical matters like creating wealth and moral issues like its distribution.

Problems of translating kinship categories: see Turnbull in Reader, pp 10–11

4 Given the kinds of problem inherent in understanding the subjective dimensions of social action, the social scientist has still to relate belief-systems to their structural context. Beliefs do not operate in a social vacuum but act on and reflect the social relationships in which they are embedded. Robert Moore expresses this kind of methodological concern in radio programme 23. After interpreting the typical meaning of Methodism for its adherents as '[giving] people a sense of their own dignity . . . a sense of purpose in life . . . whatever [job] he was doing . . . he was called to do that job conscientiously . . .,' Moore goes on: '*One had to look at the community that was Methodism and at the beliefs that were Methodism.*' We have discussed in section 5 the immediate context of beliefs in terms of their social organization. Like Weber, the social scientist may be drawn to examine a wider context, like the traditional beliefs and structures that the Protestant ethic had to break through.

5 In these methodological processes, the social scientist utilizes terms that conceptualize and suggest explanatory links between the components of his study and similar phenomena elsewhere, whether these terms are shared by a community of social scientists – millenarian cults, relative deprivation – or are conceptual innovations like Weber's 'elective affinity'. But, as we hope has been made clear, the connections between beliefs, social action and social structures are intrinsically difficult to conceptualize and evaluate. When these connections are made and a coherent theory emerges, the social scientist's work becomes 'public' knowledge available to the evaluation of his peers and the kind of critical responses that you have seen exemplified.

Now try to answer the following Self-assessment Questions in which you will need to think back to the Introduction as well as drawing on what you have just read.

SAQ 22

Why does the process of 'modernization' or 'industrialization' pose problems of understanding for social scientists in advanced societies?

SAQ 23

What are some of the problems encountered in trying to investigate and explain the links between beliefs and social action?

---

7 CONCLUSIONS

In this unit, we have explored a number of aspects of the relationship between beliefs and social action by selecting certain kinds of belief, which relate to the supra-natural, and presenting some interpretations of their consequences both for adherents and for the wider society in which these religious cultures have been located. Religious beliefs do not, of course, exhaust the whole range of beliefs. We are socialized into and operate with a multiplicity of beliefs, using different ones in order to define the different situations we meet. We interpret the world selectively in the light of our beliefs whether these constitute the commonsense knowledge of our everyday lives (discussed in Unit 19) or the more structured and complex sets of beliefs that we employ to make sense of existence. It is the latter, the systematically organized belief-systems of religion, that have concerned us in this unit.

The phenomena that we have considered span several centuries and wide cultural variations. If you spent some time on the activity (p 144) that we suggested you undertake, then one kind of linkage between these phenomena should have become apparent – that religious beliefs make sense of and legitimate social order, and create motivations that affect other areas of social life; you can extend this analysis to religious organizations in Sparkbrook and indeed to the social world around you. Another type of linkage derives from the levels of analysis that the studies share: direct or indirect observation of actual people, of their beliefs and actions, interpretations of the relationships between beliefs and actions and their consequences, and finally theoretical and methodological problems involved in evaluating such interpretations.

A third kind of linkage returns us to the unit title which implicitly suggests some kind of connection between the (religious) beliefs people hold and their situation in structures of social inequality. Section 1 indicated briefly various ways in which relationships of this kind are manifested, and in the case studies the connection was perhaps given its clearest and most explicit expression in the Rex and Moore extract. However, all the studies have been concerned in one way or another with the relationship. Weber's thesis postulated that ascetic Protestants developed a way of life that evolved into the bourgeois entrepreneurship of nineteenth century capitalism. Halévy suggested how Methodism motivated its working-class membership into a work-discipline that fitted the demands of capitalist production and into a worldview that left the political system underpinning the economy relatively stable. Cargo cults were interpreted as a millennial response to this-worldly deprivation among lower strata, and finally, the Sparkbrook study showed us the kind of relationships that can exist between social class situation and religious beliefs and affiliations in present-day Britain.

It would be useful for you to review the unit objectives before completing this week's work and to estimate how far these have been realized. Among the objectives, one in particular is worth considering a little more – the skill of learning to detach oneself from one's own cultural context in order better to understand the beliefs and values of others and how these are expressed in social action. Whether we are sympathetic or not towards religious beliefs in general or whether we may want to argue about the truth-content of particular religious belief-systems remain irrelevant to understanding the processes by which beliefs are translated into action and bring about further social consequences. Rex and Moore (1967 p 177) emphasize this principle:

> When we speak of the sociological functions of religious organizations we are not attempting to assess the truth of any one or all of the faiths, nor do we question the fact that the primary meaning of religious observances and ritual is essentially religious for adherents.

The implication of what Rex and Moore state in the second part of the quotation formed an important principle in Weber's methodology – that if as social scientists we study what others hold to be normatively valid, then we treat such beliefs as existing rather than as valid. In other words, we have to learn the skill of distinguishing between religious, political and other beliefs as matters on which we may have our own views and commitments and about which we may express value-judgements from the same beliefs as constitutive of social science explanation.

Finally, having carefully read through the unit and thought about the case-studies, you may still be tempted to ask what has the study of religious beliefs to do with making sense of society and of modern life. We hope that this question has been answered in the material you have read, seen, or listened to and that you can perceive that understanding beliefs as social phenomena goes beyond an exclusively academic concern. In addition to your own relationship to religious beliefs touched on just now, you have no doubt heard it argued that some of the significant social problems that beset us are associated with what people do or do not believe about religion. For example, while one argument runs that the population 'problem' has been aggravated by an 'irrational' attachment to religious beliefs, another suggests that it is the very loss of these beliefs that lies behind many of the crises of our time. If you considered the notion of 'secular' religion when you attempted to define religion for yourself (p 129), you perhaps debated whether Communism or certain forms of nationalism constituted religions of this kind. One does not need to spell out the implications of such a conclusion in terms of its relevance to our lives, except to point to a relationship briefly discussed in the Halévy thesis, between religious beliefs, social action and power, and it is to the study of the concept of 'power' that the course next turns.

REFERENCES

BELLAH, R. (1957) *Tokugawa religion – The values of pre-industrial Japan*, New York, Free Press.

BELLAH, R. (1971) 'Reflections on the Protestant ethic analogy in Asia' in Thompson, K. and Tunstall, J. (eds.) *Sociological perspectives*, Harmondsworth, Penguin, pp 431–8.

BENDIX, R. (1966) 'A case study in cultural and educational mobility: Japan and the Protestant ethic' in Smelser, N. J. and Lipset, S. M. (eds.) *Social structure and mobility in economic development*, London, Routledge and Kegan Paul, pp 262–79.

BENHAM, F. C. (1967) 'The social framework', in Paish, F. W. (ed.) *Economics: A general introduction*, London, Pitman, 8 ed., pp 42–56. Reprinted in Potter and Sarrre (1974) pp 202–17.

BERGER, P. and LUCKMANN, T. (1963) 'Sociology of religion and sociology of knowledge', *Sociology and Social Research*, vol. 47 (1963) pp 417–27.

BERGER, S. D. (1971) 'The sects and the breakthrough into the modern world: on the centrality of the sects in Weber's Protestant ethic thesis', *The Sociological Quarterly*, vol. 12, pp 486–99.

EISENSTADT, S. N. (1969) 'The Protestant ethic thesis' in Robertson, R. (ed.) *Sociology of religion*, Harmondsworth, Penguin, pp 297–317.

FISCHOFF, E. (1971) 'The Protestant ethic and the spirit of capitalism: The history of a controversy' in Thompson, K. and Tunstall, J. (eds.) *Sociological perspectives*, Harmondsworth, Penguin, pp 418–30.

HILL, M. (1973) 'The Halévy Thesis' in *A sociology of religion*, London, Heinemann Educational Books, pp 183–204. Reprinted in Potter and Sarre (1974) pp 405–23.

MERTON, R. (1967) *Social theory and social structure*, New York, Free Press.

MOORE, R. (1974) *Pitmen, preachers and politics*, Cambridge, Cambridge University Press.

POTTER, D. and SARRE, P. (eds.) (1974) *Dimensions of society*, London, University of London Press/The Open University Press (Course Reader).

REX, J. and MOORE, R. (1967) *Race, community, and conflict*, London, Oxford University Press (set book).

TALMON, Y. (1966) 'Millenarian movements', *European Journal of Sociology*, vol. 7, pp 159–200. Reprinted in Potter and Sarre (1974) pp 424–41.

TAWNEY, R. (1926) *Religion and the rise of capitalism*, London, John Murray.

WEBER, M. (1930) *The Protestant ethic and the spirit of capitalism*, trans. Parsons, T., London, Allen and Unwin.

WEBER, M. (1947) *Theory of social and economic organisation*, New York, Free Press.

WEBER, M. (1951) *The religion of China*, trans. Gerth, H. H., New York, Free Press.

WEBER, M. (1952) *Ancient Judaism*, trans. Gerth, H. H., and Martindale, D., New York, Free Press.

WEBER, M. (1958) *The religion of India*, trans. Gerth, H. H. and Martindale, D., New York, Free Press.

WEBER, M. (1962) 'The development of modern Western civilization' from the Author's Introduction to *The Protestant ethic and the spirit of capitalism*, London, Allen and Unwin, pp 13–31. Reprinted in Potter and Sarre (1974) pp 491–98.

WEBER, M. (1965) *The sociology of religion*, trans. Fischoff, E., London, Methuen.

WILSON, B. (1966) *Religion in secular society*, London, Watts.

WORSLEY, P. (1962) 'Progress and cults in Melanesia', *New Society*, vol. 1, no. 3, October 18, pp 16–17.

ACKNOWLEDGEMENTS

Grateful acknowledgement is made to the following sources for material used in this unit:

TEXT
New Science Publications for Peter Worsley, 'Progress and cults in Melanesia', *New Society*, 1, No. 3, October 18 1962.

FIGURES
Figures 2–5 Methodist Archives; *Figure 6* New Science Publications; *Figure 7* BBC.

ANSWERS TO SELF-ASSESSMENT QUESTIONS

SAQ 1

We cannot predict your particular response to this question. If you are widely travelled, or an amateur anthropologist, you may find nothing at all strange in the custom described. However, your reaction may correspond to one of those we have specified. If so, we should want to argue that a marriage arrangement of this kind is neither cruel nor mercenary but is highly rational from the viewpoint of the parties to the contract. The money raised from wife-purchase recompenses the girl's family for bringing her up (if you have been financially involved in the marriage of your own daughter(s), you may be particularly sympathetic), it recognizes her desirability, it ensures responsibility on the part of the husband, and it acts as a means of securing good behaviour. As in other forms of arranged marriage, conscientious parents select for their children partners they consider suitable in every way and seek to avoid incompatibilities.

If your response corresponds with any of the adjectives we have used – cruel, etc – then this probably betrays 'ethnocentrism', a view of the world in which one's own culture forms the central standard against which all others are evaluated and rated. Ethnocentrism, both of time and place, works against the detachment and empathy that we need as social scientists. These will be discussed further in section 6.

SAQ 2

B, C, E.

SAQ 3

Weber's ideas have been interpreted in a number of ways, but the essential elements of his argument seem to be as follows:

1 Modern capitalism requires that a characteristic form of rationality be adopted by members of that society, uninhibited by traditional religious or moral beliefs.
2 One particular set of beliefs Weber held to be positively associated with the development of capitalism. He called this set of beliefs the Protestant ethic. He believed such an ethic had an important role to play as a cause in the development of capitalism.
3 He attempted to demonstrate the validity of his theory by comparing the relationships between beliefs and social change in different cultural settings.
4 As a result of this comparative work, he claimed to have shown that the Protestant ethic had both preceded and had an 'elective affinity' with the spirit of capitalism. It was not *the* cause, but one of the fundamental elements in the spirit of modern capitalism based on rational business organization.

A fuller account is presented in section 2.2. Almost needless to say, Weber's ideas did not go unchallenged and some of the major criticisms are mentioned in section 2.3 which you are about to read.

SAQ 4

Some support for Weber's thesis is to be found in Unit 23 where you read Robert Merton's account of the effects of the beliefs of ascetic Protestantism on the development of science in seventeenth century England. Merton points out that although the Puritans constituted a relatively small minority in the English population, they made up sixty-two per cent of the Royal Society which 'arising about the middle of the century, provoked and stimulated scientific advance more than any other immediate agency' (Merton 1967 p 575). You have read in Unit 23 Merton's detailed account of relationship between the Protestant ethic and scientific advance.

SAQ 5

Weber's primary interest in religious beliefs was to discover ways in which they might act as a source of the dynamics of social change.

SAQ 6

This term means the capacity of both religious and secular ideologies to legitimize the development of new social institutions and individual motivations. In the work we have just considered, Weber was concerned with the *transformative capacity* of Calvinism, in the shape of the Protestant ethic, to legitimize the emergence of capitalism.

We can apply the concept of transformative capacity to other areas of social life and you can perhaps think of instances in modern times where religious or secular ideologies have played a similar role to that of the Protestant ethic, for example, the set of beliefs that express a 'social contract' between unions and government in Britain, or the ideology of 'Women's liberation'. Both of these ideologies seem to possess the potential to transform basic social institutions though we need perhaps to wait some time yet to see what shape these changes will take.

SAQ 7

Weber showed that religious beliefs can act as an independent variable in that the Protestant ethic constituted a primary source of social change. However, Weber would not argue that religious or other forms of beliefs could act as an agency of change independent of social and economic forces.

SAQ 8

Weber claimed that an adequate explanation is needed to take account of both *subjective* and *objective* dimensions of social action. Thus besides showing how the Protestant ethic appeared within an objective structural context of religious and economic institutions, broke through these, and transformed the latter into capitalistic forms, he had also to show how Calvinist beliefs themselves subjectively led to an ethic and motivation that stressed rationality and individualism and in turn to a spirit or an outlook that legitimized capitalism. The methodological principles involved here are discussed further in section 6.

SAQ 9

1   Methodism provided a channel of social/cultural mobility and thereby helped to reduce class polarization.

2   It acted as a form of social control by directing working class radicalism from revolution.

Hill discusses criticisms and elaborations of the second only:

(a)   Thompson stresses Methodism as a source of work discipline and as a retreat from political defeat for working class members.

(b)   Hobsbawm claims that the influence of Methodism has been exaggerated but in contrast to Thompson suggests a direct relationship between political and religious activism.

(c)   Kiernan adds to the thesis in terms of the response to popular disaffection by the ruling class. Methodism had stimulated the Evangelical revival in the Church of England and thereby interpenetrated the political structure. Social/political crises were able to be redefined as moral crises and matters of individual guilt. Thus the traditional social order was not fundamentally threatened.

SAQ 10

There are two main points here:

1 Both stress the independent role of beliefs and ideas in determining men's actions but reject any explanation of history based on this single cause. In fact they emphasize the interdependence between beliefs and economic and political forces in any society.

2 Both authors also point out the importance of the way in which beliefs are socially organized, in particular the very significant part played by the formation of religious sects.

Weber and Halévy are both concerned with the operation of *transitional ideologies* in social change. This concept will be taken up in section 4.2.

SAQ 11

A cargo cult is a religious movement which centres on a belief in the imminent arrival of a new age initiated by receipt of cargoes of material goods from ancestors. The cargo will consist of the desirable material goods possessed by the white man who alone has the secret power to conjure them up from across the seas.

SAQ 12

According to David Attenborough's film, the people of Tanna name their messiah John Frum who will one day bring the cargo to them from across the seas. The name, John Frum, is itself unimportant for it merely provides a focus for the beliefs of the cargo cult.

SAQ 13

In one sense such beliefs are irrational to us because we know that the cargo cult believers are mistaken about the process by which the white man acquires his material goods. Therefore, the islanders' beliefs about their forthcoming prosperity can never be achieved in the way they anticipate. On the other hand, as Worsley points out in his article, such beliefs are logical and rational given the islanders' limited knowledge. Their beliefs represent an ingenious attempt at a reasonable explanation based on very limited information about the situation. They provide both an explanation of current material inequality and a hope for change in the future.

SAQ 14

All of them.

SAQ 15

A.

SAQ 16

Because they are based on the expectation of a millenium, a new age marked by the transformation of society through supernatural intervention.

SAQ 17

Negative interpretations claim that millenarism manifests collective madness and an anti-social escapism that may lead to political extremism. Positive interpretations impute realism and rationality to millenarian movements.

SAQ 18

Positive functions include personal and social integration, providing continuity between past and present (*cf.* transitional ideologies), and facilitating political modernization.

SAQ 19

The authors list the functions of the 'churches' both at the beginning and end of Chapter VII. By amalgamating these we can summarize them as:

Pastoral: providing both material and spiritual welfare including tension-release.

Social: (re)creating group affiliations and solidarity including acting as a cultural bridge between Ireland or Jamaica and Britain.

Goal-attainment: providing a means by which individuals can attain goals.

Cognitive: transmitting sets of beliefs that give meaning to the cosmic and human worlds.

SAQ 20

Niebuhr distinguished between the 'religion of the disinherited' and the 'religion of the middle class', each with a characteristic organizational form, the sect and the denomination, respectively.

The authors provide evidence of Niebuhr's types in Sparkbrook. The sects tend to attract lower-working-class membership, reflect a culture of dispossession, but preach a future reversal of the social order. Denominations, however, include more materially successful members, teach personal piety and social responsibility, and tend to reflect an older, more stable community. Interestingly, they retain elements of their Puritan source – election and individualism. Note that in a general statement of this kind, it is easy to gloss over deviations from type, for example the Jehovah's Witnesses group. In what way did this group deviate from type?

It is also worth relating these organizations to what the authors say at the beginning of Chapter VII, that the churches have a definite 'message' which can be related to the status of the group represented by the congregation. In other words, from their original source in a single set of beliefs, Christianity, the various religious groups tend to reinterpret these beliefs or to emphasize some rather than others and thereby to give religious expression to social 'interests'.

SAQ 21

This is a difficult question to answer without our being able to follow up the empirical evidence available in Chapter VII.

Following the authors' argument and the answer to the previous question, we would probably agree that the sect/denomination dichotomy roughly corresponds to class divisions and marks the boundary between them. The mixed composition of some sects and denominations reinforces the argument that class rather than ethnicity separates the two types.

However, what weight do we attach to the statement that an unspecified number of Christ Church members left as a result of West Indians taking up 'too much of the vicar's attention'? On the other hand, the Sparkbrook Methodists acted differently and thereby created in the authors' minds the uncertainty they express in the last sentence of page 187.

In general terms, therefore, there is no single, unambiguously correct answer; if you have thought about and tried to weigh up the evidence, you will have experienced the same kind of difficulty and uncertainty that the social scientist meets – conflicting evidence, lack of consistency between findings, and similar headaches.

SAQ 22

In order to understand a process of social change such as 'modernization' or 'industrialization' we need to have a clear idea of what a 'pre-modern' or 'pre-industrialized' society is like. This may create many difficulties for the social scientist because he tends to apply the kinds of measures which are appropriate to an advanced society thereby missing out many of the factors which a member of the society under study may feel to be of central importance. This problem can be highlighted by comparing the nature of religious or supernatural beliefs in societies of each type, e.g. Christianity in modern Western Europe and the cargo cults in New Guinea.

One lesson which the social scientist may learn from this state of affairs is that it is as difficult for a member of a cargo cult to understand why we fail to interpret events in his way as it is for us to understand why he does not accept our interpretation. Such problems of communication and understanding both plague social science investigations and provide the enduring fascination of such tasks.

SAQ 23

As you have seen, there is a wide range of theoretical and methodological problems. We can attempt to summarize these problems as of three kinds:

1   The problem is often one of scale. The work of Weber and Halévy covers a very broad historical sweep making it difficult to ensure accuracy of description and interpretation.

2   Theories about such matters are difficult to conceptualize and evaluate because of the nature of the subject matter. Despite such problems, however, Weber in particular has provided us with a remarkably attractive and enduring set of ideas.

3   Finally, there is always the problem of understanding 'alien belief systems' which brings us back to the issue raised in the first Self-assessment Question but, hopefully, in the meantime we have taken an intellectual journey of interest and importance.

MAKING SENSE OF SOCIETY